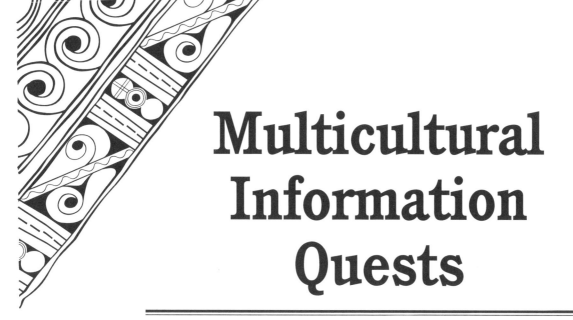

Multicultural Information Quests

Instant Research Lessons, Grades 5–8

Marie E. Rodgers

2000
Libraries Unlimited, Inc.
and Its Division
Teacher Ideas Press
Englewood, Colorado

Dedicated to Brian, to Joe, to Jeannie, and to Sam.

LIBRARIES UNLIMITED, INC.
and Its Division
Teacher Ideas Press
P.O. Box 6633
Englewood, CO 80155-6633
1-800-237-6124
www.lu.com

Library of Congress Cataloging-in-Publication Data

Rodgers, Marie E.
    Multicultural information quests : instant research lessons, grades 5–8 / Marie E. Rodgers.
       p. cm.
    Includes bibliographical references and index.
    ISBN 1-56308-686-7
    1. Pluralism (Social sciences)--United States--Study and teaching (Elementary) 2.
United States--Civilization--Study and teaching (Elementary) 3. Comparative
civilization--Study and teaching (Elementary)--United States. 4. Multicultural
education--Activity programs--United States. 5. Library orientation for school
children--United States. I. Title.

E184.A1 R63 1999
372.83´044--dc21

                                                                99-039119

Multicultural
Information
Quests

Contents

Introduction

How to Use This Book

This is a book of multicultural treasure hunts designed for use by teachers and librarians. There are several benefits of using treasure hunts or searches. The searches in this book are designed to

- develop students' awareness of cultures other than their own,

- promote student research that requires using books other than an encyclopedia,

- provide students with annotated reference lists that may be used for their own research projects,

- promote research as an educational activity that can be fun, and

- enhance the curriculum.

Students should be given copies of both reference lists and searches. They should then use the books on the reference lists to find the answers in the search. With a little imagination, educators can find many more uses for these activities. Here are a few suggestions:

- Search projects can be used to introduce students to a topic.

- Reference lists can be used independently for other assignments.

- Thematic searches can be used to celebrate or honor various events in the school year, such as Women's History Month or the birthday of Martin Luther King, Jr.

- Teachers can use these searches as part of a unit or as an independent assignment.

- Librarians can present a book talk about a reference list before students complete the searches, thus promoting the library's reference collection.

- Teachers and librarians can select questions or searches for "Jeopardy!"-style competitions.

- Teachers and librarians can use the searches to reinforce how to use a reference book or an index or how to locate information in the library.

- These searches provide an opportunity for collaboration between teachers and librarians.

- Questions can be incorporated into a bulletin board for a contest or used for Research Questions of the Week.

Tips for Using These Searches

These searches are designed to reinforce or enhance a particular topic within the curriculum. Most chapters contain several searches. This was done to accommodate the curriculum needs of teachers and librarians. For example, one teacher may wish to focus on the Holocaust, while another may wish to focus on the immigrant experience in America. Others may wish to provide students with extra assignments. (Those who like "extra credit" assignments will find these search projects useful.)

It is best to begin by reminding students how to locate books and how to use an index. It is also a good idea to demonstrate the process by doing one or two questions with the class to get them started. Once students have done a few searches, they will know exactly what to do in the future.

Not all libraries will have every book on a reference list. Answers can be provided in other ways; multiple choice, scrambled words, or clues can be given. In some cases, photographs or pictures can be used. Ready-made bulletin board materials often supply information as well. I have incorporated some information in bulletin boards. For example, a search on Black History Month may be used in conjunction with an informative bulletin board that provides answers to some questions. This is an option I actually prefer.

These searches provide excellent opportunities for using cooperative learning techniques. Depending on the size of a class, searches can be done with two to four students in a group. Having each group begin with a different question avoids having the entire class look for the same answer in the same place at one time. Another option is to use two or three searches at one time. Mix or match search questions to suit your needs.

Chapters Two through Eight coincide with the Dewey decimal system. For example, Chapter Three, Holidays, Customs, and Folklore, coincides with Dewey's 300 classification. However, it should be noted that not all books on the reference lists for these chapters will be limited to one classification.

Finally, *Multicultural Information Quests* should be viewed as a collection of more searches than you could ever use in one school year. My experience with classes scheduled for twice weekly blocks of time was that one search a month worked very well. Happy searching!

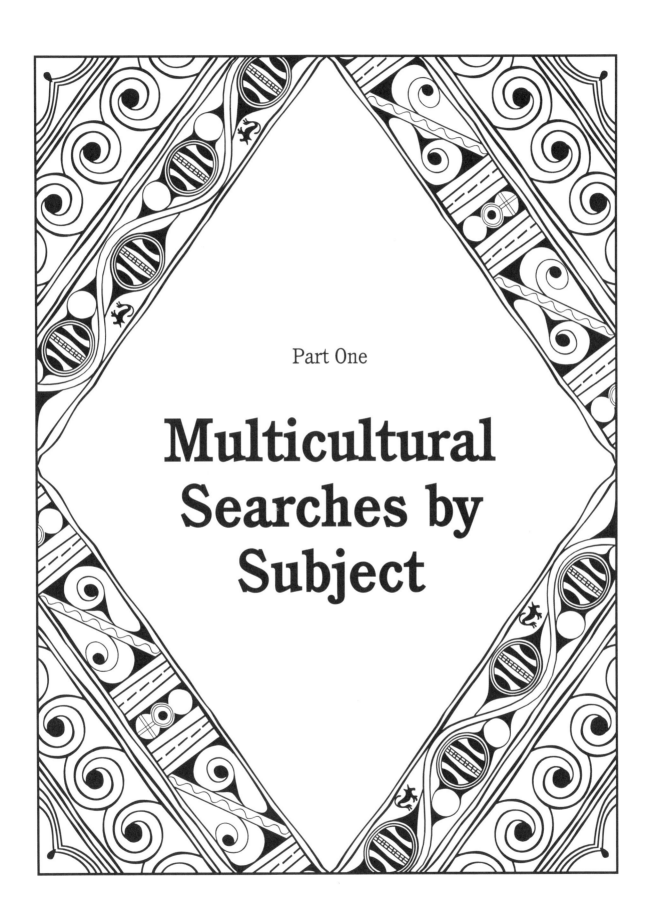

Part One

Multicultural Searches by Subject

Chapter

One

Firsts

There are a number of books of firsts. The works listed here were chosen either because they focus on an ethnic group or because they provide information about an ethnic group. As one can see by examining the list, there are single volumes devoted to the firsts achieved by Hispanics, African Americans, Native Americans, and women. There are, in fact, several volumes devoted to firsts achieved by women and African Americans. Because there are no current books of firsts for other ethnic groups, other references are used. There are two searches for multicultural firsts. The reference list may be used for both.

Reference List for Multicultural Firsts

Baron, Deborah G., and Susan B. Gall, eds. *Asian American Chronology*. New York: UXL, 1996. 173p. $39.00. ISBN 0-8103-9692-0.

Milestones in Asian American history are recorded here using a calendar arrangement. Spanning time from prehistory to 1995, entries range from a few lines to one page. Coverage includes topics such as immigration, world wars, and contributions made by Asian Americans from more than 20 countries of origin. There are more than 90 black-and-white illustrations and maps. In addition, boxes highlight important, relevant information. Cross-references, boxes with related charts and statistics, and an index provide easy access. The section Further Reading lists sources on Asian Americans in general as well as sources for specific groups. Recommended for grade 5 and above.

Bruno, Leonard C. *Science and Technology Firsts*. Detroit: Gale Research, 1997. 636p. $86.00. ISBN 0-7876-0256-6.

Twelve chapters relating to various fields of scientific endeavor such as astronomy, biology, mathematics, and transportation have been arranged in chronological order. Entries are one paragraph in length and begin with the year of discovery or breakthrough in boldface and provide details. There are also several black-and-white photographs and illustrations. Cross-references exist only within a particular chapter; however, an extensive index helps readers locate information pertaining to more than one area of science. There is also a bibliography. Written for students and general readers, this work is also appropriate for science buffs in grade 5 and above.

Kane, Joseph Nathan. *Famous First Facts*. 5th ed. Revised and expanded. New York: H. W. Wilson, 1997. 1,350p. $80.00. ISBN 0-8242-0930-3.

A popular ready reference book, *Famous First Facts* consists of more than 9,000 entries of what is listed as happenings, discoveries, and inventions in American history. Entries—arranged alphabetically by subject—are brief. One of the special features of this work is its indexes. Not only do they make the book easily accessible but they allow readers to find information by year, days of the month, geographical locations, and personal name. The work is also cross-referenced. Recommended for grade 5 and above.

Kanellos, Nicolás. *Hispanic Firsts: 500 Years of Extraordinary Achievements*. Detroit: Gale Research, 1997. 372p. $44.95. ISBN 0-7816-0517-4.

Kanellos, an award-winning expert in the field of Hispanic studies, has compiled another excellent reference. Contributions and achievements have been compiled chronologically according to fields of endeavor. Chapters include Art and Design, and Film, Labor, and Religion, as well as a Timeline, Calendar of Firsts, Bibliography, Index by Year, and General Index. There are several black-and-white photographs and illustrations. Kanellos has based his work on the premise that Hispanics have contributed greatly to U.S. civilization and that Hispanics are pioneers not only for their achievements but also for overcoming obstacles in American society that barred their success. Kanellos' work is informative and appealing; it is an excellent resource and fun to browse. Recommended for grade 5 and above.

Smith, Jessie Carney. *Black Firsts: 2,000 Years of Extraordinary Achievement*. Detroit: Visible Ink, 1994. 529p. $16.95. ISBN 0-8103-9490-1.

Smith's work is well respected, and this volume is an outstanding example. The work is arranged by topic; there are 15 in all, including civil rights and protest, religion, sports, and writers. Categories within a subject topic are used as well. For example, under Arts and Entertainment there are categories for film, music, and theater. Firsts are arranged chronologically by year in each category. Sources are listed for each entry. Included as well are several black-and-white photographs and tables. Dates of birth and death of achievers are also listed. Special features include a foldout time line, a month-by-month calendar of firsts, and an index by year. There are cross-references and a keyword index. This is an excellent resource for research and fun to browse. Recommended for grade 5 and above.

Swisher, Karen Gayton, and AnCita Benally. *Native North American Firsts*. Detroit: Gale Research, 1997. 263p. $48.55. ISBN 0-7876-0518-2.

Beginning with a month-by-month Calendar of Firsts and a Timeline, this work is arranged alphabetically by topic. Included are Education, Literature, Religious Life, Sciences, and many others. Under each topic there are also various subheadings. For example, under Military there are sections on the Civil War, World War I, and so on. Within each section, entries are listed chronologically. Also included are several black-and-white photographs, a bibliography, an index by year, and a general index. As a result, this work is very accessible. Overall, this is an excellent reference. Appropriate for grade 6 and above.

Zilboorg, Caroline, ed. *Women's Firsts*. Detroit: Gale Research, 1996. 564p. $48.55. ISBN 0-7876-0151-9.

A reference work designed to highlight women's achievements from ancient times to the present, this work is arranged by field of endeavor. Included are activism, literature, military service, science, and religion. Coverage is international, and more than 2,000 achievements are detailed here. Within each field of endeavor, achievements are listed chronologically with a citation for the source. Special features of this work include a Time Line of Events in Women's History and a bibliography. An index by day and month, index by year, and a general index provide easy access. Recommended for grade 5 and above.

Search for Multicultural Firsts

Name_____ Class_____ Date_____

Use the sources on the Reference List for Multicultural Firsts to find the answers to these questions.

1. What scientific first was achieved by German American physicist Albert A. Michelson in 1907?

    _____

    _____

    _____

2. Name the first Jewish college in America. Where and when was it founded?

    _____

    _____

    _____

3. Which scientific first in the field of communications was achieved by American inventor Chester Carlson in 1937?

    _____

    _____

    _____

4. Which first was achieved by Kristi Yamaguchi in 1992?

    _____

    _____

    _____

5. What was the first book by an African American writer to be chosen for the Book of the Month Club?

    _____

    _____

    _____

   From *Multicultural Information Quests* by Marie E. Rodgers. © 2000 Libraries Unlimited. (800) 237-6124.

6. In 1969, actor Ricardo Montalban achieved a first as president of *Nostros*. What was the purpose of this group?

_____

_____

_____

7. Who was the first Jewish person known to immigrate to America?

_____

_____

_____

8. Lt. Everett Alvarez, Jr., became the longest held prisoner of war in United States history. What first is also part of Alvarez's Vietnam experience?

_____

_____

_____

9. Constance Garnett achieved her first as a result of learning something while recuperating from a difficult childbirth. What did she learn? What was her first?

_____

_____

_____

10. Which first was achieved by Keely Smith, a Cherokee, in 1958?

_____

_____

_____

Search for More Multicultural Firsts

Name_____ Class_____ Date_____

Use the Reference List for Multicultural Firsts to find the answers to the following questions.

1. Which first was achieved by Annie Montague Alexander in 1909?

    _____

    _____

    _____

2. Which firsts were achieved by Alfred Wong in 1976?

    _____

    _____

    _____

3. Which first was achieved by author Hannah Adams?

    _____

    _____

    _____

4. In what year was the first book by a Jewish author published in the United States?

    _____

    _____

    _____

5. Which first was achieved by Fernando Valenzuela on November 11, 1981?

    _____

    _____

    _____

    From *Multicultural Information Quests* by Marie E. Rodgers. © 2000 Libraries Unlimited. (800) 237-6124.

6. A significant first in the U.S. military occurred for Native American Army scout Corux-techodish in August 1869. What was it?

_____

_____

_____

7. Which first was achieved by writer N. Scott Momaday in 1969 for his work, *House Made of Dawn*?

_____

_____

_____

8. Which first was achieved by Marjorie Stewart Joyner?

_____

_____

_____

9. Which first was achieved by John Aiso on September 25, 1953?

_____

_____

_____

10. Which first in the field of medicine was achieved by French American surgeon Alexis Carrel in 1912?

_____

_____

_____

Answer Key for Multicultural Firsts

1. In Bruno. Michelson was the first American to win a Nobel prize.
2. In Kane. Maimonides College was founded in Philadelphia, Pennsylvania on October 28, 1867.
3. In Bruno. Carlson applied for a patent for his invention, the "electro photocopy" machine, the first copy machine.
4. In Baron and Gall. She was the first Asian American to win an Olympic gold medal for women's figure skating.
5. In Smith. Richard Wright's *Native Son*.
6. In Kanellos. *Nostros*, a group of Hispanic actors, strives to promote positive images of Hispanics in television and film.
7. In Kane. Jacob Barsimson arrived on August 22, 1654.
8. In Kanellos. He was also the first U.S. serviceman shot down over North Vietnam.
9. In Zilboorg. She learned Russian and translated major Russian writers' works into English.
10. In Swisher and Benally. Smith was the first Native American woman to win a Grammy.

Answer Key for More Multicultural Firsts

1. In Zilboorg. She established the first national history museum in the United States in Berkeley, California.
2. In Baron and Gall. Wong was the first Asian Pacific American appointed U.S. marshal of the Supreme Court and the first Asian Pacific American in the White House Secret Service.
3. In Kane. She was the first woman to make writing her profession.
4. In Kane. The first book by a Jewish author was published in 1719.
5. In Kanellos. Valenzuela was the first Latino and first rookie to win the Cy Young award.
6. In Swisher and Benally. He was the first Native American to be awarded the Medal of Honor.
7. In Swisher and Benally. Momaday was the first Native American to win the Pulitzer prize.
8. In Smith. Joyner was the first African American to patent a permanent waving machine.
9. In Baron and Gall. Aiso was the first person of Nisei origin to become a judge in the continental United States.
10. In Bruno. Carrel produced the first true cell culture.

Chapter

Two

Religion and Mythology

There are many reasons to study religion. It is part of cultural tradition as well as part of the social history of a group. Religion can relate to the literature of a culture as well. Many myths and legends are based on or are linked in some way to religious or spiritual beliefs of the world's cultures.

Reference List for Religions

The questions in this search focus on the unusual or little-known facts about various belief systems. The following bibliography lists works with information on the major religions of the world; a number of the works provide information on little-known religions, cultural movements, and religions of antiquity.

Browning, W. R. F. *A Dictionary of the Bible*. Oxford: Oxford University Press, 1996. 420p. $25.00. ISBN 0-192-80060-4.

Browning's guide focuses on books of the Christian Bible as well as people, places, and ideas related to the Bible. More than 2,000 entries are provided and refer to the New Revised Standard Version. Brief essays on the land of the Bible and names for God are included in the introduction. Also included are a List of Abbreviations, Books of the Bible, Important Dates in Biblical History, Select Bibliography, and Maps. Well researched and clearly written, this work is intended for readers of all ages, so it is appropriate for students in grade 5 and above.

Bunson, Matthew. *The Pope Encyclopedia: An A to Z of the Holy See.* New York: Crown Trade Paperbacks, 1995. 390p. $17.00. ISBN 0-517-88256-6.

More than 2,000 entries provide details on the lives of the popes, including original names, dates of birth and death, and election histories. Information on other topics related to the papacy has been included as well; topics include the Swiss Guard, Good Friday, and Vatican locations. Arrangement is alphabetical, and black-and-white illustrations have been included. Bunson writes in a lively, straightforward style. Of special interest to anyone studying or researching the papacy, this work is also appealing to anyone who is browsing. Appropriate for grade 6 and above.

Fischer-Schreiber, Ingrid, et al. *The Encyclopedia of Eastern Philosophy and Religion.* Boston: Shambhala, 1994. 468p. $25.00. ISBN 0-87773-980-3.

Limited to four Eastern philosophies—Buddhism, Taoism, Zen, and Hinduism—this work is intended to familiarize the general reader with terminologies and concepts of these religions. The work is arranged alphabetically. The letters *B, H, T,* or *Z* identify each entry as Buddhist, Hindu, Taoist, or Zen. Included is a pronunciation key, a Zen lineage chart, and a bibliography of primary and secondary sources for each of the four religions. Written for adults, this work is also recommended for grade 7 and above.

Gaer, Joseph. *How the Great Religions Began.* New York: Dodd, Mead, 1981. 424p. $6.95. ISBN 0-396-07985-7.

Gaer's work, a classic originally published in 1929, is still available in paperback. What makes this work so appealing is Gaer's thoughtful, straightforward approach to his subject. The work is arranged in three sections: Book One, The Religions of India; Book Two, The Religions of China and Japan; and Book Three, The Advance of One God. Gaer presents such information as the founder of the religion, date and place of origin, sacred books, and number of followers (updated). In addition, life stories of founders of religions are provided. Gaer's narrative style simplifies the complexities of his subject and should be appealing to students in grade 5 and above.

Gross, David C. *1,001 Questions and Answers About Judaism.* Revised ed. New York: Hippocrene Books, 1990. 322p. $9.95. ISBN 0-87052-626-X.

Gross' work consists of 10 chapters arranged by topic. Personal Life, The Synagogue, The Sabbath, Jewish History, and Israel are a few. Additionally, there are 100 questions and answers for the 1990s, a bibliography, a glossary, and an index. The question-and-answer format makes this work interesting to browse. However, Gross has provided readers with a vast amount of information. His work serves as a reference and handbook for anyone interested in Judaism. The index makes the book easily accessible. Recommended for grade 5 and above.

Littleton, C. Scott, gen. ed. *Eastern Wisdom*. New York: Henry Holt, 1996. 176p. $30.00. ISBN 0-8050-4647-X.

While this work is not comprehensive—it limits coverage to five major Eastern religions—it is appealing. The text explains practices of Hinduism, Buddhism, Confucianism, Daoism, and Shinto. More than 100 color illustrations and maps add to the appeal of this work. Festivals and holidays, various sects, history, and modern practice are explained in this work. The explanations clarify ideas that may seem complicated in religious texts. Littleton also offers explanations of the impact of these religions on one another and on culture. Recommended for grade 6 and above.

Nanji, Azimli. *The Muslim Almanac*. Detroit: Gale Research, 1995. 581p. $107.00. ISBN 0-8103-8924-X.

The goal of this work is to provide an in-depth look at various aspects of Islam. Arranged in 12 parts, topics covered include Beginnings and Foundations of Islam, Diversity in Islam, Islamic Law, Literary Expressions in Islam, and Contemporary Developments in Islam. Included are several black-and-white illustrations, a glossary, a bibliography, and an index. Appendixes include Islamic Calendar, Bosnia Herzegovina, and Muslim Life-Cycle. Written for students, this is a good source for anyone interested in learning more about Islam. Recommended for grade 5 and above.

Nielson, Jr., Niels C., et al. *Religions of the World*. New York: St. Martin's Press, 1993. 536p. $60.00. ISBN 0-312-05023-2.

This volume describes principal doctrines and issues of religions from antiquity to modern times. The introduction discusses religious traditions, calendar rituals, and cultural traditions. There is also an explanation of how to use the book. The work is arranged in eight sections; discussions include primal religions, Hinduism, Buddhism, religions of Japan and China, Judaism, Christianity, and Islam. Special features include time lines, comparison boxes that enable readers to compare and contrast aspects of different religions, and a glossary. There are also black-and-white photographs and illustrations, an extensive bibliography, and an index. Recommended for students in grade 8 and above.

Robinson, Francis. *Atlas of the Islamic World Since 1500*. New York: Facts on File, 1992. 238p. $45.00. ISBN 0-87196-629-8.

According to Robinson, more than 20 percent of the world population practices Islam. Robinson's narrative begins in 1500 in Part One and traces Muslim history through the twentieth century. The work includes 53 maps, 302 illustrations—almost 200 in color—a chronology, and a list of rulers. Other special features include political cartoons, Belief and Practice, and Islam in the West. Part Two consists of three topics: Religious Life, Arts of Islam, and Society and the Modern World. The book provides a list of maps, a glossary, a bibliography, a gazetteer, and an index. Recommended for grade 6 and above.

Snelling, John. *The Buddhist Handbook: A Complete Guide to Buddhist Schools, Teaching, Practice and History*. Rochester, VT: Inner Traditions, 1991. 537p. $14.95. ISBN 0-89281-319-9.

Snelling has compiled a handbook that discusses not only various aspects of Buddhism but also provides information on the Buddha and background on how Buddhism spread from India to the rest of the world. There are six parts to the book, some of which also cover basic teachings and the spread and practice of Buddhism in the West. Appendixes offer useful addresses, major Buddhist festivals, and a section titled Further Reading. A useful resource written for adults but also appropriate for students in grade 8 and above.

Search for Religions

Name_____ Class_____ Date_____

Use the Reference List for Religions to find the answers to the questions below. It is possible that some answers can be found in more than one of the listed sources.

1. What is Gammarelli's? Why do popes go there?

   _____

   _____

   _____

2. Why do bookbinders traditionally take a vacation during Passover?

   _____

   _____

   _____

3. The Mihrab is a central figure in a mosque. What is it?

   _____

   _____

   _____

4. What is a *zensu*?

   _____

   _____

   _____

5. Islamic author Furuzan's writing makes a comment on the lives of women in her culture. What kind of women does she write about?

   _____

   _____

   _____

6. What was Solomon's Porch?

_____

_____

_____

7. In Jainism there are several heavens and hells. How many of each are there?

_____

_____

_____

8. Today in Taiwan, Daoists are classified as Blackheads or Redheads. Why?

_____

_____

_____

9. What, according to most Chinese religions, is the goal of life?

_____

_____

_____

10. When is Buddha day?

_____

_____

_____

From _Multicultural Information Quests_ by Marie E. Rodgers. © 2000 Libraries Unlimited. (800) 237-6124.

Reference List for Deities

This search focuses on deities rather than on religious practice. The search will present a fascinating list of deities.

Browning, W. R. F. *A Dictionary of the Bible*. Oxford: Oxford University Press, 1996. 420p. $25.00. ISBN 0-192-80060-4.

Browning's guide focuses on books of the Christian Bible as well as people, places, and ideas related to the Bible. More than 2,000 entries are provided and refer to the New Revised Standard Version. Brief essays on the land of the Bible and names for God are included in the introduction. Also included are a List of Abbreviations, Books of the Bible, Important Dates in Biblical History, Select Bibliography, and Maps. Well researched and clearly written, this work is intended for readers of all ages, so it is appropriate for students in grade 5 and above.

Fischer-Schreiber, Ingrid, et al. *The Encyclopedia of Eastern Philosophy and Religion*. Boston: Shambhala, 1994. 468p. $25.00. ISBN 0-87773-980-3.

Limited to four Eastern philosophies—Buddhism, Taoism, Zen, and Hinduism—this work is intended to familiarize the general reader with terminologies and concepts of these religions. The work is arranged alphabetically. The letters *B, H, T,* or *Z* identify each entry as Buddhist, Hindu, Taoist, or Zen. Included is a pronunciation key, a Zen lineage chart, and a bibliography of primary and secondary sources for each of the four religions. Written for adults, this work is also recommended for grade 7 and above.

Gill, Sam D., and Irene Sullivan. *Dictionary of Native American Mythology*. New York: Oxford University Press, 1992. 425p. $15.95. ISBN 0-19-508602-3.

More than 100 Native American cultures are represented in more than 1,000 alphabetically arranged entries. Information on names, phrases, images, and symbols is provided in this comprehensive work. There are several black-and-white photographs and illustrations, an extensive bibliography, and an index by tribe. Entries range from a few sentences to a full page. The authors' intent is to introduce readers to Native American tradition and hopefully spark an interest that leads to further study. When possible, tribe and culture area (such as the Southwest) associated with a particular entry are identified. Cross-references and bibliographic references are provided as well. Several maps are also provided. Recommended for grade 7 and above.

Jordan, Michael. *Encyclopedia of the Gods*. New York: Facts on File, 1993. 337p. $40.00. ISBN 0-8160-2909-1.

Information on deities from antiquity to modern times is presented in Jordan's work. The introduction offers a historical perspective. Entries are listed alphabetically with major deities printed in bold capitals. The original cultural source, the role of the deity, and brief explanations are listed as well. The work begins with a chronology of principal religions and cultures and ends with a subject index and civilization index, which allows the reader to focus on deities of a particular civilization. Recommended for grade 6 and above.

Leeming, David Adams, with Margaret Leeming. *The Encyclopedia of Creation Myths*. Santa Barbara, CA: ABC-CLIO, 1994. 330p. $60.00. ISBN 0-87436-739-5.

Based on the idea that all cultures have creation myths, this work lists them alphabetically. Included are creation myths of ancient and obscure civilizations. Entries are not limited to religions or cultural theories; scientific theories are included as well. Each entry identifies and retells the creation story. There are also several black-and-white photographs and illustrations. The introduction presents a discussion of creation myths and the elements found in them. This is an excellent resource for students of mythology and religion as well as for general readers. Recommended for grade 7 and above.

MacGregor, Geddes. *The Dictionary of Religion and Philosophy*. New York: Paragon House, 1989. 696p. $35.00. ISBN 1-55778-019-6.

MacGregor's main focus is on Judeo-Christian religions. Many entries cover philosophical topics. Included are notes on Sanskrit pronunciations and selected bibliographies, which are grouped under types of religion. Topics such as Afterlife and Modern Religious Movements are included as well. MacGregor's work is fairly comprehensive and includes more than 3,000 entries. Written specifically for students and researchers interested in religious studies, this is a useful single-volume reference for general readers as well. Recommended for grade 7 and above.

Nielson, Jr., Niels C., et al. *Religions of the World*. New York: St. Martin's Press, 1993. 536p. $60.00. ISBN 0-312-05023-2.

This volume describes principal doctrines and issues of religions from antiquity to modern times. The introduction discusses religious traditions, calendar rituals, and cultural traditions. There is also an explanation of how to use the book. The work is arranged in eight sections; discussions include primal religions, Hinduism, Buddhism, religions of Japan and China, Judaism, Christianity, and Islam. Special features include time lines, comparison boxes that enable readers to compare and contrast aspects of different religions, and a glossary. There are also black-and-white photographs and illustrations, an extensive bibliography, and an index. Recommended for students in grade 8 and above.

Search for Deities

Name_____ Class_____ Date_____

Use the Reference List for Deities to find the answers to the following questions. It is possible that some answers can be found in more than one of the listed sources.

1. Who was the Lion of Judah? What does the word *lion* mean in this title?

_____

_____

_____

2. Who are the Buddhas of the Three times?

_____

_____

_____

3. According to Zulu creation, who is the creator, and where is he now?

_____

_____

_____

4. If you were a Polynesian dancer, why might Laka be important to you?

_____

_____

_____

5. Someone who can't sleep at night might know of Nidra. Who is Nidra? With which religious philosophy is Nidra associated?

_____

_____

_____

6. Who is Kaahkwa in Seneca mythology?

_____

_____

_____

7. Who is Sugriva?

_____

_____

_____

8. Use a map of China in Confucius' day to find the name of the sacred mountain in one of the states visited by Confucius.

_____

_____

_____

9. What is the significance of the letters _I. H. S.?_

_____

_____

_____

10. What is the month and year of Muhammad's Farewell Pilgrimage?

_____

_____

_____

Mythology

Mythology is fascinating study. Probably the most popular myths are Greek and Roman. However, there are a number of works on mythology of various other cultures. Choosing sources on the mythology of individual groups would be difficult because there are so many excellent titles. Rather than eliminate some worthy collections, the books listed here tend to be references or anthologies that provide information on several cultures.

Reference List for Mythology

Cottrell, Arthur. *The Macmillan Illustrated Encyclopedia of Myths and Legends*. New York: Macmillan, 1989. 260p. $29.95. ISBN 0-02-580181-3.

Entries for more than 1,250 characters of myth and legend comprise this work. Divided in two parts, the work first discusses various cultures, then provides the alphabetically arranged list. Cross-references are used as is a micropedia of more than 1,000 short entries. Symbols are used to identify the culture of each entry. The index allows for further cross-referencing. There are several color and black-and-white photographs and illustrations on nearly every page. Also discussed are such themes as Heroes, Giants, Creation, Demons, Saviors, and Trickster Gods. Intended as a reference for general readers, this work is appealing and appropriate for grade 5 and above.

Hirsch, Jr., E. D., Joseph Kett, and James Trefil. *The Dictionary of Cultural Literacy*. 2nd ed. Revised and updated. Boston: Houghton Mifflin, 1993. 619p. $24.95. ISBN 0-395-65597-8.

Hirsch and his colleagues compiled what they have identified as shared common knowledge of literate Americans. This information is categorized into 23 subject sections. Sections include The Bible, World History, Mythology and Folklore, American Geography, Medicine and Health, and Technology. Entries within these sections are arranged alphabetically. Included are more than 250 illustrations, maps, and charts. Entries offer definitions as well as current cultural connotations. Cross-references and a pronunciation key are provided. Hirsch also presents an essay, "The Theory Behind the Dictionary." Written for general readers and students, this work is appropriate for grade 5 and above.

Jordan, Michael. *Encyclopedia of the Gods*. New York: Facts on File, 1993. 337p. $40.00. ISBN 0-8160-2909-1.

Information on deities from antiquity to modern times is presented in Jordan's work. The introduction offers historical perspective. Entries are listed alphabetically with major deities printed in bold capitals. The original cultural source, the role of the deity, and brief explanations are listed as well. The work begins with a chronology of principal religions and cultures and ends with a subject index and civilization index, which allows the reader to focus on deities of a particular civilization. Recommended for grade 6 and above.

Leeming, David Adams, with Margaret Leeming. *The Encyclopedia of Creation Myths*. Santa Barbara, CA: ABC-CLIO, 1994. 330p. $60.00. ISBN 0-87436-739-5.

Based on the idea that all cultures have creation myths, this work lists them alphabetically. Included are creation myths of ancient and obscure civilizations. Entries are not limited to religions or cultural theories; scientific theories are included as well. Each entry identifies and retells the creation story. There are also several black-and-white photographs and illustrations. The introduction presents a discussion of creation myths and the elements found in them. This is an excellent resource for students of mythology and religion as well as for general readers. Recommended for grade 7 and above.

Mercante, Anthony S. *The Facts on File Encyclopedia of World Mythology and Legend*. New York: Facts on File, 1988. 807p. $95.00. ISBN 0-8160-1049-8.

Consisting of more than 3,000 entries, Mercante's work is a collection of ancient and modern myths, fables, and legends. The introduction provides discussions of myth, legend, folktale, fairy tale, and fable. Religions and historical traditions are represented as well as botanical and zoological references. Entries are listed under most used spelling; however, a key to variant spellings is provided. Each entry consists of a brief definition and a description of its influence on art, literature, and music of the time. Indexes by subject and culture make this work easily accessible. The author's intention is to provide general readers with a ready reference on mythology. Appropriate for grade 5 and above.

Monaghan, Patricia. *The Book of Goddesses and Heroines*. Revised and enlarged ed. St. Paul, MN: Llewellyn Publications, 1993. 421p. $17.95. ISBN 0-87542-573-9.

Monaghan lists more than 1,000 goddesses and heroines in alphabetical order. The work opens with a chart of families of goddesses and heroines from several cultures. The entries are then presented and followed by a Calendar of Goddess Feasts and an Index of Associations, which is actually a listing of goddesses associated with various elements, such as air, beauty, and summer. A list of alternative names for minor goddesses is included as is a bibliography. Each entry includes origin and when possible, the myth, legend, or tale associated with the goddess. Written for general readers, this work is appropriate for grade 7 and above.

Search for Mythology

Name_____ Class_____ Date_____

Use the Reference List for Mythology to find the answers to the following questions about mythology. It is possible that some answers can be found in more than one of the listed sources.

1. In Germanic and Scandinavian mythology, swan maidens flew through the air in bird disguises. According to myth, how could the maidens be captured? How could they escape?

    _____

    _____

    _____

2. In Egypt, people were forbidden to harm a cat. To do so would be punishable by death. When their cats died, however, Egyptians went into mourning. How could one tell by looking at an Egyptian family that their cat had died?

    _____

    _____

    _____

3. What is Yggdrasil? With which creation myth is it associated?

    _____

    _____

    _____

4. Bobbi-Bobbi is a god to which group of people?

    _____

    _____

    _____

5. Does Sherwood Forest, the home of Robin Hood, hero of English legend, really exist?

    _____

    _____

    _____

6. Who is Ate?

_____

_____

_____

7. According to *Farmers Almanac Creation*, when did the world begin?

_____

_____

_____

8. What is Zamzam?

_____

_____

_____

9. Mother Friday is a Russian harvest goddess who is very particular about keeping her feast days sacred. What happens to those who do not comply?

_____

_____

_____

10. What do the Elysian fields symbolize? Write the name and location of a famous street named after the Elysian fields.

_____

_____

_____

Answer Key for Religions

1. In Bunson. Gammarelli's is the pope's tailor.
2. In Gross. Glue used in books has ingredients that are forbidden on Passover.
3. In Robinson. It is a niche built into the wall of the mosque facing in the direction of Mecca.
4. In Fischer-Schreiber. A *zensu* is a student of Zen who is being guided by a Zen master.
5. In Nanji. She writes short stories about women who are self-sufficient and independent.
6. In Browning. It was part of Jerusalem Temple that was added to the temple by Herod the Great.
7. In Gaer. There are 26 heavens and seven hells.
8. In Littleton. The names are based on color of headdress. Black signifies orthodox, and red is unorthodox.
9. In Nielson. Harmony in the world is the goal.
10. In Snelling. It is on the full moon in May.

Answer Key for Deities

1. In Browning. It is a term for Jesus Christ who was seen as the Messiah. The lion signifies strength and preeminence.
2. In Fischer-Schreiber. Buddhas of three times signify past, present, and future.
3. In Leeming and Leeming. Unkulunkulu is the creator, and no one knows where he is.
4. In Jordan. She is the Polynesian goddess of dancing.
5. In Fischer-Schreiber. She is the Hindu goddess of sleep.
6. In Gill and Sullivan. Kaahkwa is the sun who lives in a lodge in the sky and is commanded to give light.
7. In Jordan. Sugriva is the Hindu monkey god and leader of the monkey army.
8. In Littleton. Taishan is the sacred mountain.
9. In MacGregor. It is believed to be the acronym for *Iesus Hominum Salvator* (Jesus Christ the Savior).
10. In Nielson. March 632.

Answer Key for Mythology

1. In Monaghan. Swan maidens removed their bird cloaks to dance. When their cloaks were removed, they could be captured. If they later found their bird cloaks, the swan maidens could put them on and fly away.
2. In Mercante. Egyptian families shaved their eyebrows if their cat died.
3. In Leeming and Leeming. It is the world tree and is associated with Norse or Icelandic creation.
4. In Cottrell. Bobbi-Bobbi is a god to the Aboriginal people of northern Australia.
5. In Hirsch, Kett, and Trefil. Sherwood Forest is real.
6. In Jordan. A minor goddess of misfortune in Greek mythology, Ate is a daughter of Zeus. She signifies blind folly leading to disaster.
7. In Leeming and Leeming. 9:00 A.M. on Wednesday, October 26, 4004 B.C. James Ussher, an Irish bishop, made this determination.
8. In Mercante. According to Islamic legend, it is a sacred well at Mecca.
9. In Monaghan. Women who swept or used a spinning wheel would be blinded by dust.
10. In Hirsch, Kett, and Trefil. They represent a place of ultimate bliss. Champs-Elysées is a boulevard in Paris.

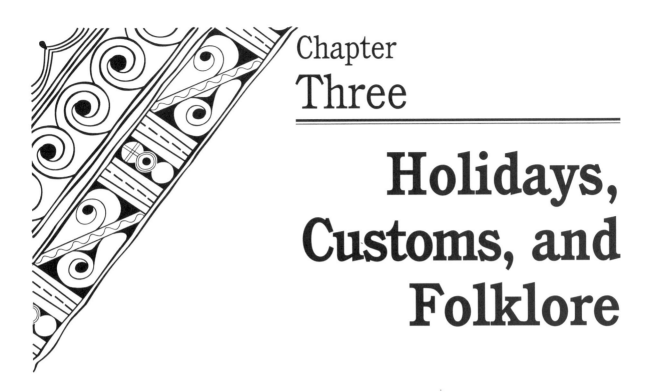

Chapter
Three

Holidays, Customs, and Folklore

These are popular areas of interest for students in middle school and general readers alike. Folklore, like religion and mythology, is part of virtually every culture. Many customs and holidays are linked to folklore. For our purposes, however, there will be three hunts. Each one will focus on different aspects of each of these topics. As with other sections, the purpose is to introduce students to various reference books. Most works used will be references, anthologies, or cultural celebrations.

Reference List for Customs and Traditions

Barillo, Madeline. *The Wedding Sourcebook*. Los Angeles: Lowell House, 1998. 322p. $18.00. ISBN 1-56565-650-4.

Anyone who is planning a wedding would find Barillo's guide valuable. She covers every aspect of weddings from cake, flowers, receptions, parties, and clothing to honeymoons, budgets, and wedding stress. There are tips and ideas here for every part of a wedding from beginning to end. Wedding anecdotes, including Wedding Horror Stories, are used effectively throughout the book. An appendix provides several lists: consultants, publications, jewelers, cakes, ceremonies, and music to name a few. There is also an index.

The reason for this book's inclusion here is that Barillo goes a step further. Throughout the book, Barillo has listed several wedding traditions, myths, and customs. The author provides details on various ethnic ceremonies and traditions. This in itself is interesting reading—even to those who are not marriage minded. Recommended for grade 5 and above.

Berg, Elizabeth. *Family Traditions: Celebrations for Holidays and Everyday*. Pleasantville, NY: Reader's Digest Association, 1992. 287p. $12.95. ISBN 0-895-77626-X.

Berg, while she recognizes the need for traditions, devotes much of her work to creating new traditions. She has compiled a list of activities and rituals that she feels may become family traditions. The focus here is on family, and in her introduction, Berg addresses what "family" may mean in today's world. Sections are devoted to everyday traditions, seasonal celebrations, family holidays, weddings, birthdays, and births. There are directions and recipes for many celebrations, including ideas for block parties, reunions, and milestones in school. Recipes and activities also appear in sidebars, and there are several sepia-toned illustrations. Recommended for grade 5 and above.

Coffin, Tristram Potter. *The Book of Christmas Folklore*. New York: Seabury Press, 1973. 192p. $22.00. ISBN 0-8164-9158-5.

Coffin is a well-known folklorist, and although this book is more than 20 years old, it is still on the shelves of many public and school libraries. The book consists of eight chapters dealing with many aspects of Christmas. Separate indexes for persons (real and fictional), places and subjects, and various titles make this work easily accessible. Coffin covers several themes, including superstition, the Christmas tree, cards, and food and drink. The work is well researched, and Coffin's writing is lively and engaging. Recommended for grade 5 and above.

Cohen, Henning, and Tristram Potter Coffin, eds. *The Folklore of American Holidays*. Detroit: Gale Research, 1987. 431p. $80.00. ISBN 0-8103-2126-2.

Folklore related to given holidays whether old or new, religious or secular, well-known or obscure is the focus of this work. Chronologically arranged, each entry contains the name of the holiday, its date or time frame, its origin, historical background, and other pertinent information. Entries also contain source and comment sections that provide bibliographic and collection information, cross-references, and related commentary. There are several indexes in this work that provide easy access. They include Subject Index; Ethnic or Geographical Index; Collectors, Informants, and Translators Index; Song Titles and First Significant Lines Index; and, finally, Motifs and Tale

Types Index. The introduction discusses development of calendars, festivals, and customs. Coffin is a widely known and well-respected folklorist. This work is a credit to his expertise in the subject. It reflects a diversity of ethnic and religious celebrations, making it not only a "day" book but also an excellent multicultural collection of folklore and a fairly comprehensive reference. Many specific references are made to such things as Thanksgiving Day parades in various cities, recipes for food served at a Hindu celebration, and many ethnic folktales. The editors even describe ethnic holidays as celebrated in a particular city or community. This is also fun to browse. Recommended for grade 5 and above.

Post, Elizabeth L. *Emily Post's Etiquette*. 15th ed. New York: HarperCollins, 1992. 783p. $23.80. ISBN 0-06-270047-2.

A classic, this guide to formalities and manners has been updated to reflect today's code of behavior. Post offers rules for proper procedure in business and social situations, a guide to correct communications, correct forms of address and interaction in today's family relationships, and new rules for wedding etiquette. Also included are standards for dining, entertaining, and traveling. Written for all ages. Recommended for grade 5 and above.

Silverthorne, Elizabeth. *Fiesta! Mexico's Great Celebrations*. Brookfield, CT: Millbrook Press, 1992. 64p. $6.95. ISBN 1-56294-836-9.

Opening with a discussion of three cultures in Mexico—Indian, Spanish, and Mexican—the following chapters in this book focus on religious, patriotic, and seasonal fiestas. The book ends with a calendar of Mexican fiestas, a bibliography, and an index. Color illustrations and directions for making piñatas, masks, and Mexican food are also included. Recommended for grades 5 through 8.

Thompson, Sue Ellen, ed. *Holiday Symbols*. Detroit: Omnigraphics, 1998. 558p. $55.00. ISBN 0-7808-0072-9.

Symbols associated with 200 popular holidays are arranged alphabetically by holiday name. Each entry consists of the name of holiday and an alternate name or spelling if any, type of holiday, date of observation, and where the holiday is celebrated. Origins and symbols are discussed, and works for further reading are listed. Cross-references, a general index, and a symbol index provide easy access. This work is unique in that the symbols are the major focus. Many holidays are based on legend, folklore, or tradition, and the essays in this book trace their evolution to modern times. Secular, religious, and cultural holidays are included. Written for general readers, this work is useful to students, teachers, and librarians. Recommended for grade 5 and above.

Tuleja, Ted. *Curious Customs: The Stories Behind 296 Popular American Rituals.* New York: Harmony Books, 1987. 210p. $15.00. ISBN 0-517-56653-2.

Tuleja has compiled and categorized a selection of rituals and customs practiced in everyday life. Categories covered include Etiquette, Holidays, Superstitions, Foodways, and Entertainment. Also included is a bibliography. When possible, origins of customs are included. Tuleja uses a lively narrative and offers his personal conclusions on the origins of some customs. For that reason it may not be considered a historically accurate reference, but it is still interesting, informative, and fun to browse. There is no index, but the table of contents is helpful in locating particular items. Recommended for grade 6 and above.

Search for Customs and Traditions

Name_____ Class_____ Date_____

Use the Reference List for Customs and Traditions to find the answers to the following questions.

1. When is St. Anthony's Day, and how is it usually celebrated in Mexico?

   _____

   _____

   _____

2. How did gift wrapping presents become a custom in America?

   _____

   _____

   _____

3. According to Chinese tradition, why may a bride wear a red dress on her wedding day?

   _____

   _____

   _____

4. If your family wanted to create a new tradition marking your milestones in school, they might decide to use a learning jar. Describe how this can be used as an everyday family tradition.

   _____

   _____

   _____

5. Which popular Christmas tradition is part of midwinter celebrations in *Sir Gawain and the Green Knight*?

   _____

   _____

   _____

6. According to tradition, what must one do on St. Patrick's Day to make cabbage grow?

_____

_____

_____

7. Why is a large rope or rosary wrapped in a figure eight around the shoulders of a Hispanic couple at their wedding?

_____

_____

_____

8. What are the simple guidelines for correct behavior at public places of recreation?

_____

_____

_____

9. What is Colcannon? How is it associated with Halloween?

_____

_____

_____

10. When and why was the custom of singing telegrams started?

_____

_____

_____

Little-Known or
Unusual Celebrations

Some of the special days in this search are important to a specific group or culture. Others are just for fun. Are there any here that you will start celebrating?

Reference List for Little-Known or Unusual Celebrations

Anyike, James C. *African American Holidays*. Chicago: Popular Truth, 1991. 102p. $7.95. ISBN 0-9631547-0-2.

Anyike's work devotes each chapter to a specific celebration with one exception—Chapter One presents a historical perspective on several holidays that came about during slavery. Chapters Two through Eight focus on celebrations for Black History Month, Malcolm X Day, and Juneteenth National Freedom Day, to name a few. Biographic and historical information are presented for each holiday, and suggestions for celebrating them are offered. Appendixes include Important Dates in African American History, the Historic Origin of Popular American Holidays, a Bibliography, and Organizations. As the author points out, many of these celebrations are unknown to mainstream Americans. Anyike's work presents insightful information about these holidays. Recommended for grade 5 and above.

Barkin, Carol, and Elizabeth James. *The Holiday Handbook*. New York: Clarion, 1994. 241p. $16.95. ISBN 0-395-65011-9.

Barkin and James have written several books together. In this one, they present information on secular holidays and suggest activities for celebration. Along with more well-known holidays—such as Martin Luther King Day and Flag Day—the authors provide details and activities for National Grouch Day, International Lefthanders Day, and Mother Goose Day. The book is arranged by seasons beginning with autumn. The introductions for each season provide information on various religious holidays that are celebrated at that time. There is an appendix of sources where one may write for further information on various holidays. Also provided are a selective bibliography and an index. Written for students, this book is recommended for grade 5 and above.

Dunkling, Leslie. *A Dictionary of Days*. New York: Facts on File, 1988. 156p. $18.95. ISBN 0-8160-1916-9.

Many days alluded to in American and British literature are found in Dunkling's work, particularly in her introduction. Though not as comprehensive as other books of days, this work makes mention of ethnic events, folkloric events, and food and drink days. There is also a section on generic terms and verbal expressions. There are black-and-white illustrations, a calendar, and cross-references. However, there is no index. Literary allusions make this a unique book of days. Written for a general audience but appropriate for grade 5 and above.

Hatch, Jane M., comp. and ed. *The American Book of Days*. 3rd ed. New York: H. W. Wilson, 1978. 1,214p. $102.75. ISBN 0-8242-0593-6.

This well-known reference was first published in 1937. It lists American holidays, describes religious traditions, and provides commemorative dates. Also included are articles on the history of states in the union, coverage of wars, and a selection of biographies of presidents of the United States. Information on celebrations, festivals, and observances is provided as well. A day-by-day table of contents and an index make this work easily accessible. There is also a lengthy appendix that discusses calendars, eras, days of the week, and signs of the zodiac. An excellent reference written for general readers, this work is appropriate for grade 5 and above.

MacDonald, Margaret Read, ed. *The Folklore of World Holidays*. Detroit: Gale Research, 1992. 739p. $110.00. ISBN 0-8103-7577-X.

Arranged according to the calendar, this work covers various religious, seasonal, and agricultural holidays. Entries are arranged by country for holidays celebrated worldwide. Sources are listed for each section, and direct quotations are used whenever possible. A detailed subject index provides easy access. The introduction discusses various calendars used throughout history. This is a unique resource for world holidays and a splendid collection of folklore. It is an excellent reference and fun to browse. Recommended for grade 5 and above.

Thompson, Sue Ellen, and Barbara W. Carlson, comp. *Holidays, Festivals, and Celebrations of the World Dictionary*. 2nd ed. Detroit: Omnigraphics, 1997. 822p. $88.00. ISBN 0-7808-0074-5.

Intended for use in school and public libraries, this work details more than 1,400 holidays, rituals, and other important events. Most entries are one or two paragraphs, with major holidays such as Christmas receiving a full page of coverage. In addition to its alphabetical listing of holidays, there are listings of legal holidays by state and country, a discussion of calendar systems around the world, and a bibliography. A special subject index lists folkloric, historic, calendar, sporting, ancient and pagan, and promotional events. Other indexes cover fixed and movable days and major religious groups. There are extensive general and keyword indexes. Comprehensive and highly recommended, this work is recommended for grade 5 and above.

Search for Little-Known or Unusual Celebrations

Name_____ Class_____ Date_____

Use the Reference List for Little-Known or Unusual Celebrations to find answers to questions about these celebrations.

1. Why do Jewish people celebrate the Blessing of the Sun only once every 28 years on a Wednesday?

_____

_____

_____

2. Where is a Daffodil Festival held? Why is it held there?

_____

_____

_____

3. What is significant about how long Juneteenth has been celebrated? When is it celebrated?

_____

_____

_____

4. When is Dictionary Day? Why is it celebrated on that particular day?

_____

_____

_____

5. Chester Greenwood Day is celebrated on the first Saturday in December in Farmington, Maine. Why and how is Chester Greenwood honored?

_____

_____

_____

6. Find the name of the author who refers to Unbirthday in his work.

_____

_____

_____

7. Chinese and Korean people celebrate an unusual feast on March 5. Name it.

_____

_____

_____

8. Khamis al-Amuwat is celebrated by Muslims. By what other name is this day known?

_____

_____

_____

9. What is Multitude's Idle Day? When is it celebrated?

_____

_____

_____

10. Which group of Samoans is honored on the second Sunday in October?

_____

_____

_____

Mysterious and Notorious

Many of the works listed for this search can be found in the 300 section of the library. They were discovered while looking for works related to folklore and holidays. The one thing these works have in common is that they all deal with villainous or notorious characters. A few titles found in other areas of the library have been added to the list. As in most other areas, the focus is multicultural. This list consists of only a few reference books; others circulate, making these books available for home use. For those interested in vampires, werewolves, ghosts, and other unsavory or otherworldly characters, this search should be fun.

Reference List for Mysterious and Notorious

Bannatyne, Lesley Pratt. *Halloween: An American Holiday, An American History*. New York: Facts on File, 1990. 180p. $21.95. ISBN 0-8160-1846-4.

Halloween is truly a holiday with customs and traditions from many cultures. This becomes obvious after examining Bannatyne's work. She traces the history of Halloween in this volume and cites traditions brought to America by Irish immigrants as well as customs followed by the Puritans and traditions observed in the Ozarks and Appalachians. Various chapters in the book deal with these customs and traditions. Other topics discussed include the Victorian era and the twentieth century. Also included are several black-and-white illustrations, poems, stories, and an extensive bibliography. Recommended for general readers and students in grade 8 and above.

Bunson, Matthew. *The Vampire Encyclopedia*. New York: Crown Trade Paperbacks, 1993. 303p. $16.00. ISBN 0-517-88100-4.

Intended as a handy reference source on vampires, this work provides information on vampires and related material. Areas covered include literature, folklore, poetry, art, medicine, religion, and comedy. The book is arranged alphabetically and has three appendixes of related reading, a list of societies and organizations, and several black-and-white photographs and illustrations. Intended for general readers, this work is also fun to browse. Recommended for grade 8 and above.

Cohen, Daniel. *The Encyclopedia of Ghosts*. New York: Avon, 1991. 260p. $4.99. ISBN 0-380-71484-1.

Cohen has authored several works on what is referred to as parapsychology. This one is a collection of ghost stories, some of which date back 400 years. Cohen uses eight categories to arrange his collection; among them are Famous Ghosts and Ghosts of the Famous, Animal Ghosts, Hauntings, and Ghostly Legends. There is a section of black-and-white photographs and illustrations and an annotated bibliography. There is no index;

only the table of contents provides accessibility. The title is misleading in that this work, a paperback, is a collection of ghost stories rather than an A-to-Z collection of material and terms related to ghosts. However, Cohen is a popular young adult author, and this work should be enjoyed by his fans as well as by those who enjoy ghost stories. Recommended for grade 7 and above.

————. *Werewolves*. New York: Dutton, 1996. 117p. $14.95. ISBN 0-525-65207-8.

Cohen presents an interesting discussion of werewolves in his introduction, touching on Hollywood and literary treatments of the subject. Also discussed are medical and scientific explanations of werewolves. Chapters retell various werewolf stories, such as "The Christmas Werewolf" and "The Werewolf in Washington Square." There is even a chapter on werewolves on the Internet. Like many other of Cohen's works, this one is written for young adults. A selected bibliography has been included. Recommended for grade 7 and above.

De Sola, Ralph. *Crime Dictionary*. New York: Facts on File, 1988. 223p. $24.95. ISBN 0-8160-1872-3.

A compilation of more than 10,000 terms used by criminals and those who catch them, this work consists of legal, medical, and law-enforcement terms as well as slang. Also included are acronyms, abbreviations, nicknames, and historical entries. The entries are in bold print and followed by a definition. Foreign terms and place-name nicknames are found in a separate section. Also included is an annotated bibliography. This work is a must-have for crime buffs but also a fun-to-browse book for general readers. Recommended for grade 7 and above.

Long, Kim. *The Almanac of Anniversaries*. Santa Barbara, CA: ABC-CLIO, 1992. 270p. $40.00. ISBN 0-87436-675-5.

This unique book is not devoted solely to notorious or mysterious characters; however, it does mark anniversaries of a wide selection of events. The chronological arrangement allows readers to select a year and see which anniversaries occur in that year. For example, 1996 marked the 25-year ban on radio and television advertisement of cigarettes. The years covered are 1993 through 2001, but anniversaries date back 500 years and more. The bulk of information relates to events in the United States, but significant international events have been included as well. Topics include U.S. history, births and deaths of famous people, business, inventions, music, literature, and unusual events. The user's guide is clear, explaining the book's special features, such as Significant Anniversary Milestones and Milestone Stars. There is a Calendar Locator, an index, and a bibliography. Written for general readers, this work should appeal to interested readers in grade 6 and above.

Mahoney, M. H. *Women in Espionage: A Biographical Dictionary*. Santa Barbara, CA: ABC-CLIO, 1993. 253p. $65.00. ISBN 0-87436-743-3.

Arranged alphabetically, this volume lists biographical sketches of more than 150 women involved in espionage. Most entries range from half a page to two pages. Entries list given name, other names used, and places and dates of birth and death. Sketches provide details of the subject's early life, family life, and circumstances that led to her activities in espionage. Mahoney's narrative is straightforward and lively. Sources and related publications are listed at the end of each sketch. Several black-and-white photographs, a bibliography, a list of acronyms and abbreviations, and an index are provided as well. Written for general readers, this book is recommended for grade 7 and above.

Marley, David L. *Pirates and Privateers of the Americas*. Santa Barbara, CA: ABC-CLIO, 1994. 458p. $75.00. ISBN 0-874-367514.

A biographical encyclopedia, this work contains an A-to-Z listing of well-known and lesser-known buccaneers of the mid-seventeenth to early eighteenth centuries. Included as well are entries on battles, weapons, and ship terms. Entries include explanations as well as excerpts of journals and letters. There are cross-references, an index, and a bibliography. Also included is a section of black-and-white illustrations. Recommended for grade 7 and above.

Platt, Richard. Photographed by Tina Chambers. *Pirate*. (Eyewitness Books). New York: Alfred A. Knopf, 1995. 64p. $19.00. ISBN 0-679-87255-8.

Eyewitness Books are popular with readers because of the numerous illustrations. This one is no exception. There are many excellent illustrations in color and black-and-white of authentic memorabilia related to piracy. The book is arranged so that one or two pages are devoted to an aspect of the subject. Text and illustrations are used to present an accurate representation of each aspect chosen. Among topics discussed in this book are "Pirates in Film and Theatre," "Food on Board," "Women Pirates," and "Pirates in Literature." The quality and quantity of the illustrations make this series fascinating for readers of all ages. Recommended for grade 5 and above.

Wilcox, Charlotte. *Mummies and Their Mysteries*. Minneapolis, MN: Carolrhoda Books, 1993. 64p. $7.95. ISBN 0-87614-767-8.

Although it is only 64 pages long, this work presents a look at mummies around the world. There are color and black-and-white photographs and illustrations on every page. Wilcox discusses mummies around the world and mummies preserved in ice and even provides instructions on how to make an Egyptian mummy. There is a glossary, an index, and a list of places where mummies can be seen in the United States. Recommended for grade 5 and above.

Search for Mysterious and Notorious

Name_____ Class_____ Date_____

Use the Reference List for Mysterious and Notorious to find answers to questions about notorious or villainous characters.

1. In what three states have mummies been found?

    _____

    _____

    _____

2. What is a wooden kimono?

    _____

    _____

    _____

3. Ghosts of famous people are believed to return to various New York City locations on Halloween. What does the ghost of Aaron Burr do?

    _____

    _____

    _____

4. Where was the geographic location of the Spanish Main, a term for waters often sailed by pirates?

    _____

    _____

    _____

5. How and why are fishnets used to protect people from vampires?

    _____

    _____

    _____

From *Multicultural Information Quests* by Marie E. Rodgers. © 2000 Libraries Unlimited. (800) 237-6124.

6. Marie Laveau, a voodoo queen of New Orleans, has been said to appear near the cemetery where her body is buried. According to one story, what did her ghost do to someone who failed to recognize her?

_____

_____

_____

7. How do a person's fingers or hands indicate that he or she is a werewolf?

_____

_____

_____

8. The year 2000 marks the 300-year anniversary of the trial of William Kidd. Of what crime was he convicted, and by what other name is he known?

_____

_____

_____

9. Jesse Jordan, a Scot, was married to a German during World War II. What type of business did she use to hide her espionage activities?

_____

_____

_____

10. The skull and crossbones was usually found on the flag of a pirate ship. However, there was an even more fearful flag. Describe it, and tell what it meant.

_____

_____

_____

Superstitions and Curiosities

When students think of folklore, they usually focus on tales and stories. There are many anthologies of folklore, and students may recognize them readily. However, folklore also consists of superstitions, old wives' tales, traditions, and other curious bits of information. The books on this list reflect this aspect of folklore. The list includes a few familiar standard references on folklore as well as collections of folklore on flowers, food, and medicine.

Reference List for Superstitions and Curiosities

American Folklore and Legend. Pleasantville, NY: Reader's Digest Association, 1979. 448p. ISBN 0-8957-7045-8

Folklore and legend make up only part of this book. Fact, fiction, and tradition are included here as well. Arranged chronologically, this work is an anthology of popular American stories, poems, tales, songs, and other information. There are several black-and-white and color illustrations. There is also a guide to folk events in the United States. Sidebar articles called Folkways and Fact and Fiction provide information on related topics. Recommended for grade 5 and above.

Gay, Kathlyn. Debbie Palon, ill. *Keep the Buttered Side Up: Food Superstitions from Around the World*. New York: Walker and Company, 1995. 102p. $15.95. ISBN 0-8027-8228-0.

Customs, beliefs, and superstitions related to food are the focus of this book. There are numerous bits of food trivia from around the world. For example, there is a section on the origin of the fortunes in fortune cookies. There are 13 chapters in all, each devoted to a specific type of food or a particular aspect of eating. There are chapters on beef, cakes and cookies, vegetables, nuts, and dairy food. There is a chapter on Table Talk and another that asks Are You Superstitious? Special features include Tidbits, which are sidebars containing food facts, myths, and trivia. The black-and-white illustrations are lively and enhance the text. This is a fascinating book for all ages even though it is written for students. Recommended for grade 5 and above.

Leach, Maria, ed. *Funk and Wagnalls Standard Dictionary of Folklore, Mythology, and Legend*. San Francisco: HarperSanFrancisco, 1984. 1,236p. $44.00. ISBN 0-06-250511-4.

This classic reference work, originally published in two volumes, is now a single volume. Arranged alphabetically, it contains information on gods, folk heroes, cultural heroes, and tricksters as well as the folklore of animals, plants, gems, dances, festivals, foods, customs, and games. There are several lengthy survey articles on various topics and cultures. There is a key to countries, regions, cultures, and ethnic groups. This is a well-known and popular reference, appealing to scholar and general reader alike. It is clearly written and easily accessible. Recommended for grade 5 and above.

Opie, Iona, and Moira Tatem, eds. *A Dictionary of Superstitions*. New York: Oxford University Press, 1989. 494p. $30.00. ISBN 0-19-211597-9.

Superstitions are an important part of folklore. This volume has a wide range of entries relating to cures, spells, and signs; the significance of color, plants, stones, and animals; and the lore of sailors, actors, and farmers. Many seasonal customs are also discussed. Superstitions are arranged alphabetically with quotations and sources listed when possible. There is a select bibliography and an analytical index that contains cross-references and thematic entries. Written for general readers but appropriate for grade 6 and above.

Powell, Claire. *The Meaning of Flowers*. London: Jupiter Books, 1977. 182p. ISBN 0-904041-87-5.

Powell traces the meaning or sentiment attached to specific flowers in this work. Her introduction provides a historical perspective. The work is arranged alphabetically, and each entry offers not only the flower's meaning but also its historical significance. Powell provides information on how the plant or flower may be or has been used. There is also a section on sentiments that flowers may express. Illustrations are red or green in color and designed from woodcuts. This book is written for adults, but the content should appeal to students as well. While most of the book is devoted to the alphabetical list of flowers and the meanings attached to them, lore, poetry, mythology, and botany all play an important role in the content of this book. Recommended for grade 6 and above.

Rinzler, Carol Ann. *Feed a Cold, Starve a Fever: A Dictionary of Medical Folklore*. New York: Ballantine Books, 1991. 286p. $4.99. ISBN 0-345-38012-6.

As the title suggests, this book is devoted to folklore as it relates to common ailments. Home remedies, folk cures, old wives' tales, and other beliefs are all listed alphabetically. For example, under hiccups several cures are listed. The author presents information on why the cure may or may not work. While browsing through the book, one finds many familiar home remedies. This work is fun to read and informative. Written for general readers but appropriate for grade 6 and above.

Search for Superstitions and Curiosities

Name_____ Class_____ Date_____

Use the Reference List for Superstitions and Curiosities to find the answers to these questions about traditions and superstitions.

1. According to Cajun superstition, what happens to a person who falls asleep in the moonlight?

   _____

   _____

   _____

2. Is it true that lemon juice, buttermilk, or yogurt can make freckles disappear?

   _____

   _____

   _____

3. With which part of the body is the gem opal associated? According to folklore, what effect does the opal have?

   _____

   _____

   _____

4. According to superstition, why should a person never use his or her left hand to stir with a spoon in a cup?

   _____

   _____

   _____

5. What does the flower lily of the valley signify?

   _____

   _____

   _____

6. According to American folklore, is it a fact or myth that pirates walked the plank?

_____

_____

_____

7. How did the belief that red cars are lucky come about?

_____

_____

_____

8. Use a list of attributes associated with flowers to describe three to five aspects of your personality.

_____

_____

_____

9. What is a superstition among sailors regarding the presence of children on a ship?

_____

_____

_____

10. Why, according to folklore, should one never kick a cat?

_____

_____

_____

Holiday Celebrations in Multicultural America

The concept that America is a mosaic of cultures is never more evident than in the observance of holidays. Religious and cultural holiday celebrations reflect the diversity of Americans. The references and questions in this section illustrate not only various cultural traditions but also provide information on such truly American holidays as Independence Day and Flag Day.

Reference List for Holiday Celebrations

Anyike, James C. *African American Holidays*. Chicago: Popular Truth, 1991. 102p. $7.95. ISBN 0-9631547-0-2.

Anyike's work devotes each chapter to a specific celebration with one exception. Chapter One presents a historical perspective on several holidays that came about during slavery. Chapters Two through Eight focus on celebrations for Black History Month, Malcolm X Day, and Juneteenth National Freedom Day, to name a few. Biographic and historical information are presented for each holiday, and suggestions for celebrating them are offered. Appendixes include Important Dates in African American History, the Historic Origin of Popular American Holidays, a Bibliography, and Organizations. As the author points out, many of these celebrations are unknown to mainstream Americans. Anyike's work presents insightful information about these holidays. Recommended for grade 5 and above.

Appelbaum, Diane Karter. *Thanksgiving: An American Holiday, An American History*. New York: Facts on File, 1984. 305p. $15.95. ISBN 0-87196-794-2.

Appelbaum traces the history of Thanksgiving and the various ways it has been observed in America. Starting with the first Thanksgiving, the author describes the holiday as celebrated in New England—A Yankee Army Camp—and in the West by pioneers. The author parallels the evolution of the holiday with the growth of the country. The work presents several little-known facts, includes black-and-white photographs and illustrations, and presents a culinary history in an appendix. There is an annotated bibliography for each chapter and an index. Appelbaum has compiled an impressive set of facts and details on a favorite American holiday. Recommended for grade 6 and above.

Bannatyne, Lesley Pratt. *Halloween: An American Holiday, An American History*. New York: Facts on File, 1990. 180p. $21.95. ISBN 0-8160-1846-4.

Halloween is truly a holiday with customs and traditions from many cultures. This becomes obvious after examining Bannatyne's work. She traces the history of Halloween in this volume and cites traditions brought to America by Irish immigrants as well as customs followed by the Puritans and traditions observed in the Ozarks and Appalachians. Various chapters in the book deal with these customs and traditions. Other topics discussed include the Victorian era and the twentieth century. Also included are several black-and-white illustrations, poems, stories, and an extensive bibliography. Recommended for general readers and students in grade 8 and above.

Barkin, Carol, and Elizabeth James. *The Holiday Handbook*. New York: Clarion, 1994. 241p. $16.95. ISBN 0-395-65011-9.

Barkin and James have written several books together. In this one, they present information on secular holidays and suggest activities for celebration. Along with more well-known holidays—such as Martin Luther King Day and Flag Day—the authors provide details and activities for National Grouch Day, International Lefthanders Day, and Mother Goose Day. The book is arranged by seasons beginning with autumn. The introductions for each season provide information on various religious holidays that are celebrated at that time. There is an appendix of sources where one may write for further information on various holidays. Also provided are a selective bibliography and an index. Written for students, this book is recommended for grade 5 and above.

Berg, Elizabeth. *Family Traditions: Celebrations for Holidays and Everyday*. Pleasantville, NY: Reader's Digest Association, 1992. 287p. $12.95. ISBN 0-895-77626-X.

Berg, while she recognizes the need for traditions, devotes much of her work to creating new traditions. She has compiled a list of activities and rituals that she feels may become family traditions. The focus here is on family, and in her introduction, Berg addresses what "family" may mean in today's world. Sections are devoted to everyday traditions, seasonal celebrations, family holidays, weddings, birthdays, and births. There are directions and recipes for many celebrations, including ideas for block parties, reunions, and milestones in school. Recipes and activities also appear in sidebars, and there are several sepia-toned illustrations. Recommended for grade 5 and above.

Coffin, Tristram Potter. *The Book of Christmas Folklore*. New York: Seabury Press, 1973. 192p. $22.00. ISBN 0-8164-9158-5.

Coffin is a well-known folklorist, and although this book is more than 20 years old, it is still on the shelves of many public and school libraries. The book consists of eight chapters dealing with many aspects of Christmas. Separate indexes for persons (real and fictional), places and subjects, and various titles make this work easily accessible. Coffin covers several themes, including superstition, the Christmas tree, cards, and food and drink. The work is well researched, and Coffin's writing is lively and engaging. Recommended for grade 5 and above.

Cohen, Henning, and Tristram Potter Coffin, eds. *The Folklore of American Holidays*. Detroit: Gale Research, 1987. 431p. $80.00. ISBN 0-8103-2126-2.

Folklore related to given holidays whether old or new, religious or secular, well-known or obscure is the focus of this work. Chronologically arranged, each entry contains the name of the holiday, its date or time frame, its origin, historical background, and other pertinent information. Entries also contain source and comment sections that provide bibliographic and collection information, cross-references, and related commentary. There are several indexes in this work that provide easy access. They include Subject Index; Ethnic or Geographical Index; Collectors, Informants, and Translators Index; Song Titles and First Significant Lines Index; and, finally, Motifs and Tale Types Index. The introduction discusses development of calendars, festivals, and customs. Coffin is a widely known and well-respected folklorist. This work is a credit to his expertise in the subject. It reflects a diversity of ethnic and religious celebrations, making it not only a "day" book but also an excellent multicultural collection of folklore and a fairly comprehensive reference. Many specific references are made to such things as Thanksgiving Day parades in various cities, recipes for food served at a Hindu celebration, and many ethnic folktales. The editors even describe ethnic holidays as celebrated in a particular city or community. This is also fun to browse. Recommended for grade 5 and above.

Gross, David C. *1,001 Questions and Answers About Judaism*. Revised ed. New York: Hippocrene Books, 1990. 322p. $9.95. ISBN 0-87052-626-X.

Gross' work consists of 10 chapters arranged by topic. Personal Life, The Synagogue, The Sabbath, Jewish History, and Israel are a few. Additionally, there are 100 questions and answers for the 1990s, a bibliography, a glossary, and an index. The question-and-answer format makes this work interesting to browse. However, Gross has provided readers with a vast amount of information. His work serves as a reference and handbook for anyone interested in Judaism. The index makes the book easily accessible. Recommended for grade 5 and above.

Hatch, Jane M., comp. and ed. *The American Book of Days*. 3rd ed. New York: H. W. Wilson, 1978. 1,214p. $102.75. ISBN 0-8242-0593-6.

This well-known reference was first published in 1937. It lists American holidays, describes religious traditions, and provides commemorative dates. Also included are articles on the history of the states in the union, coverage of wars, and a selection of biographies of presidents of the United States. Information on celebrations, festivals, and observances is provided as well. A day-by-day table of contents and an index make this work easily accessible. There is also a lengthy appendix that discusses calendars, eras, days of the week, and signs of the zodiac. An excellent reference written for general readers, this work is appropriate for grade 5 and above.

Thompson. Sue Ellen, ed. *Holiday Symbols*. Detroit: Omnigraphics, 1998. 558p. $55.00. ISBN 0-7808-0072-9.

Symbols associated with 200 popular holidays are arranged alphabetically by holiday name. Each entry consists of the name of the holiday and an alternate name or spelling if any, type of holiday, date of observation, and where the holiday is celebrated. Origins and symbols are discussed, and works for further reading are listed. Cross-references, a general index, and a symbol index provide easy access. This work is unique in that the symbols are the major focus. Many holidays are based on legend, folklore, or tradition, and the essays in this book trace their evolution to modern times. Secular, religious, and cultural holidays are included. Written for general readers, this work is useful to students, teachers, and librarians. Recommended for grade 5 and above.

Search for Holiday Celebrations

Name_____ Class_____ Date_____

Use the Reference List for Holiday Celebrations to find answers to these questions. The answers may be found in more than one source.

1. During Rosh Hashanah some Jewish people eat carrots. Why?

   _____

   _____

   _____

2. When and why was Umoja Karamou, an African American holiday, conceived?

   _____

   _____

   _____

3. President Franklin Delano Roosevelt issued a proclamation that changed the day when Thanksgiving is observed. Which organization successfully requested that the holiday be moved ahead one week? Why was the request made?

   _____

   _____

   _____

4. When and where did Memorial Day begin?

   _____

   _____

   _____

5. Over the years, Independence Day has developed into a weeklong celebration in Philadelphia. What is the name of this weeklong celebration?

   _____

   _____

   _____

6. What city holds a Fantasy Festival on Halloween?

_____

_____

_____

7. May 5 is marked by celebrations of many ethnic groups. Name the celebration and ethnicity of each group who celebrates on this day.

_____

_____

_____

8. Who founded Labor Day?

_____

_____

_____

9. Tet, a seven-day festival, is celebrated by which ethnic group? What is the full-moon name of the celebration? What is celebrated?

_____

_____

_____

10. First footing is a New Year's Day tradition originating in Scotland. What is the significance?

_____

_____

_____

Celebrations of Light

This search focuses on only four holidays: Diwali or Divali, Hanukkah, Kwanzaa, and Christmas. These celebrations all have at least two things in common: They occur around the same time of year, and light is a significant part of the celebration. Many students are probably familiar with this aspect of these holidays. Therefore, with one exception, the questions in this search focus on various other aspects of the celebrations.

Reference List for Celebrations of Light

Bragdon, Allen. *Joy Through the World*. New York: Dodd, Mead, 1985. 167p. $19.95. ISBN 0-916410-26-9.

Fifteen celebrations around the world are detailed in this work. Most of them relate to Christmas, but there are sections on Hanukkah, Kwanzaa, and Diwali. Each holiday is detailed with a brief history followed by sections such as Celebration, Feasting, and Giving. There are several color and black-and-white photographs and illustrations, recipes, and directions for crafts associated with the holiday. An index is provided as well. Written for the general reader, this work should also appeal to grade 5 and above.

Coffin, Tristram Potter. *The Book of Christmas Folklore*. New York: Seabury Press, 1973. 192p. $22.00. ISBN 0-8164-9158-5.

Coffin is a well-known folklorist, and although this book is more than 20 years old, it is still on the shelves of many public and school libraries. The book consists of eight chapters dealing with many aspects of Christmas. Separate indexes for persons (real and fictional), places and subjects, and various titles make this work easily accessible. Coffin covers several themes, including superstition, the Christmas tree, cards, and food and drink. The work is well researched, and Coffin's writing is lively and engaging. Recommended for grade 5 and above.

Cohen, Henning, and Tristram Potter Coffin, eds. *The Folklore of American Holidays*. Detroit: Gale Research, 1987. 431p. $80.00. ISBN 0-8103-2126-2.

Folklore related to given holidays whether old or new, religious or secular, well-known or obscure is the focus of this work. Chronologically arranged, each entry contains the name of the holiday, its date or time frame, its origin, historical background, and other pertinent information. Entries also contain source and comment sections that provide bibliographic and collection information, cross-references, and related commentary. There are several indexes in this work that provide easy access. They include Subject Index;

Ethnic or Geographical Index; Collectors, Informants, and Translators Index; Song Titles and First Significant Lines Index; and, finally, Motifs and Tale Types Index. The introduction discusses development of calendars, festivals, and customs. Coffin is a widely known and well-respected folklorist. This work is a credit to his expertise in the subject. It reflects a diversity of ethnic and religious celebrations, making it not only a "day" book but also an excellent multicultural collection of folklore and a fairly comprehensive reference. Many specific references are made to such things as Thanksgiving Day parades in various cities, recipes for food served at a Hindu celebration, and many ethnic folktales. The editors even describe ethnic holidays as celebrated in a particular city or community. This is also fun to browse. Recommended for grade 5 and above.

Copiage, Eric V. *Kwanzaa: An African-American Celebration of Culture and Cooking*. New York: Quill, 1991. 356p. $12.00. ISBN 0-688-12835-1.

Copiage has compiled a fascinating array of information and recipes. His introduction explains not only how his family came to celebrate Kwanzaa but also how the family celebration has evolved over the years. Chapters are arranged by category of food, such as Appetizers, Main Dishes, and Beverages. Vignettes explaining the origins of recipes are interspersed throughout the book. Each chapter begins with an explanation of the seven principles and provides stories that illustrate them. Copiage's work is excellent as a cultural resource and as a cookbook. It should appeal to anyone interested in either. An epilogue explains how the meaning of Kwanzaa may vary from child to adult to elder. In addition, there is a section of menus, a glossary of foods, and an index. Recommended reading for grade 6 and above.

Gross, David C. *1,001 Questions and Answers About Judaism*. Revised ed. New York: Hippocrene Books, 1990. 322p. $9.95. ISBN 0-87052-626-X.

Gross' work consists of 10 chapters arranged by topic. Personal Life, The Synagogue, The Sabbath, Jewish History, and Israel are a few. Additionally, there are 100 questions and answers for the 1990s, a bibliography, a glossary, and an index. The question-and-answer format makes this work interesting to browse. However, Gross has provided readers with a vast amount of information. His work serves as a reference and handbook for anyone interested in Judaism. The index makes the book easily accessible. Recommended for grade 5 and above.

Harris, Jessica B. *A Kwanzaa Keepsake: Celebrating the Holiday with New Traditions and Feasts*. New York: Simon & Schuster, 1995. 176p. $22.00. ISBN 0-684-80045-4.

This day-by-day guide presents an explanation of the principles of Kwanzaa. Chapter One explains the celebration, Chapter Two tells how to prepare for it, and the remainder of the book has a chapter devoted to each of the seven days of Kwanzaa. Each chapter opens with an explanation of the meaning behind that day's celebration. Harris then presents biographical sketches of famous or historical figures that demonstrate the principle. For example, on the fifth night *Nia* ("purpose") is celebrated. Sketches on Toussaint L'Ouverture and Thurgood Marshall demonstrate purpose. Following these sketches is a menu with recipes for that night's feast. Finally, each chapter ends with a project that also focuses on the principle being celebrated. Blank pages are provided for one's own family recipes. Recommended for grade 5 and above.

Schauss, Hayim. *The Jewish Festivals: A Guide to Their History and Observance.* New York: Schocken Books, 1996. 317p. $15.00. ISBN 0-805-20937-9.

Beginning with the Sabbath and moving chronologically through the year, Schauss devotes several chapters to each celebration. Ancient Times, Development, Modern Times, and Custom and Ceremony are detailed. This work is very comprehensive. There is a chapter devoted to minor festivals and an index. Not only does this work provide information on Jewish celebrations, it also serves as an introduction to ideas and values found in Judaism. Recommended for grade 6 and above.

Search for Celebrations of Light

Name_____ Class_____ Date_____

Use the Reference List for Celebrations of Light to find answers to these questions about holidays you or your friends may observe. It is likely that more than one source will have the answer to some questions.

1. Why are cheese dishes served for Hanukkah?

   _____

   _____

   _____

2. Who designed the first Christmas card?

   _____

   _____

   _____

3. Diwali, sometimes spelled Divali, is a festival of light celebrated in India. Name the small lamps used in this festival.

   _____

   _____

   _____

4. Why is the number seven significant in the celebration of Kwanzaa?

   _____

   _____

   _____

5. According to folklore, what special talent does a child born on Christmas day have?

   _____

   _____

   _____

6. When was the first Hanukkah celebration held?

_____

_____

_____

7. In one source on Kwanzaa, the author prints an excerpt from Malcolm X's autobiography. What principles of Kwanzaa does it illustrate?

_____

_____

_____

8. How do people in India prepare their homes for Diwali?

_____

_____

_____

9. In Israel there is a public observance of Hanukkah. What is it?

_____

_____

_____

10. What is celebrated on the sixth night of Kwanzaa?

_____

_____

_____

Answer Key for Customs and Traditions

1. In Silverthorne. January 17 is St. Anthony's Day. Ribbons and flowers are placed on pets, which are taken to the church to be blessed.
2. In Tuleja. Retailers began this custom when store-bought gifts replaced handmade gifts. They felt it would make up for the lack of the personal touch.
3. In Barillo. Red symbolizes love and joy.
4. In Berg. Each day after school, the child writes down one thing he or she learned that day. At the end of the school year, the jar is emptied, and everyone takes turns reading the contents of the jar aloud.
5. In Coffin. Singing carols is mentioned.
6. In Cohen and Coffin. One must sow cabbage seed in pajamas or bed clothing.
7. In Barillo. It symbolizes the union between them.
8. In Post. Don't crowd other people. Clean up after yourself. Keep all noises, including radios, to your own space.
9. In Thompson. Made of mashed potatoes, parsnips, and onions, it is served in Ireland. Items hidden in it include coins, which bring wealth to the finder; rings, which indicate marriage; a doll, which indicates children; and a thimble, which indicates spinsterhood.
10. In Tuleja. The Postal Telegraph Company started it in 1933 as a way of improving their business during the Great Depression.

Answer Key for Little-Known or Unusual Celebrations

1. In Thompson and Carlson. The sun returns to the same position it held during the fourth day of creation once every 28 years. The last Blessing of the Sun was observed on April 8, 1981.
2. In Hatch. It is held in Puyallup Valley, near Tacoma, Washington. There are more than 30 million daffodils in the valley every spring.
3. In Anyike. It is the oldest African American observance. It is held on June 19.
4. In Barkin and James. It is October 16. It is the birthday of Noah Webster, who wrote the first dictionary.
5. In Thompson and Carlson. Greenwood invented earmuffs and is remembered with a parade, a flag-raising ceremony, and a footrace.
6. In Dunkling. Lewis Carroll refers to it. Any day other than one's birthday may be celebrated as one's Unbirthday.
7. In MacDonald. It is the Feast of Excited Insects.
8. In Thompson and Carlson. It is also known as Dead Remembrance Day.
9. In Dunkling. It was an alternative name for Christmas used by Puritans.
10. In MacDonald. Known as "White Sunday," it honors children.

Answer Key for Mysterious and Notorious

1. In Wilcox. They have been found in Arizona, Kentucky, and Colorado.
2. In De Sola. A wooden kimono is a coffin.
3. In Bannatyne. Burr's ghost supposedly walks the seawall in Battery Park City looking for his daughter Theodosia.
4. In Marley. The Spanish Main included the northern coast of Panama, Colombia, and the western coast of Venezuela.
5. In Bunson. Fishnets are used in windows, on doors, or in graves to distract vampires. Vampires are obsessive about untangling things.
6. In Cohen, *Ghosts*. The ghost of Laveau supposedly hit the person in the face.
7. In Cohen, *Werewolves*. Two signs are hairy palms and a third finger that is longer than a middle finger.
8. In Long. He was convicted of piracy and murder and is better known as Captain Kidd.
9. In Mahoney. She used a beauty parlor.
10. In Platt. A solid red flag meant death to all who saw it.

Answer Key for Superstitions and Curiosities

1. In *American Folklore*. People who fall asleep in moonlight go crazy.
2. In Rinzler. No.
3. In Leach. Opal strengthens the eyes. It was also called the patron of thieves because it supposedly made anyone wearing it invisible.
4. In Gay. Seven years will be lost from his or her life.
5. In Powell. It signifies the return of happiness.
6. In *American Folklore*. It is probably a myth. It is more likely that the undesirable were merely thrown overboard.
7. In Opie and Tatem. According to a safety report, red cars were in fewer accidents than any other.
8. In Powell. Answers will vary.
9. In Opie and Tatem. Children on a ship bring good luck.
10. In Leach. People who kick cats get rheumatism.

Answer Key for Holiday Celebrations

1. In Gross. In Yiddish the word for carrots, *meren*, means "to increase." Hopefully, one's good deeds will increase in the New Year.
2. In Anyike. Edward Simms, Jr. introduced this day in 1971, and it is observed on the fourth Sunday in November. Its purpose is to reaffirm meaning in African American family life.
3. In Appelbaum. The National Retail Dry Goods Association requested the change so that the holiday shopping season could be extended, resulting in a post-Depression rise in the economy.
4. In Berg. Memorial Day, also called Decoration Day, began two years after the Civil War ended in Columbus, Mississippi.
5. In Hatch. It is called Freedom Week.
6. In Bannatyne. Key West holds the festival.
7. In Cohen and Coffin. Cinquo De Mayo is celebrated by Mexicans and Mexican Americans; Boys Festival, or Festival of Flags and Banners, is celebrated by Japanese and Japanese Americans; and Double Five Day or Dragon Boat Festival is celebrated by Chinese and Chinese Americans.
8. In Barkin and James. Peter McGuire founded the holiday.
9. In Cohen and Coffin. Tet is a Vietnamese celebration of the New Year and the beginning of spring. The full-moon name is Nguyen-Dan.
10. In Thompson. The first person who sets foot in the door after midnight determines the family's luck over the New Year. Fair-haired or redheaded people or women were said to bring bad luck.

Answer Key for Celebrations of Light

1. In Schauss. Eating cheese traces back to the story of Judith, who served cheese to the leader of the enemies of the Jews. As a result, he became thirsty and drank too much wine. When he became drunk, she beheaded him.
2. In Coffin. It was designed by J. C. Horsley in 1843.
3. In Bragdon. Dipa lamps are used.
4. In Harris. There are seven days, seven principles, and seven symbols.
5. In Cohen and Coffin. They can understand the speech of animals.
6. In Gross. It was held in 165 B.C.
7. In Copiage. It illustrates Creativity, *Kuumba*, and Purpose, *Nia*.
8. In Bragdon. Everything in the home is cleaned and polished. The house is decorated with flowers and lights.
9. In Gross and in Bragdon. There is a torchlight race from Modin to Jerusalem.
10. In Copiage and in Harris. *Kuumba*, or creativity, is celebrated.

Chapter Four

Dictionaries and Slang

American language is fascinating and fun to study. The works in this section all deal with some aspect of our language: slang, origin, usage, and idioms. Using these books should be fun. In addition, those who use them will see how colorful our language is and recognize its multicultural origins. The dictionaries used here are only a small sample of the many specialized dictionaries that can be found in the library. The same list may be used for both searches.

Reference List for Dictionaries and Slang

Allen, Irving Lewis. *The City in Slang: New York Life and Popular Speech*. New York: Oxford University Press, 1993. 307p. $12.95. ISBN 0-19-509265-1.

Many words in use today evolved from urban slang. Familiar words include *rush hour* and *hot dog*. This work traces the origin of these words and hundreds of others. Whenever possible, origins are provided for expressions. The work is an excellent source of social history as well. Also included are black-and-white illustrations, references, a bibliography, and indexes of words and phrases and author and subject. The work is not arranged as a dictionary, but the indexes to words and phrases and subject make it easily accessible. Topics include Tall Buildings, Sporting Life, and Contempt for Provincial Life. This work is informative and fun to browse. Recommended for grade 6 and above.

Bernstein, Theodore. *Bernstein's Reverse Dictionary*. 2nd ed. Revised and expanded by David Grambs. New York: Times Books, 1988. 351p. $19.95. ISBN 0-8129-1593-3.

Bernstein's work has been popular with word buffs since its publication. Definitions are listed alphabetically. Grambs has added 2,500 entries. Bernstein's introduction explains how to use his work. There are omnibus listings for phobias, manias, and creature terms as well as for medical terms and U.S. state nicknames. Anyone who has ever asked the question, "What do you call that thing?" will find the answer in this special dictionary. An index to target words helps readers find the answers. Written for general readers, this work is appropriate for grade 6 and above.

Blevins, Winfred. *Dictionary of the American West*. New York: Facts on File, 1993. 400p. $35.00. ISBN 0-8160-2031-0.

More than 5,000 entries related to the American West are presented in alphabetical order. Many ethnic groups made up the American West, and all are represented here. Terms and expressions related to cowboys, Native Americans, ranchers, and gamblers as well as those of various ethnic groups, including African Americans, Hispanics, and immigrants, are presented. There are black-and-white photographs and illustrations and a bibliography as well. The introduction presents an example of a fur trapper whose vocabulary is a mixture of French, English, and Spanish. Entries include a short definition and origin (when possible) as well as a pronunciation key (when necessary). This lively collection is written for general readers, but it is also appropriate for students in grade 6 and above.

De Sola, Ralph, Dean Stahl, and Karen Kerchilich. *Abbreviation Dictionary*. 9th ed. Boca Raton, FL: CRC Press, 1995. 1,347p. $135.00. ISBN 0-8493-8944-5.

Abbreviations, contractions, eponyms, and acronyms are only part of this reference. A broad range of other information is included as well. Computer jargon, ports of the world, railroads, winds of the world, and birthstones of the month are other kinds of information available in this work. A section on superlatives relates mostly to places, but it is worth noting. Also notable is a section titled Bafflegab. Ambiguous and euphemistic expressions fall into this category. For example, in Bafflegab a Baltimore beefsteak is really broiled liver. In the section on how to use the book, there is a list of definitions as well as an explanation of arrangement, capitalization, and punctuation. Written for the general reader, this is an excellent source of information for students in grade 7 and above.

Hendrickson, Robert. *The Facts on File Encyclopedia of Word and Phrase Origins*. Revised and expanded. New York: Facts on File, 1997. 754p. $65.00. ISBN 0-8160-3266-1.

The more than 9,000 entries in this work include slang, animal and plant names, nicknames, historical expressions, and phrases from literature. Most entries range from a few sentences to a paragraph. Hendrickson's writing is lively, and his work appears to be well researched. Entries include plausible theories about words of unknown origin as well as their first recorded use. This is an excellent reference and should appeal to anyone interested in word origins. Recommended for grade 6 and above.

Maggio, Rosalie. *The Dictionary of Bias-Free Usage: A Guide to Nondiscriminatory Language*. Phoenix, AZ: Oryx Press, 1991. 294p. $25.00. ISBN 0-89774-653-8.

The author has compiled 5,000 entries that are in some way considered biased and presents readers with 15,000 alternatives. Categories include terms that refer to various biases against people's race, age, disability, gender, or ethnic origin. Biases in writing are also discussed, and guidelines are presented to help identify and correct them. Under a section called General Rules, the author discusses parallel treatment, feminine endings, and hidden biases. Maggio's work is thorough and thought provoking. Several types of entries are included. Definition entries, occupation entries, and key concept entries are a few. Written for general readers but appropriate for grade 6 and above.

Major, Clarence, comp. and ed. *Juba to Jive: The Dictionary of African American Slang*. New York: Penguin, 1994. 548p. $14.95. ISBN 0-14-051306-X.

Major, a well-respected scholar, has compiled a lexicon of African American slang that includes early rural Southern slang, musician slang, street slang, and working-class slang. Entries include parts of speech, date of origin, and definition. Major presents an informative introduction on slang and African American language in general. Explanatory notes identify geographic locations. There is also an extensive bibliography. This is a fascinating work not only as a slang dictionary but also for its historical information. For example, there is a lengthy entry on the origin of the word *jazz*. Written for anyone interested in slang, African American studies, or language, this work is also recommended for students in grade 6 and above.

Mariani, John. *The Dictionary of American Food and Drink*. New York: Hearst, 1994. 379p. $19.95. ISBN 0-688-10139-9.

Mariani's work consists of more than 2,000 entries about food. The introduction traces the evolution of American cuisine. Mariani explains dish night at movie theaters, describes nouvelle cuisine, and provides hundreds of recipes from New Bedford Pudding to Rice Krispies Treats®. Items related to food slang, anecdotes, and history are included as well. There is a bibliographic guide and an index. The work is written in a lively narrative and is well researched. This is an excellent source of history and lore related to food. Written for food buffs but recommended for grade 6 and above.

Speake, Jennifer, ed. *The Oxford Dictionary of Foreign Words and Phrases*. New York: Oxford University Press, 1997. 512p. $30.00. ISBN 0-19-863159-6.

More than 8,000 entries from more than 40 languages have been covered in this updated work. The emphasis is on words introduced in this century. A pronunciation guide and an appendix that breaks down headwords by country of origin and century of introduction are included. Entries provide pronunciation, part of speech, origin, and definition. This work is informative and fun to browse. Written for general readers, but recommended for grade 5 and above.

Spears, Richard A. *Straight from the Horse's Mouth: And 8,500 Other Colorful Idioms*. Lincolnwood, IL: NTC Publishing, 1996. 532p. $12.95. ISBN 0-8442-0901-5.

Spears' work is limited to idiomatic phrases. A section titled To the User explains entries, and a Phrase-Finder Index is helpful for those who are not sure of the phrase. Entries include meaning, cross-references, comments, and examples. The work is equally useful to native and new speakers of English. Not as comprehensive as other sources, but the Phrase-Finder is an interesting feature. Written for general readers, but appropriate for grade 6 and above.

Search for Dictionaries

Name_____ Class_____ Date_____

Use the Reference List for Dictionaries and Slang to locate the answers to the following questions. You may find answers in more than one source.

1. What do you call the plastic thing at the end of a shoelace?

   _____

   _____

   _____

2. At one time elevators were called birdcages. How did this come about?

   _____

   _____

   _____

3. *Posole* was used in the West. What is it? What is the origin of the word?

   _____

   _____

   _____

4. JLA is an abbreviation of four different library associations. What does the "J" stand for in each?

   _____

   _____

   _____

5. What is the origin of cherry soup?

   _____

   _____

   _____

6. What is the origin of the term Night of the Long Knives?

_____

_____

_____

7. Describe a sweet treat called *linzertorte*.

_____

_____

_____

8. What does it mean to burn with a low blue flame?

_____

_____

_____

9. What is the origin of the term more better or mo' better?

_____

_____

_____

10. What other terms may be used in place of the word fisherman?

_____

_____

_____

Search for Slang

Name_____ Class_____ Date_____

Use the Reference List for Dictionaries and Slang to locate the answers to the following questions. You may find answers in more than one source. There is even one question that has a different answer in a few sources. See if you can find which one it is.

1. What is a nonsexist version of the term lounge lizard?

   _____

   _____

   _____

2. What is the food-related term for the period of one's youthful inexperience?

   _____

   _____

   _____

3. What is a sidewalk superintendent?

   _____

   _____

   _____

4. If someone has been dry gulched, what has happened to that person?

   _____

   _____

   _____

5. What is a cookie pusher?

   _____

   _____

   _____

6. Towel Town is a nickname for what city? Why?

_____

_____

_____

7. What is the first recorded use of the expression relating to a cat's having nine lives?

_____

_____

_____

8. List phrases that make use of the word beans.

_____

_____

_____

9. To what does the slang term Mister Hawkins refer?

_____

_____

_____

10. What are the ingredients in a Hoboken special?

_____

_____

_____

Answer Key for Dictionaries

1. In Bernstein. The plastic end on a shoelace is called an aglet.
2. In Allen. It came about because of the grilled and ornate open ironwork on early elevators.
3. In Blevins. *Posole* is boiled corn and meat cooked to a mush. It is of Spanish origin.
4. In De Sola, Stahl, and Kerchilich. "J" stands for Jamaica, Japan, Jewish, and Jordan.
5. In Mariani. Cherry soup is popular in the Midwest and is probably Scandinavian or Eastern European in origin.
6. In Hendrickson. The original Night of the Long Knives was June 29, 1934, when Hitler jailed or murdered his enemies. It has come to describe any conspiracy created to deal with those whose loyalty is in question.
7. In Speake. It is a pastry with jam filling and a lattice top design.
8. In Spears. It refers to someone who is extremely angry.
9. In Major. It is of Gullah origin.
10. In Maggio. Fisher, angler, fish catcher or fishing licensee are acceptable.

Answer Key for Slang

1. In Maggio. A lounge lizard may be called a social parasite.
2. In Bernstein. It is salad days.
3. In Allen. The term refers to someone watching a construction site.
4. In Blevins. The person has been ambushed by someone who hid and shot him or her in the back after he or she rode by.
5. In Mariani. It is a waitress. However, in other sources a cookie pusher has been defined as a low-level diplomatic employee.
6. In De Sola, Stahl, and Kerchilich. It is a nickname for Kannapolis, North Carolina, location of the Cannon towel factory.
7. In Hendrickson. It was in 1546.
8. In Spears. Some phrases are "full of beans," "don't know beans about," "spill the beans," and "hill of beans."
9. In Major. It refers to a cold winter wind.
10. In Mariani. It is not a slang term but a pineapple soda with a scoop of chocolate ice cream.

Chapter
Five

Great Scientists

This search provides a multicultural focus on great scientists. Several of the books used for this search rank the top 100 names within an ethnic group or gender. The questions in this search highlight achievements of these contributors in the field of science.

Reference List for Great Scientists

Bruno, Leonard C. *Science and Technology Firsts*. Detroit: Gale Research, 1997. 636p. $86.00. ISBN 0-7876-0256-6.

Twelve chapters relating to various fields of scientific endeavor such as astronomy, biology, mathematics, and transportation have been arranged in chronological order. Entries are one paragraph in length and begin with the year of discovery or breakthrough in boldface and provide details. There are also several black-and-white photographs and illustrations. Cross-references exist only within a particular chapter; however, an extensive index helps readers locate information pertaining to more than one area of science. There is also a bibliography. Written for students and general readers, this work is also appropriate for science buffs in grade 5 and above.

Felder, Deborah G. *The 100 Most Influential Women of All Time: A Ranking Past and Present*. New York: Citadel Press, 1996. 374p. $24.95. ISBN 0-8065-1726-3.

Felder has ranked her subjects according to importance. This alone makes her work interesting and provocative. Readers are likely to debate the rankings. Whether or not they agree with the ranking order, readers will recognize that the women here have all made great contributions to the world. Among those listed are Rosa Parks, Freda Kahlo, Bessie Smith, Joan of Arc, and Lucille Ball. The list was compiled by means of a survey sent to Women's Studies departments of American colleges and universities. Using the surveys, Felder devised her list based on whom she felt had the greatest impact on the world. Profiles of the 100 subjects begin with dates of birth and death, a quotation by or about the subject, and a black-and-white photograph or illustration. Most profiles are two to three pages in length. Also included are career highlights, achievements, and personal information. There is an index and a bibliography as well. Recommended for grade 7 and above.

Novas, Himilce. *The Hispanic 100: A Ranking of Latino Men and Women Who Have Most Influenced Thought and Culture*. New York: Citadel Press, 1995. 495p. $24.95. ISBN 0-8065-1651-8.

Hispanic men and women from all fields of endeavor have been ranked according to degree of impact. For the author's purposes, they also had to be considered trailblazers. The introduction provides an explanation of the use of the terms Latino and Hispanic as well as a brief discussion of Latinos in the United States. Entries are two-and-a-half to three pages. A black-and-white photograph or illustration with dates of birth and death begin each entry. Details of childhood, family life, education, career highlights, and honors and awards are also provided. Additionally, a brief discussion of each entrant's influence is presented. There is an index. Novas' writing is clear and straightforward. Recommended for grade 5 and above.

Saari, Peggy, and Stephen Allison, eds. *Scientists: The Lives and Works of 150 Scientists*. Detroit: Gale Research, 1996. 3 vols. $105.00. ISBN 0-7876-0960-9.

Biographical information in this work focuses on personal life as well as on scientific contribution. Each sketch includes black-and-white photographs or illustrations of the scientist, dates of birth and death, early life, contributions, and an Impact box that details the scientific discovery and its impact on the world. There are also bibliographies on each subject and biographical boxes of major influences on a particular scientist's life. The scope of the work is from the Industrial Revolution to the present day. Each volume begins with a complete list of Scientists by Field of Specialization, a Timeline of Scientific Breakthroughs, and Words to Know. There is also a general index. Written for students, this is an excellent reference for grade 5 and above.

Salley, Columbus. *The Black 100: A Ranking of the Most Influential African Americans, Past and Present.* New York: Citadel Press, 1993. 384p. $18.95. ISBN 0-8065-1550-3.

The 100 most influential African Americans are profiled by Salley, who also provides reasons for his rankings. All have been chosen because they greatly changed the lives of all Americans. Each profile begins with a black-and-white photograph, dates of birth and death, and a quotation by or about the subject or his or her contribution. Details of personal life and professional achievements are provided as well as a brief discussion of the entrant's impact on the United States. Salley's writing is clear and insightful. There is also a bibliography and an index. Recommended for grade 5 and above.

Shapiro, Michael. *The Jewish 100: A Ranking of the Most Influential Jews of All Time.* New York: Citadel Press, 1994. 387p. $22.95. ISBN 0-8065-1492-2.

As with the other "100" books in this series, this work ranks its subjects according to degree of impact. Shapiro's list consists of Jewish people who influenced the world as well as those whose influence may have only been felt by Jewish people themselves. Included are Jewish people from all walks of life and those from the Bible. There are black-and-white photographs or illustrations, dates of birth and death, and a two- to three-page sketch for each entrant. Sketches provide details of childhood, education, contributions, and honors and awards. Shapiro also provides a brief explanation of each entrant's rank on the list. There is an index. Recommended for grade 5 and above.

Simmons, John. *The Scientific 100: A Ranking of the Most Influential Scientists, Past and Present.* New York: Citadel Press, 1996. 504p. $29.95. ISBN 0-8065-1749-2.

Scientific writer Simmons ranks the top 100 scientists of all time according to their overall influence on the world. Sketches are two to three pages in length and begin with a black-and-white photograph of the subject, field of endeavor, and dates of birth and death. Details of early life and education are presented, but sketches focus on career highlights and achievements. Simmons also discusses why each subject was chosen and ranked. Also included is an essay, Inexcusable Omissions, Honorable Mentions, and Also Rans; a bibliography; and an index. Written for general readers, but appropriate for grade 6 and above.

Search for Great Scientists

Name_____ Class_____ Date_____

Use the Reference List for Great Scientists to find the answers to these questions. You may find the answer to a question in more than one source on the list.

1. Native American nuclear physicist Fred Begay achieved a first in his education in 1971. What was it?

   _____

   _____

   _____

2. Elizabeth Blackwell, the first woman to obtain a medical degree, graduated from Geneva College in New York. How many schools turned her down before she was accepted at Geneva?

   _____

   _____

   _____

3. Luis W. Alvarez designed an invention used by a U.S. president. Name the invention, and name the president.

   _____

   _____

   _____

4. What scientific discovery is credited to Selman Waksman?

   _____

   _____

   _____

5. Jonas Salk developed a vaccine for polio. What other diseases did he research later in life?

   _____

   _____

   _____

6. Chinese-born American virologist Flossie Wong-Staal is credited with the discovery of what virus?

_____

_____

_____

7. Austrian American physicist Wolfgang Pauli is responsible for a scientific first in 1931. What was it?

_____

_____

_____

8. What is significant about a wooden clock made by African American inventor and astronomer Benjamin Banneker?

_____

_____

_____

9. In 1983 geneticist Barbara McClintock won a Nobel prize. She was not the first woman to win, but a first is linked to her prize. What is it?

_____

_____

_____

10. An important scientific first occurred on January 13, 1942, for Russian American aeronautical engineer Igor Sikorsky. What was it?

_____

_____

_____

Answer Key for Great Scientists

1. In Saari and Allison. Begay was the first Navajo to receive a doctorate degree in physics.
2. In Felder. Blackwell was turned down by 28 schools.
3. In Novas. Alvarez invented an electric indoor training device for golfers. President Dwight D. Eisenhower used it.
4. In Shapiro. Waksman is credited with the discovery of antibiotics.
5. In Simmons. Salk also worked on cures for multiple sclerosis, cancer, and human immunodeficiency virus (HIV).
6. In Saari and Allison. Wong-Staal is credited with the discovery of the HIV virus.
7. In Bruno. Pauli first suggested the existence of neutrons, uncharged particles.
8. In Salley. Banneker's clock was the first clock made in America, and it kept perfect time for more than 40 years.
9. In Felder. McClintock was the first woman to win an unshared Nobel prize.
10. In Bruno. The first successful flight of a single-rotor helicopter was recorded. Sikorsky built it.

Chapter Six

Fun Food Facts

Americans love to dine out, try new cuisine, and celebrate their ethnic heritage with traditional meals. That is the focus of these two searches. One search consists of fun facts about foods. The other highlights ethnic cuisine as part of a daily meal and as part of a holiday celebration. Although there are hundreds of excellent ethnic cookbooks, the intention here is not to present a list of ethnic recipes. The books on these lists were limited to those that had a historical or cultural focus. As a result, some of the books on this list are cookbooks, and others are not. All provide information on ethnic foods or celebrations.

Reference List for Fun Food Facts

Albyn, Carole Lisa, and Lois S. Webb. *The Multicultural Cookbook for Students*. Phoenix, AZ: Oryx Press, 1994. 287p. $26.95. ISBN 0-89774-735-6.

Arranged geographically by continent, this work provides 337 recipes from 122 countries. Each section opens with an introductory description of the region. Outline maps are included as well. Many recipes begin with information on the origin of the dish. For those interested, recipes are clearly written and easy to follow. Special features include a glossary and a comprehensive index of recipes, countries, and ingredients. Recommended for grade 5 and above.

America A to Z: People, Places, Customs, Culture. Pleasantville, NY: Reader's
Digest Association, 1997. 416p. $30.00. ISBN 0-89577-900-5.

People, places, historical events, notable occasions, inventions, facts, and milestones in American social history make up more than 1,000 entries in this chronicle of American culture. The work is arranged alphabetically, and there are two or three color or black-and-white illustrations on each page. Fads and trivia are listed along with famous names and places. There are entries for charm bracelets and Jell-O as well as for Monticello and robber barons. Most entries are one paragraph in length. Fun to browse, this book presents a vivid record of American culture past and present. Recommended for grade 5 and above.

Anderson, Jean. *The American Century Cookbook*. New York: Clarkson Potter,
1997. 548p. $35.00. ISBN 0-517-70576-1.

Anderson has compiled more than 500 recipes in this work. However, this book is also a social history of American cooking. There is a time line on right-facing pages. Many sidebars provide various kinds of information, including recipe origins, foreign influence in American cooking, profiles of famous food personalities, and reproductions of advertisements for food products, appliances, cookbooks, and gadgets. The author's intent was to compile the most popular recipes in America and to chronicle the evolution of American tastes and eating during the twentieth century. Anderson's work is a treat for those who love to cook and eat as well as for those interested in Americana. There are many fascinating food facts, an extensive bibliography, and an index. Written for those interested in cooking, but appropriate for grade 6 and above.

Galens, Judy, Anna Sheets, and Robin V. Young, eds. *Gale Encyclopedia of
Multicultural America*. Detroit: Gale Research, 1995. 1,477p. $125.00.
ISBN 0-8103-9163-5.

More than 100 alphabetically arranged signed essays have been compiled in this work. Articles, ranging from 5,000 to 20,000 words, have been written by experts in their fields. Essays focus on the experiences of each ethnic group discussed. Entries begin with an overview and a history and provide information on each group's individual contributions to American society. Also discussed are language, religion, politics, organizations, and achievers from each group. There are several black-and-white photographs and illustrations, a general bibliography, and an index. Recommended for grade 5 and above.

Gay, Kathlyn. Debbie Pallon, illus. *Keep the Buttered Side Up: Food Superstitions from Around the World*. New York: Walker and Company, 1995. 102p. $15.95. ISBN 0-8027-8228-0.

Customs, beliefs, and superstitions related to food are the focus of this book. There are numerous bits of food trivia from around the world. For example, there is a section on the origin of the fortunes in fortune cookies. There are 13 chapters in all, each devoted to a specific type of food or a particular aspect of eating. There are chapters on beef, cakes and cookies, vegetables, nuts, and dairy food. There is a chapter on Table Talk and another that asks Are You Superstitious? Special features include Tidbits, which are sidebars containing food facts, myths, and trivia. The black-and-white illustrations are lively and enhance the text. This is a fascinating book for all ages even though it is written for students. Recommended for grade 5 and above.

The Guinness Book of World Records: 1998. New York: Bantam Books, 1998. 750p. $6.99. ISBN 0-553-57895-2.

Originally designed to settle disputes, this is a popular reference for all ages. It enables readers to find the longest, the shortest, oldest, fastest, biggest, and smallest. All kinds of records and achievements are recorded. Also included are black-and-white photographs as well as tips and hints from achievers. The book is arranged by topic, and there is an index for easy access. Recommended for grade 5 and above.

Smith, Jeff. *The Frugal Gourmet on Our Immigrant Ancestors*. New York: Avon, 1990. 619p. $6.50. ISBN 0-380-71708-5.

Smith is widely known for his television show and cookbooks. This volume focuses on ethnic recipes. There are recipes from 35 groups. The book opens with a glossary of hints, kitchen equipment, special equipment, and cooking methods and terms, and a list of herbs and spices. Smith presents an essay on the immigrant experience that includes several anecdotes about Ellis Island. Each section of recipes opens with a map of the country and a brief history of the group in their homeland and in America. This is followed by recipes. Smith's narrative is engaging. Written for those who love to cook but appropriate reading for grade 5 and above.

Search for Fun Food Facts

Name_____ Class_____ Date_____

Use the Reference List for Fun Food Facts to find the answers to these questions. It is possible that you will find answers to the questions in more than one of the listed sources.

1. What's a feather fowlie? Who eats it?

    _____

    _____

    _____

2. Slovenians eat a treat called *krofi*. What would this treat be called in America?

    _____

    _____

    _____

3. What are the three favorite sandwich fillings of American schoolchildren?

    _____

    _____

    _____

4. What is the country of origin of an ethnic dish called Cullen Skink? What kind of dish is it?

    _____

    _____

    _____

5. When and where was the longest sushi roll created?

    _____

    _____

    _____

6. Iced tea, ice cream, and cotton candy all share a common first. What is it?

_____

_____

_____

7. Who was Duncan Hines? Did he invent cake mixes?

_____

_____

_____

8. Why are M&M's® called M&M's®?

_____

_____

_____

9. Tuskegee ice cream was created by George Washington Carver. What are the ingredients?

_____

_____

_____

10. When did animal crackers first appear? Why was the string originally placed on the box?

_____

_____

_____

Ethnic Foods

Among our favorite dishes are ethnic foods. International cuisine is more popular than ever. However, in our homes, many of us enjoy traditional foods made from recipes of our parents and grandparents who brought them from their homeland. This search celebrates ethnic cuisine.

Reference List for Ethnic Foods

Albyn, Carole Lisa, and Lois S. Webb. *The Multicultural Cookbook for Students*. Phoenix, AZ: Oryx Press, 1994. 287p. $30.75. ISBN 0-89774-735-6.
Arranged geographically by continent, this work provides 337 recipes from 122 countries. Each section opens with an introductory description of the region. Outline maps are included as well. Many recipes begin with information on the origin of the dish. For those interested, recipes are clearly written and easy to follow. Special features include a glossary and a comprehensive index of recipes, countries, and ingredients. Recommended for grade 5 and above.

Cao, Lan, and Himilce Novas. *Everything You Need to Know About Asian American History*. New York: Plume, 1996. 366p. $12.95. ISBN 0-452-27315-3.
Written in a question-and-answer format, this book devotes one chapter to each of seven groups: Chinese, Japanese, Filipino, Southeast Asian, Korean, Asian Indians, and Pacific Islanders. The introduction is in part also written in a question-and-answer format. Information boxes are placed in relevant areas throughout the book. Examples include Asian American Heartthrobs, Thirteen Asian American Women Who Made a Difference, and Some Popular Asian American Dishes. There is a recommended reading list for each ethnic group and an index. Although the question-and-answer format makes this book fun to browse, it is also an excellent source of information. Recommended for grade 5 and above.

Cohen, Henning, and Tristram Potter Coffin, eds. *The Folklore of American Holidays*. Detroit: Gale Research, 1987. 431p. $80.00. ISBN 0-8103-2126-2.
Folklore related to given holidays whether old or new, religious or secular, well-known or obscure is the focus of this work. Chronologically arranged, each entry contains the name of the holiday, its date or time frame, its origin, historical background, and other pertinent information. Entries also contain source and comment sections that provide bibliographic and collection information, cross-references, and related commentary. There are several indexes in this work that provide easy access. They include Subject Index; Ethnic or Geographical Index; Collectors, Informants, and Translators Index; Song Titles and First Significant Lines Index; and, finally, Motifs and Tale Types Index. The introduction discusses development of calendars,

festivals, and customs. Coffin is a widely known and well-respected folklorist. This work is a credit to his expertise in the subject. It reflects a diversity of ethnic and religious celebrations, making it not only a "day" book but also an excellent multicultural collection of folklore and a fairly comprehensive reference. Many specific references are made to such things as Thanksgiving Day parades in various cities, recipes for food served at a Hindu celebration, and many ethnic folktales. The editors even describe ethnic holidays as celebrated in a particular city or community. This is also fun to browse. Recommended for grade 5 and above.

Galens, Judy, Anna Sheets, and Robin V. Young, eds. *Gale Encyclopedia of Multicultural America*. Detroit: Gale Research, 1995. 1,477p. $125.00. ISBN 0-8103-9163-5.

More than 100 alphabetically arranged signed essays have been compiled in this work. Articles, ranging from 5,000 to 20,000 words, have been written by experts in their field. Essays focus on the experiences of each ethnic group discussed. Entries begin with an overview and a history and provide information on each group's individual contributions to American society. Also discussed are language, religion, politics, organizations, and achievers from each group. There are several black-and-white photographs and illustrations, a general bibliography, and an index. Recommended for grade 5 and above.

Mariani, John. *The Dictionary of American Food and Drink*. New York: Hearst, 1994. 379p. $19.95. ISBN 0-688-10139-9.

Mariani's work consists of more than 2,000 entries about food. The introduction traces the evolution of American cuisine. Mariani explains dish night at movie theaters, describes nouvelle cuisine, and provides hundreds of recipes from New Bedford Pudding to Rice Krispies Treats®. Items related to food slang, anecdotes, and history are included as well. There is a bibliographic guide and an index. The work is written in a lively narrative and is well researched. This is an excellent source of history and lore related to food. Written for food buffs but recommended for grade 6 and above.

Smith, Jeff. *The Frugal Gourmet on Our Immigrant Ancestors*. New York: Avon, 1990. 619p. $6.50. ISBN 0-380-71708-5.

Smith is widely known for his television show and cookbooks. This volume focuses on ethnic recipes. There are recipes from 35 groups. The book opens with a glossary of hints, kitchen equipment, special equipment, and cooking methods and terms, and a list of herbs and spices. Smith presents an essay on the immigrant experience that includes several anecdotes about Ellis Island. Each section of recipes opens with a map of the country and a brief history of the group in their homeland and in America. This is followed by recipes. Smith's narrative is engaging. Written for those who love to cook but appropriate reading for grade 5 and above.

Zibart, Eve, Muriel Stevens, and Terrell Vermont. *The Unofficial Guide to Ethnic Cuisine and Dining in America*. New York: Macmillan, 1995. 425p. $13.00. ISBN 0-02-860067-3.

Zibart, Stevens, and Vermont present information on a variety of cuisines from Europe, Africa, Asia, and the Americas. Although there are recipes, this work is not so much a cookbook as a guide. The authors present a brief history of various cuisines as well as key ingredients pertinent to each cuisine. Also included are menu suggestions and tips on how to eat ethnic dishes. A few recipes for each cuisine have been included for home preparation. However, the focus is on restaurant dining. In each section after a brief discussion of the country, its history, and its cuisine, there is a discussion of the main ingredients and main dishes, instructions on how to order like a native, and a section on cooking at home that includes recipes. Special features include sidebars listing basic cuisine in which menu items, key flavors, eating utensils, cost, nutritional information, and a list of ethnic restaurants in major American cities are cited. Recommended for grade 5 and above.

Search for Ethnic Foods

Name_____ Class_____ Date_____

Use the Reference List for Ethnic Foods to find the answers to these questions. It is possible that you may find the answers in more than one source.

1. Part of Chinese cuisine is a delicacy called 100-Year-Old Eggs. Are the eggs really 100 years old? How are they made?

   _____

   _____

   _____

2. According to one guide, what are the key flavors of the cuisine in Russia, Poland, and Eastern Europe?

   _____

   _____

   _____

3. If you lived in Bulgaria, you might enjoy a drink called a *lassi*. What is it?

   _____

   _____

   _____

4. What foods traditionally are served at a Polish Christmas Eve supper?

   _____

   _____

   _____

5. What is vegetable liver?

   _____

   _____

   _____

6. What cuisine would you be eating if you had Codfish Pil Pil for dinner?

_____

_____

_____

7. What ingredients are used to make Pueblo Bread?

_____

_____

_____

8. What are some traditional foods enjoyed by African Americans on New Year's Day? What significance is attached to these foods?

_____

_____

_____

9. What are the ingredients in Tie-Me-Up, a popular dessert in the Caribbean?

_____

_____

_____

10. What are some typical desserts enjoyed by Portugese Americans?

_____

_____

_____

Answer Key for Fun Food Facts

1. In Albyn and Webb. It is Scottish chicken soup.
2. In Galens, Sheets, and Young. A *krofi* is a doughnut.
3. In Gay. Turkey, ham, and peanut butter and jelly are the favorites of American school-children.
4. In Smith. Cullen Skink is a soup from Scotland made of fish, potatoes, and onions.
5. In *Guinness*. At the Seattle Cherry Blossom and Cultural Festival the world's longest sushi roll was created on April 26, 1997.
6. In *America A to Z*. Each was first served at the 1904 World's Fair in St. Louis.
7. In Anderson. Hines did not invent cake mixes. He was a traveling salesman who kept a list of his favorite restaurants. Eventually it became a guide, and establishments were eager to display the seal, "Recommended by Duncan Hines."
8. In Anderson. M&M's® are named for the two men who created them, Forrest Mars and Bruce Muries.
9. In Albyn. One quart of softened vanilla or lemon ice cream mixed with one quarter pound of peanut brittle make Tuskegee ice cream.
10. In *America A to Z*. Animal crackers were first sold around Christmastime in 1902. The string was placed on the box so that it could be hung on the family Christmas tree.

Answer Key for Ethnic Foods

1. In Cao and Novas. The eggs are preserved for about 100 days until the yolk turns gray.
2. In Zibart, Stevens, and Vermont. Sour cream, paprika, smoked and salted fish are flavors popular in these countries.
3. In Albyn and Webb. *Lassi* is an iced yogurt drink.
4. In Cohen and Coffin. *Pierogi*, which are made of dough and filled with cabbage, potatoes, or other fillings; *babka*, a sweet bread; and *mazurek*, which are cookies, are a few of the dishes enjoyed by Polish people at Christmas.
5. In Mariani. It is a Jewish American dish made of eggplant and spices served on certain Jewish holy days.
6. In Smith. This dish is from Basque cuisine.
7. In Mariani. Pueblo Bread is made from flour, salt, yeast, and water.
8. In Galens, Sheets, and Young. Black-eyed peas for good fortune, rice for prosperity, greens for money, and fish for an increase of wealth are some of the dishes enjoyed by African Americans on January 1.
9. In Zibart, Stevens, and Vermont. A Tie-Me-Up is a dish of cornmeal mush tied up in a banana leaf.
10. In Galens, Sheets, and Young. A baked custard called *pudim flan*, almond cake called *toucinho do ceu*, and dried figs stuffed with almonds and chocolate called *fizos recheados* are a few desserts on the menus of Portugese Americans.

Chapter
Seven

Sports
Heroes

Sports heroes are always popular, and discussion is often generated regarding who is the best in a given sport. In this search all the athletes mentioned are truly great. Each is a credit to his or her sport and a source of pride to his or her ethnic group as well.

Reference List for Sports Heroes

Galens, Judy, Anna Sheets, and Robin V. Young, eds. *Gale Encyclopedia of Multicultural America*. Detroit: Gale Research, 1995. 1,477p. $125.00. ISBN 0-8103-9163-5.

More than 100 alphabetically arranged signed essays have been compiled in this work. Articles, ranging from 5,000 to 20,000 words, have been written by experts in their field. Essays focus on the experiences of each ethnic group discussed. Entries begin with an overview and a history and provide information on each group's individual contributions to American society. Also discussed are language, religion, politics, organizations, and achievers from each group. There are several black-and-white photographs and illustrations, a general bibliography, and an index. Recommended for grade 5 and above.

Grolier Library of International Biographies. Danbury, CT: Grolier Education Corp., 1996. 10 vols. $299.00. ISBN 0-7172-7527-2.

Twentieth-century achievers from various fields of endeavor are profiled in this 10-volume set. Each entry provides personal information ranging from childhood events to career highlights to values and beliefs. Achievements are detailed as well. Written for students, this work is written in clear, straightforward language. Each volume is devoted to a particular field of endeavor, covering areas such as scientists, performing artists, writers, and explorers. Boldface is used to indicate that the word and its definition will be found in a glossary specific to each volume's subject area. Black-and-white photographs, bibliographies, and indexes for each volume and a general index by subject, country, and name are included. Recommended for grade 5 and above.

Herzog, Brad. *The Sports 100: The 100 Most Important People in Sports History*. New York: Macmillan, 1995. 418p. $16.95. ISBN 0-02-860402-4.

Not all profiles in this work are devoted to athletes. A few have been included for those who pioneered, changed, or influenced sports. The ranking is the author's, and in his introduction he discusses the difficulties he encountered in devising the list and lists another 100 greats who did not make his list. The profiles include details of birth and death, early life, career highlights, and a discussion of the subject's influence on sports. Special features include an appendix of tables on the top 100: when and where they were born, the sport in which they excelled (most in baseball), race and gender, and period of peak performance. Another special feature is the occasional sidebars containing anecdotes, statistics, and little-known facts. Herzog's writing is clear and engaging. There is a bibliography but no index. This book should be a treat for all sports fans in grade 5 and above.

Moss, Joyce, and George Wilson. *Peoples of the World*: *North Americans*. 1st ed. Detroit: Gale Research, 1991. 441p. $45.00. ISBN 0-8103-7768-3.

The Peoples of the World series profiles various ethnic groups. The authors have made the focus of their work the people of a country rather than the country itself. The premise of the work is that governments and other world events affect change in many countries, but culture and tradition do not change. Separate volumes have been devoted to North Americans and to Latin Americans as well as to other areas around the world. Each entry is introduced with phonetic spelling and definition. Information on population, location, language, and geographical setting is also included. Other sections for each culture include historical background and culture today. Special features include maps for each culture that indicate current location. While political and economic information may not be current, this work is a good source of cultural and historical information. Also included are black-and-white illustrations and photographs, a glossary, and an index. This set is written especially for students in junior high school, making it appropriate for students in grade 7 and above.

Rust, Edna, and Art Rust, Jr. *Art Rust's Illustrated History of the Black Athlete.* Garden City, NY: Doubleday, 1985. 435p. $15.95. ISBN 0-385-15140-3.

Arranged by sport, this volume traces the history of African American Athletes in nine sports. The Rusts present a historical overview of each sport and then profile African Americans who excelled in the sport. Profiles include black-and-white photographs and quotations by or about each subject. Many profiles are one to one-and-a-half pages in length, although such true greats as Joe Louis, Jackie Robinson, and Jesse Owens receive lengthier coverage. Several black-and-white photographs enhance the Rusts' clearly written and appealing narrative. There are sections on the Harlem Globetrotters and Olympic Gold Medalists. More than a series of profiles or a list of facts, dates, and statistics, this work is a social history rich in detail. It provides insight into the history of sports in the United States and chronicles obstacles overcome, injustices, and the impact of African Americans on American sports. Written for general readers, this work is also recommended for grade 5 and above.

Slater, Robert. *Great Jews in Sports.* Revised and expanded. Midvale Village, NY: Jonathan David Publishers, 1992. 331p. $22.95. ISBN 0-8246-0285-4.

More than 100 profiles make up the bulk of this work. There are also more than 50 thumbnail sketches and a section of Israeli sports figures. Most sketches are one to three pages in length. They include details of birth, early life, achievements in sports and other areas, and honors and awards. A black-and-white photograph of each subject is included as well. Written for general readers, Slater's book is clearly written and should appeal to sports fans in grade 5 and above.

Zia, Helen, and Susan B. Gall, eds. *Notable Asian Americans.* Detroit: Gale Research, 1995. 468p. $75.00. ISBN 0-8103-9623-8.

Biographical sketches of 250 Asian Americans from various fields of endeavor—many of which have been taken from personal interviews—are listed alphabetically in this volume. Most entries are accompanied by black-and-white photographs. Sketches include field of endeavor, personal and professional information, and honors and awards. Sources are listed at the end of each signed sketch. Also included are Occupational Index, Ethnicity Index, and Subject Index. Recommended for grade 5 and above.

Search for Sports Heroes

Name_____ Class_____ Date_____

Use the Reference List for Sports Heroes to find the answers to these questions. It is possible that the answers to some questions may be found in more than one source.

1. Native American athlete Jim Thorpe was voted greatest athlete of the first half of the century in a 1950 poll taken by the Associated Press. How many votes did he receive? Who came in second?

_____

_____

_____

2. Morten Andersen, a Danish immigrant, came to the United States as a high-school exchange student. He distinguished himself on the football field. For what team and in what position did he play?

_____

_____

_____

3. What sports first was achieved by African American athlete Isaac Murphy?

_____

_____

_____

4. Asian American Olympic athlete Duke Kahanamoku once performed a daring rescue of a group of people in a capsized boat. What athletic equipment did he use for the rescue?

_____

_____

_____

5. Oksana Baiul, Ukranian-born figure skater, won an Olympic Gold Medal in 1994. How old was she when she won?

_____

_____

_____

6. British Canadian track star Terry Fox raised several million dollars for cancer research. How and why did he do it?

_____

_____

_____

7. Croation-born NBA star Toni Kukoc was a champion in his age group in another sport when he was 14. Name the sport.

_____

_____

_____

8. Austrian-born basketball coach Harry Litwak produced four all-American players while a coach at Temple University. Name the four players.

_____

_____

_____

9. Acadian baseball player Ron Guidry led the New York Yankees to victory at the 1978 World Series. What award did he win that year? Answer your question using one of his two nicknames.

_____

_____

_____

10. What was Danny Biasone's contribution to basketball?

_____

_____

_____

Answer Key for Sports Heroes

1. In Herzog. Thorpe won with 875 votes. Babe Ruth came in second with 539 votes.
2. In Galens, Sheets, and Young. Andersen was a kicker for the New Orleans Saints.
3. In Rust and Rust. Murphy was the first jockey to ride three Kentucky Derby winners.
4. In Zia and Gall. Kahanamoku used a surfboard for the rescue.
5. In *Grolier*. Baiul was 16 years old.
6. In Moss and Wilson. Fox, stricken with cancer himself, decided to run from one Canadian coast to the other to raise money for cancer research.
7. In *Grolier*. Kukoc was a table-tennis champion at age 14.
8. In Slater. Litwak's all-American players were Guy Rogers, Hal Lear, Bill Kennedy, and John Baum.
9. In Galens, Sheets, and Young. "Louisiana Lightnin' " or "Ragin' Cajun" won the Cy Young award for pitching that year.
10. In Herzog. Biasone's contribution was the 24-second shot clock.

Chapter
Eight

Literature

Three searches for literature have been included in this section. All searches have to do with books and authors. The reference lists vary. The first search uses a reference list of books that pertain to literature in general rather than to a specific group of writers; the second uses a reference list of books related to writers in a specific ethnic group, such as African Americans or Native Americans; and the third search uses books that either rank the 100 most influential people within a specific group, such as Women or Hispanics, or books that identify great individuals.

Reference List for Literature

Bradbury, Malcolm, ed. *The Atlas of Literature*. London: De Agostini Editions, 1996. 352p. $35.00. ISBN 1-899883-68-1.
    A unique form of literary and social history is presented in this work. Maps show real places such as houses, communities, theaters, and even cafes that are associated with authors. The work consists of eight parts, including Middle Ages, Age of Reason, The Modern World, and The World Today. Settings of literary works are shown as well. Also discussed is the impact of certain literary works on particular locations. There is a key to maps that indicates whether a place still exists. A bibliography, a section on authors and their works, a list of places to visit (includes address, hours, and phone number), and an index are included. Written for adults, this work should appeal to anyone who loves literature in grade 7 and above.

Dunkling, Leslie. *A Dictionary of Days*. New York: Facts on File, 1988. 156p. $18.95. ISBN 0-8160-1916-9.

Many days alluded to in American and British literature are found in Dunkling's work, particularly in her introduction. Though not as comprehensive as other books of days, this work makes mention of ethnic events, folkloric events, and food and drink days. There is also a section on generic terms and verbal expressions. There are black-and-white illustrations, a calendar, and cross-references. However, there is no index. Literary allusions make this a unique book of days. Written for a general audience but appropriate for grade 5 and above.

Hart, James D. *The Oxford Companion to American Literature*. 6th ed. Revisions and additions by Phillip W. Leininger. New York: Oxford University Press, 1995. 779p. $65.00. ISBN 0-19-506548-4.

With more than 5,000 entries—2,000 of them biographical—this classic reference profiles authors, American and foreign, who have had an impact on American literature. Entries cover several other aspects of American literature as well. Information on literary movements, awards, periodicals, and summaries of more than 1,000 literary works can be found. Entries range from a paragraph to half a page. The work is arranged alphabetically and provides cross-references and a chronological index. Written for students and general readers, this work is appropriate for grade 6 and above.

The Literary Almanac: The Best of the Printed Word 1900 to the Present. Kansas City: High Tide Press, 1997. 288p. $16.95. ISBN 0-8362-3701-3.

Arranged chronologically, this work lists significant births and deaths, best-sellers, and prize winners for each year. There are also one or two brief biographical sketches for each year and black-and-white photographs. Excerpts from reviews and brief author quotes frequently are included in sidebars. The section, The Prizes, provides the history and descriptions of eight literary prizes or awards. Required Reading is a chronological list of 99 Best Novels compiled by Anthony Burgess. A section titled Controversial Books provides a list of banned books that includes author, title, reason, and censors. Other special features include a list of America's poet laureates; the Astrological Author; Alternative Occupations; Literary Love Affairs; and, finally, Writing Undercover, which is a list of pen names. A treat for book lovers, this work is an excellent reference and fun to browse. Written for general readers but appropriate for book lovers in grade 7 and above.

Olendorf, Donna, ed. *Something About the Author*. Detroit: Gale Research, 1998. 94 vols. $85.00 per vol. ISBN 0-8103-2279-X.

This popular ongoing series details lives and works of children's and young-adult authors. Early and contemporary, well-known and lesser-known authors are profiled. Odd-numbered volumes include author and illustrator indexes. Entries include personal information such as dates of birth and death, names of relatives, affiliations, and degrees. Addresses and career information are provided as are awards, writings, and works in progress. Sidelights for authors contain a biographical sketch of the author, some of which are written by the authors themselves. Included as well are several black-and-white photographs and illustrations. This series is an excellent reference for grade 5 and above.

Siepman, Katherine Baker, ed. *Benet's Reader's Encyclopedia*. 3rd ed. New York: HarperCollins, 1987. 1,091p. $45.00. ISBN 0-06-181088-6.

A standard ready reference, this work contains more than 9,000 entries related to all aspects of literature. In addition to biographical sketches of authors and plot summaries, there are sketches of literary characters, terms, awards, and literary movements. The scope is international and covers classic and contemporary literature. Recommended for grade 5 and above.

Search for Literature

Name_____ Class_____ Date_____

Use the Reference List for Literature to find the answers to the following questions. It is possible that you may find the answers to some questions in more than one of the sources on the list.

1. Award-winning author Alan Say emigrated from Japan to the United States. Name the awards he won for his book, *The Boy of the Three-Year Map*.

    _____

    _____

    _____

2. Who was the peasant bard?

    _____

    _____

    _____

3. Find a literary map of writers from the Caribbean. On which islands were writers Jean Rhyss, Derek Walcott, and Jamaica Kincaid born?

    _____

    _____

    _____

4. Jacob Riis, a Danish-born writer, immigrated to New York City in the late 1800s. He wrote several books describing social conditions he worked hard to improve. To what causes did he devote his work?

    _____

    _____

    _____

5. Name the author and the title of the book and the Academy Award-winning film in which Halloween is significant.

    _____

    _____

    _____

6. What was another occupation of writer Anne Sexton?

_____

_____

_____

7. Which paperback book by Jim Davis was a best-seller in 1982?

_____

_____

_____

8. German writer Thomas Mann came to America and eventually became an American citizen. Why did he leave Germany?

_____

_____

_____

9. Where did writer Nella Larsen live during the Harlem Renaissance?

_____

_____

_____

10. What is R. L. Stine's birth date?

_____

_____

_____

Reference List for Ethnic Writers

Galens, Judy, Anna Sheets, and Robin V. Young, eds. *The Gale Encyclopedia of Multicultural America.* Detroit: Gale Research, 1995. 2 vols. $125.00. ISBN 0-8103-9163-5.

More than 100 alphabetically arranged signed essays have been compiled in this work. Articles, ranging from 5,000 words to 20,000 words, have been written by experts in their field. Essays focus on the experiences of each ethnic group discussed. Entries begin with an overview and a history and provide information on each group's individual contributions to American society. Also discussed are language, religion, politics, organizations, and achievers from each group. There are several black-and-white photographs and illustrations, a general bibliography, and an index. Recommended for grade 5 and above.

Malinowski, Sharon, ed. *Black Writers: A Selection of Sketches from Contemporary Authors.* 2nd ed. Detroit: Gale Research, 1994. 721p. $95.00. ISBN 0-8103-7788-8.

Metzger, Linda. *Black Writers: A Selection of Sketches from Contemporary Authors.* Detroit: Gale Research, 1989. 619p. $89.00. ISBN 0-8103-7772-4.

Each volume contains more than 400 profiles. Entries provide biographical as well as bibliographical material. Writers from artistic, journalistic, political, and scholarly backgrounds have been included. Information provided includes dates and places of birth and death, parents' names and occupations, names and dates pertaining to spouse and children, colleges and degrees, affiliations, address, career highlights, honors and awards, and chronological bibliography. Volume Two has a cumulative index to both editions as well as nationality and gender indexes. Special features include Sidelights, a section containing further biographical information, career and critical commentary, and in many cases comments by the author. Finally, biographical and critical sources list books, articles, and reviews of the author's work. Recommended for grade 5 and above.

Malinowski, Sharon, ed., and George Abrams. *Notable Native Americans.* Detroit: Gale Research, 1994. 492p. $80.00. ISBN 0-8103-9638-6.

More than 265 Native Americans from historical times to the present are featured in this biobibliography. Entrants from all fields of endeavor are listed alphabetically. Signed essays one to three pages in length include tribal name, field of endeavor, dates of birth and death, and when possible, a black-and-white photograph. Sketches include details of family and early life, education, career highlights, honors and awards, a list of works when applicable, and a list of sources for further reading. Special features include a list of entries according to tribal group and a list according to occupation. Abrams provides an insightful introduction, Race, Culture, and Law: The Question of American Indian Identity. Written for students, teachers, librarians, and general readers, this book is appropriate for grade 5 and above.

Moss, Joyce, and George Wilson. *Peoples of the World: North Americans*. 1st ed. Detroit: Gale Research, 1991. 441p. $45.00. ISBN 0-8103-7768-3.

The series Peoples of the World profiles various ethnic groups. The authors have made the focus of their work the people of a country rather than the country itself. The premise of the work is that governments and other world events affect change in many countries, but culture and tradition do not change. Separate volumes have been devoted to North Americans and to Latin Americans as well as to other areas around the world. Each entry is introduced with phonetic spelling and definition. Information on population, location, language, and geographic setting is also included. Other sections for each culture include historical background and culture today. Special features include maps for each culture that indicate current location. While political and economic information may not be current, this work is a good source of cultural and historical information. Also included are black-and-white illustrations and photographs, a glossary, and an index. This set is written especially for students in junior high school, making it appropriate for students in grade 7 and above.

Ryan, Bryan, ed. *Hispanic Writers: A Selection of Sketches from Contemporary Authors*. Detroit: Gale Research, 1991. 514p. $90.00. ISBN 0-8103-7688-1.

More than 400 entries on twentieth-century Hispanic writers have been compiled for this work. Works of Hispanic writers who are social and political figures, scholars, historians, journalists, and literary figures have been included. Entries provide personal information, including address, career highlights, awards, honors, and biographical and critical sources as well as a chronological list of writings and work in progress. Also included is a guide to authors and a nationality index. This is an excellent source for anyone interested in Hispanic writers. Recommended for grade 5 and above.

Shapiro, Ann R., editor in chief, et al. *Jewish American Women Writers*. Westport, CT: Greenwood Press, 1994. 557p. $89.50. ISBN 0-313-28437-7.

Arranged alphabetically by writer, this reference provides biographical sketches, a discussion of major themes in each author's work, and a survey of criticism of the author's work. Included after each essay are a bibliography of each author's works and a bibliography of writings about the author. An essay, Jewish American Women's Autobiography, and a list of suggestions for further reading have been included. A glossary and an index are provided. This is a reference written for adults but is suitable for grade 7 and above.

Zia, Helen, and Susan B. Gall, eds. *Notable Asian Americans*. Detroit: Gale Research, 1995. 468p. $75.00. ISBN 0-8103-9623-8.

Biographical sketches of 250 Asian Americans from various fields of endeavor, many of which have been taken from personal interviews, are listed alphabetically in this volume. Most entries are accompanied by black-and-white photographs. Sketches include field of endeavor, personal and professional information, and honors and awards. Sources are listed at the end of each signed sketch. Also included are Occupational Index, Ethnicity Index, and Subject Index. Recommended for grade 5 and above.

Search for Ethnic Writers

Name_____ Class_____ Date_____

Use the Reference List for Ethnic Writers provided to find the answers to the following questions about these writers of various ethnic backgrounds.

1. Asian American writer Lawrence Yep was named by his older brother. Why did Yep's brother choose the name Lawrence?

   _____

   _____

   _____

2. Native American writer Paula Gunn Allen is recognized as a prominent scholar of Native American literature. However, her ancestry is varied. What is it?

   _____

   _____

   _____

3. In what way is Jewish American writer Bella Spewack associated with the Girl Scouts of America?

   _____

   _____

   _____

4. Norwegian American author Kathryn Forbes' best-seller *Mama's Bank Account* became a hit as a film, a Broadway play, and a television series under another title. What was the other title?

   _____

   _____

   _____

5. Which of Italian American author Pietro DiDonato's books is considered a classic novel of the Italian immigrant experience in America?

   _____

   _____

   _____

   From *Multicultural Information Quests* by Marie E. Rodgers. © 2000 Libraries Unlimited. (800) 237-6124.

6. What do Jewish American writers Isaac Bashevis Singer and Saul Bellow have in common?

_____

_____

_____

7. If you wanted to write to Hispanic author Denise Chavez, where would you find her address? What is it?

_____

_____

_____

8. When and where was African American writer Ralph Ellison born?

_____

_____

_____

9. Filipino writer Jose Aruego is a widely recognized author of children's books. He once said his work must have a certain element to inspire him and please his readers. What is that element?

_____

_____

_____

10. In what field of endeavor did German-speaking Hungarian Joseph Pulitzer distinguish himself?

_____

_____

_____

Reference List for the Best Writers

Bullock, Allan, ed. *Great Lives of the 20th Century*. Secaucus, NJ: Chartwell Books, 1988. 184p. ISBN 1-55521-305-7.

More than 250 brief biographical sketches are arranged alphabetically. Most sketches are two to three paragraphs in length and include dates of birth and death, field of endeavor, place of birth, and when applicable, place of residence. This is helpful in identifying those who immigrated to this country. Included in sketches is information on the subject's early life, career highlights, and honors and awards. The introduction discusses omissions as well. There are color and black-and-white photographs on each page. Written for general readers, but appropriate for grade 5 and above.

Felder, Deborah G. *The 100 Most Influential Women of All Time: A Ranking Past and Present*. New York: Citadel Press, 1996. 374p. $24.95. ISBN 0-8065-1726-3.

Felder has ranked her subjects according to importance. This alone makes her work interesting and provocative. Readers are likely to debate the rankings. Whether or not they agree with the ranking order, readers will recognize that the women here have all made great contributions to the world. Among those listed are Rosa Parks, Freda Kahlo, Bessie Smith, Joan of Arc, and Lucille Ball. The list was compiled by means of a survey sent to Women's Studies departments of American colleges and universities. Using the surveys, Felder devised her list based on whom she felt had the greatest impact on the world. Profiles of the 100 subjects begin with dates of birth and death, a quotation by or about the subject, and a black-and-white photograph or illustration. Most profiles are two to three pages in length. Also included are career highlights, achievements, and personal information. There is an index and a bibliography as well. Recommended for grade 7 and above.

Malinowski, Sharon, ed., and George Abrams. *Notable Native Americans*. Detroit: Gale Research, 1994. 492p. $80.00. ISBN 0-8103-9638-6.

More than 265 Native Americans from historical times to the present are featured in this biobibliography. Entrants from all fields of endeavor are listed alphabetically. Signed essays one to three pages in length include tribal name, field of endeavor, dates of birth and death, and when possible, a black-and-white photograph. Sketches include details of family and early life, education, career highlights, honors and awards, a list of works when applicable, and a list of sources for further reading. Special features include a list of entries according to tribal group and a list according to occupation. Abrams provides an insightful introduction, Race, Culture, and Law: The Question of American Indian Identity. Written for students, teachers, librarians, and general readers, this book is appropriate for grade 5 and above.

Novas, Himilce. *The Hispanic 100: A Ranking of Latino Men and Women Who Have Most Influenced Thought and Culture.* New York: Citadel Press, 1995. 495p. $24.95. ISBN 0-8065-1651-8.

Hispanic men and women from all fields of endeavor have been ranked according to degree of impact. For the author's purposes, they also had to be considered trailblazers. The introduction provides an explanation of the use of the terms Latino and Hispanic as well as a brief discussion of Latinos in the United States. Entries are two-and-a-half to three pages. A black-and-white photograph or illustration with dates of birth and death begin each entry. Details of childhood, family life, education, career highlights, and honors and awards are also provided. Additionally, a brief discussion of each entrant's influence is presented. There is an index. Novas' writing is clear and straightforward. Recommended for grade 5 and above.

Salley, Columbus. *The Black 100: A Ranking of the Most Influential African Americans, Past and Present.* New York: Citadel Press, 1993. 384p. $18.95. ISBN 0-8065-1550-3.

The 100 most influential African Americans are profiled by Salley, who also provides reasons for his rankings. All have been chosen because they greatly changed the lives of all Americans. Each profile begins with a black-and-white photograph, dates of birth and death, and a quotation by or about the subject or his or her contribution. Details of personal life and professional achievements are provided as well as a brief discussion of the entrant's impact on the United States. Salley's writing is clear and insightful. There is also a bibliography and an index. Recommended for grade 5 and above.

Shapiro, Michael. *The Jewish 100: A Ranking of the Most Influential Jews of All Time.* New York: Citadel Press, 1994. 387p. $22.95. ISBN 0-8065-1492-2.

As with the other "100" books in this series, this work ranks its subjects according to degree of impact. Shapiro's list consists of Jewish people who influenced the world as well as those whose influence may have only been felt by Jewish people themselves. Included are Jewish people from all walks of life and those from the Bible. There are black-and-white photographs or illustrations, dates of birth and death, and a two- to three-page sketch for each entrant. Sketches provide details of childhood, education, contributions, and honors and awards. Shapiro also provides a brief explanation of each entrant's rank on the list. There is an index. Recommended for grade 5 and above.

Search for the Best Writers

Name_____ Class_____ Date_____

Use the Reference List for the Best Writers to find the answers to the following questions. It is possible that many answers will be found in more than one source. Great writers are listed in sources by both ethnicity and gender.

1. Latino author Piri Thomas, best known for his autobiography, *Down These Mean Streets*, has written two sequels to that book. Name them.

   _____

   _____

   _____

2. In 1950 Lorraine Hansberry worked as a reporter on a newspaper called *Freedom*. Who owned the newspaper?

   _____

   _____

   _____

3. Which fictional hero was created by Jerry Siegal and Joe Shuster, two 19-year-old friends who lived in Cleveland?

   _____

   _____

   _____

4. In what way is Native American writer Louise Erdrich connected to the author of *Yellow Raft in Blue Water*?

   _____

   _____

   _____

5. In terms of his writing, why did British writer W. H. Auden come to live in the United States?

   _____

   _____

   _____

      From *Multicultural Information Quests* by Marie E. Rodgers. © 2000 Libraries Unlimited. (800) 237-6124.

6. Murasaki Shikibu, a lady of the Japanese court in the eleventh century, is credited with a first in writing. What is it?

_____

_____

_____

7. Name two works by Jewish American writer Arthur Miller that are identified with his second wife.

_____

_____

_____

8. What well-known book by African American writer Lerone Bennett, Jr. originally appeared as a series of articles in _Ebony_ magazine?

_____

_____

_____

9. Historian Barbara Tuchman has written history as if it were a story. Although she has won two Pulitzer prizes, she has no Ph.D. in her field. Why did she consider this a plus?

_____

_____

_____

10. How old was Gwendolyn Brooks when her first poem was published?

_____

_____

_____

Answer Key for Literature

1. In Olendorf. Say's book won the Boston Globe/Horn Book Award and was chosen American Library Association's Notable Children's Book and the Caldecott Honor Book.
2. In Siepman. It was Robert Burns.
3. In Bradbury. Jean Rhyss was born on Dominica, Derek Walcott on St. Lucia, and Jamaica Kincaid on Antigua.
4. In Hart. Riis wrote about tenement conditions, slum life, and child labor, all issues Riis tried to remedy.
5. In Dunkling. In *To Kill a Mockingbird*, the novel by Harper Lee, Halloween is significant.
6. In *Literary Almanac*. Sexton was also a door-to-door cosmetics salesperson.
7. In *Literary Almanac*. *Garfield Weighs In* was a paperback best-seller in 1982.
8. In Siepman. Mann was exiled from Germany by the Nazis.
9. In Bradbury. Larsen lived on 135th Street between 7th and 8th Avenues.
10. In Olendorf. Stine was born on October 8, 1943.

Answer Key for Ethnic Writers

1. In Zia and Gall. Yep's 10-year-old brother wasn't sure he wanted a baby brother, so he chose the name of a saint who died a horrible death.
2. In Malinowski. Her ancestry is Pueblo-Sioux-Lebanese-Scottish-American.
3. In Shapiro. Spewack claims to have come up with the idea for Girl Scout cookies.
4. In Galens, Sheets, and Young. The play, film, and television series were called *I Remember Mama*.
5. In Galens, Sheets, and Young. DiDonato's classic is *Christ in Concrete*.
6. In Moss and Wilson. Singer and Bellow both received a Nobel Prize in literature.
7. In Ryan. Chavez's address is listed as 1524 Sul Ross, Houston, TX 77006.
8. In Malinowski. Ralph Ellison was born on March 1, 1914, in Oklahoma City, Oklahoma.
9. In Zia and Gall. Humor is the most important element to Jose Aruego in his work.
10. In Moss and Wilson. Pulitzer was a newspaper publisher.

Answer Key for the Best Writers

1. In Novas. Thomas' sequels are *Savior, Hold My Hand*, and *Seven Long Times*.
2. In Salley. *Freedom* was owned by Paul Robeson.
3. In Shapiro. They created Superman.
4. In Malinowski. Erdrich married Michael Dorris, Native American author of *Yellow Raft in Blue Water* in 1981. They often collaborated until shortly before his death.
5. In Bullock. Auden felt that because society was more open in America, he could write more freely.
6. In Felder. Lady Murasaki Shikibu is credited with writing the first great novel in world literature.
7. In Shapiro. Miller's plays *After the Fall* and *The Misfits* both starred his second wife, Marilyn Monroe.
8. In Salley. *Before the Mayflower* first appeared in *Ebony* as a series of articles.
9. In Felder. Tuchman felt that having a Ph.D. would have probably stifled her writing.
10. In Felder. Brooks was 13 when her first work was published.

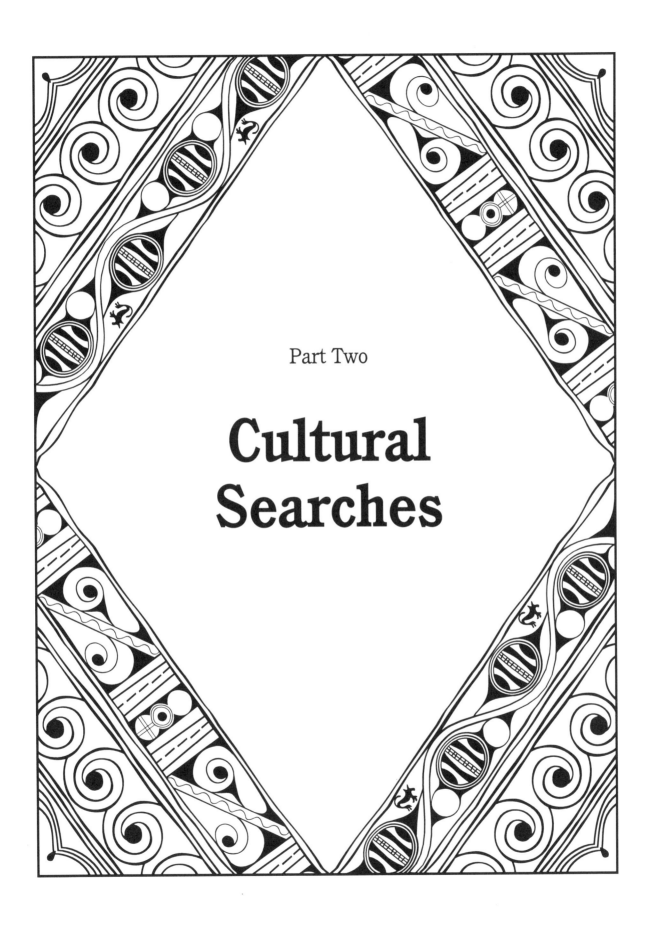

Part Two

Cultural Searches

Chapter
Nine

Hispanics

These searches will provide insight into contributions made by Hispanics to the United States. Many Hispanics come here to provide a better life for themselves and their families. In spite of a language barrier and other obstacles, many Hispanics have excelled in all fields of endeavor.

Latino Language and Culture

This search highlights language as it relates to everyday words and cultural terms. Some questions relate solely to Latino culture, while others demonstrate how many everyday words in our language are derived from Hispanic words.

Reference List for
Latino Language and Culture

Albyn, Carole Lisa, and Lois S. Webb. *The Multicultural Cookbook for Students.* Phoenix, AZ: Oryx Press, 1994. 287p. $26.95. ISBN 0-89774-735-6.
  Arranged geographically by continent, this work provides 337 recipes from 122 countries. Each section opens with an introductory description of the region. Outline maps are included as well. Many recipes begin with information on the origin of the dish. For those interested, recipes are clearly written and easy to follow. Special features include a glossary and a comprehensive index of recipes, countries, and ingredients. Recommended for grade 5 and above.

Ayto, John. *Dictionary of Word Origins*. New York: Little Brown, and Company, 1990. 583p. $16.95. ISBN 1-55970-133-1.

Ayto presents a historical perspective of approximately 800 words used in the English language. His purpose is to trace the history of words and to show connections between them. Ayto's introduction highlights significant events in history that had the greatest impact on our language. The work is arranged alphabetically. Entries show the word in bold followed by a number in brackets that denotes the century in which the word came into use. When the century is not indicated, the letters *OE* are used to indicate Old English origin. Each entry consists of a brief history of the word. This work should be appealing to anyone interested in etymology. Recommended for grade 6 and above.

Corbeil, Jean-Claude, and Ariane Archamboult. *The Facts on File English/ Spanish Visual Dictionary*. New York: Facts on File, 1992. 924p. $39.95. ISBN 0-8160-1546-5.

More than 3,000 illustrations with terminology in English and Spanish have been arranged according to subject in this work. Subjects include The Human Body, The Animal Kingdom, Food, Clothing, Music, and Hobbies. The work does not provide definitions; instead, it is a dictionary of illustrated terminology. The editors identified two goals in their work: to list terms one needs to know in everyday life and to provide representations of each term. There are general and thematic indexes in English and Spanish as well as a bibliography. Written for the average reader, this work is appealing to students of English and Spanish language, and to anyone interested in visual representations of items necessary in everyday life. The illustrations are well-done, easy to read, and cover many areas of interest. Recommended for grade 5 and above.

Kanellos, Nicolás. *Hispanic Firsts: 500 Years of Extraordinary Achievements*. Detroit: Gale Research, 1997. 372p. $44.95. ISBN 0-7816-0517-4.

Kanellos, an award-winning expert in the field of Hispanic studies, has compiled another excellent reference. Contributions and achievements have been compiled chronologically according to fields of endeavor. Chapters include Art and Design, and Film, Labor, and Religion, as well as a Timeline, Calendar of Firsts, Bibliography, Index by Year, and General Index. There are several black-and-white photographs and illustrations. Kanellos has based his work on the premise that Hispanics have contributed greatly to U.S. civilization and that Hispanics are pioneers not only for their achievements but also for overcoming obstacles in American society that barred their success. Kanellos' work is informative and appealing; it is an excellent resource and fun to browse. Recommended for grade 5 and above.

Kanellos, Nicolás, and Claudio Esteva-Fabregat, general eds. *Handbook of Hispanic Cultures in the United States*. Houston: Arte Público Press, 1994. 4 vols. $200.00. ISBN 1-55885-103-8.

Each volume in this set deals with a different aspect of Hispanic culture. Volume One, *Sociology*, traces the immigration of Mexicans, Puerto Ricans, and Cubans; discusses Latinos in American politics; and provides information on mass communications among Hispanics. Volume Two, *Literature and Art*, discusses Latino literature, art, theater, cinema, and the press. Volume Three, *Anthropology*, discusses language, family, health, religion, food, and many other related topics. Volume Four, *History*, presents a chronological history of Hispanics in the United States. This set is a treasury of information for students and adult readers. Each volume begins with a general introduction and ends with an index. There are also several black-and-white photographs and illustrations. Bibliographies specific to subject are also found throughout the four volumes. Recommended for grade 6 and above.

Moss, Joyce, and George Wilson. *Peoples of the World: Latin Americans*. 1st ed. Detroit: Gale Research, 1991. 323p. $45.00. ISBN 0-8103-7445-5.

The series Peoples of the World profiles various ethnic groups. The authors have made the focus of their work the people of a country rather than the country itself. The premise of the work is that governments and other world events affect change in many countries, but culture and tradition do not change. Separate volumes have been devoted to North Americans and to Latin Americans as well as to other areas around the world. Each entry is introduced with phonetic spelling and definition. Information on population, location, language, and geographical setting is also included. Other sections for each culture include historical background and culture today. Special features include maps for each culture that indicate current location. While political and economic information may not be current, this work is a good source of cultural and historical information. Also included are black-and-white illustrations and photographs, a glossary, and an index. This set is written especially for students in junior high school, making it appropriate for students in grade 7 and above.

Nagel, Rob, and Sharon Rose. *Hispanic American Biography*. New York: UXL, 1995. 2 vols. $60.00. ISBN 0-8103-9808-1.

More than 90 prominent Hispanic Americans from all fields of endeavor are profiled in this set. Black-and-white photographs are provided for each entry as well as a list of sources for further reading. A quotation by or about the subject introduces each entry. Fields of endeavor, dates, and places of birth and death are listed. Entries provide personal and professional information, career highlights, achievements, and awards. Arranged alphabetically, the work lists subjects in a table of contents and has an index by field of endeavor. Published for students, this work is both informative and appealing. Recommended for grade 5 and above.

Tenenbaum, Barbara A., ed. *The Encyclopedia of Latin American History and Culture*. New York: Charles Scribner's Sons, 1996. 5 vols. $485.00. ISBN 0-684-19253-5.

Nearly 5,300 alphabetically arranged articles cover persons, places, and things related to Latin American history and culture. Articles range from a paragraph to a page and are signed. However, certain topics are often given more coverage. There are several black-and-white photographs and illustrations. Cross-references are listed in an appendix. Other appendixes list biographies according to field of endeavor. There is also an index. Recommended for grade 6 and above.

Search for Latino
Language and Culture

Name_____ Class_____ Date_____

Use the Reference List for Latino Language and Culture to find the answers to these questions.

1. What names are given to second- and third-generation Puerto Ricans who renew their ties to Puerto Rico by moving there from the mainland?

    _____

    _____

    _____

2. What is the origin of the word alligator?

    _____

    _____

    _____

3. Find a visual illustration of a salad spinner. What is the Spanish word for this kitchen utensil?

    _____

    _____

    _____

4. What is a *jicara*?

    _____

    _____

    _____

5. What is a *molinillo*?

    _____

    _____

    _____

6. What are Huichols?

_____

_____

_____

7. What is the origin of the word *renegade*?

_____

_____

_____

8. Gazpacho, a chilled tomato vegetable soup, is a popular menu item in many restaurants. What were the ingredients of the original version eaten by Spanish peasants?

_____

_____

_____

9. Find a visual representation of a seventeenth-century cannon. List Spanish names for the projectiles known as chain shot and grape shot.

_____

_____

_____

10. Values shared among many Panamanians are *personalismo* and *machismo*. Define these terms.

_____

_____

_____

Hispanics in
Arts and Entertainment

Many Hispanics have attained success in fine and performing arts as painters, actors, singers, and dancers. Others have excelled in sports. This search highlights achievements in these fields.

Reference List for
Hispanics in Arts and Entertainment

Grolier Library of International Biographies. Danbury, CT: Grolier Education Corp., 1996. 10 vols. $299.00. ISBN 0-7172-7527-2.

Twentieth-century achievers from various fields of endeavor are profiled in this 10-volume set. Each entry provides personal information ranging from childhood events to career highlights to values and beliefs. Achievements are detailed as well. Written for students, this work is written in clear, straightforward language. Each volume is devoted to a particular field of endeavor, covering areas such as scientists, performing artists, writers, and explorers. Boldface is used to indicate that the word and its definition will be found in a glossary specific to each volume's subject area. Black-and-white photographs, bibliographies, and indexes for each volume and a general index by subject, country, and name are included. Recommended for grade 5 and above.

Kanellos, Nicolás. *Hispanic Firsts: 500 Years of Extraordinary Achievements.* Detroit: Gale Research, 1997. 372p. $44.95. ISBN 0-7816-0517-4.

Kanellos, an award-winning expert in the field of Hispanic studies, has compiled another excellent reference. Contributions and achievements have been compiled chronologically according to fields of endeavor. Chapters include Art and Design, and Film, Labor, and Religion, as well as a Timeline, Calendar of Firsts, Bibliography, Index by Year, and General Index. There are several black-and-white photographs and illustrations. Kanellos has based his work on the premise that Hispanics have contributed greatly to U.S. civilization and that Hispanics are pioneers not only for their achievements but also for overcoming obstacles in American society that barred their success. Kanellos' work is informative and appealing; it is an excellent resource and fun to browse. Recommended for grade 5 and above.

Nagel, Rob, and Sharon Rose. *Hispanic American Biography.* New York: UXL, 1995. 2 vols. $60.00. ISBN 0-8103-9808-1.

More than 90 prominent Hispanic Americans from all fields of endeavor are profiled in this set. Black-and-white photographs are provided for each entry as well as a list of sources for further reading. A quotation by or about the subject introduces each entry. Fields of endeavor, dates, and places of birth and death are listed. Entries provide personal and professional information, career highlights, achievements, and awards. Arranged alphabetically, the work lists subjects in a table of contents and has an index by field of endeavor. Published for students, this work is both informative and appealing. Recommended for grade 5 and above.

Novas, Himilce. *The Hispanic 100: A Ranking of Latino Men and Women Who Have Most Influenced Thought and Culture*. New York: Citadel Press, 1995. 495p. $24.95. ISBN 0-8065-1651-8.

Hispanic men and women from all fields of endeavor have been ranked according to degree of impact. For the author's purposes, they also had to be considered trailblazers. The introduction provides an explanation of the use of the terms Latino and Hispanic as well as a brief discussion of Latinos in the United States. Entries are two-and-a-half to three pages. A black-and-white photograph or illustration with dates of birth and death begin each entry. Details of childhood, family life, education, career highlights, and honors and awards are also provided. Additionally, a brief discussion of each entrant's influence is presented. There is an index. Novas' writing is clear and straightforward. Recommended for grade 5 and above.

Telgen, Diane, and Jim Camp, eds. *Notable Hispanic Women*. Detroit: Gale Research, 1993. 448p. $59.95. ISBN 0-8103-7578-8.

Nearly 300 alphabetically arranged entries comprise this work. Entrants were chosen by an advisory board of experts. After evaluation and selection, many subjects were interviewed by telephone. Entries range from 500 to 2,500 words and include personal, family, and career highlights. Longer entries also provide a black-and-white photograph. The work is cross-referenced for locating compound surnames. In addition to alphabetical listings of the subjects, there are listings by ethnicity and field of endeavor. This is an excellent resource for students in grade 5 and above.

Tenenbaum, Barbara A., ed. *The Encyclopedia of Latin American History and Culture*. New York: Charles Scribner's Sons, 1996. 5 vols. $485.00. ISBN 0-684-19253-5.

Nearly 5,300 alphabetically arranged articles cover persons, places, and things related to Latin American history and culture. Articles range from a paragraph to a page and are signed. However, certain topics are often given more coverage. There are several black-and-white photographs and illustrations. Cross-references are listed in an appendix. Other appendixes list biographies according to field of endeavor. There is also an index. Recommended for grade 6 and above.

Search for Hispanics in Arts and Entertainment

Name_____ Class_____ Date_____

Use the Reference List for Hispanics in Arts and Entertainment to find the answers to these questions. You may find answers for some questions in more than one source.

1. Martin Dihigo was a Cuban baseball player who never made it to the major leagues. Use an international reference to find out why he is notable.

    _____

    _____

    _____

2. Why did actress Elizabeth Peña's parents name her Elizabeth?

    _____

    _____

    _____

3. Celia Cruz is known as the Queen of Salsa. However, this was not her original plan. What was her original goal?

    _____

    _____

    _____

4. In 1923, Adolfo Luque achieved a first in baseball. What was it?

    _____

    _____

    _____

5. Judith Baca, artist and teacher, is best-known for her mural, *The Great Wall of Los Angeles.* What is significant about this mural? How long did it take Baca to complete?

    _____

    _____

    _____

6. Carlos Santana and his group were the first musicians to experiment with the fusion of rock and salsa. How many gold and platinum albums have been awarded to Santana?

_____

_____

_____

7. Diego Rivera, a Mexican artist, produced a work called *The Mathematician*. The work shows Rivera's involvement with another artist. Who is the other artist?

_____

_____

_____

8. Felipé Alou, a native of the Dominican Republic, debuted for the Giants in 1958. Which honor did he receive in 1994?

_____

_____

_____

9. What is notable about Dolores Del Rio? What was her real name?

_____

_____

_____

10. What first was achieved by Rudy Galindo in 1996?

_____

_____

_____

Hispanic Literature

Many Hispanics have excelled in writing. This search focuses on writers who are Hispanic and Hispanic Americans. Not only have these writers excelled in their field, many of them have also won numerous awards for their work. A few questions also relate to Hispanic literature.

Reference List for Hispanic Literature

Kanellos, Nicolás. *Hispanic Firsts: 500 Years of Extraordinary Achievements*. Detroit: Gale Research, 1997. 372p. $44.95. ISBN 0-7816-0517-4.

Kanellos, an award-winning expert in the field of Hispanic studies, has compiled another excellent reference. Contributions and achievements have been compiled chronologically according to fields of endeavor. Chapters include Art and Design, and Film, Labor, and Religion, as well as a Timeline, Calendar of Firsts, Bibliography, Index by Year, and General Index. There are several black-and-white photographs and illustrations. Kanellos has based his work on the premise that Hispanics have contributed greatly to U.S. civilization and that Hispanics are pioneers not only for their achievements but also for overcoming obstacles in American society that barred their success. Kanellos' work is informative and appealing; it is an excellent resource and fun to browse. Recommended for grade 5 and above.

Magill, Frank N., ed. *Masterpieces of Latino Literature*. New York: HarperCollins, 1994. 655p. $45.00. ISBN 0-06-270106-1.

Part of Magill's Masterpieces series, this work presents 140 essays on works of Latino literature and 33 essays on poetry, prose, and drama. Essays are arranged alphabetically by title of work. Information in each essay follows a format that includes author, type of work, setting, date published, character description, plot summary, analysis, and a critical context, which evaluates the impact and contribution of the work. The general essays examine authors' works, list major works, and discuss the author's themes and imagery. There are title and author indexes. A useful resource for students and teachers, this work serves as a guide to Latino literature. Recommended for grade 7 and above.

Nagel, Rob, and Sharon Rose. *Hispanic American Biography*. New York: UXL, 1995. 2 vols. $60.00. ISBN 0-8103-9808-1.

More than 90 prominent Hispanic Americans from all fields of endeavor are profiled in this set. Black-and-white photographs are provided for each entry as well as a list of sources for further reading. A quotation by or about the subject introduces each entry. Fields of endeavor, dates, and places of birth and death are listed. Entries provide personal and professional information, career highlights, achievements, and awards. Arranged alphabetically, the work lists subjects in a table of contents and has an index by field of endeavor. Published for students, this work is both informative and appealing. Recommended for grade 5 and above.

Ryan, Bryan, ed. *Hispanic Writers: A Selection of Sketches from Contemporary Authors*. Detroit: Gale Research, 1991. 514p. $90.00. ISBN 0-8103-7688-1.

More than 400 entries on twentieth-century Hispanic writers have been compiled for this work. Works of Hispanic writers who are social and political figures, scholars, historians, journalists, and literary figures have been included. Entries provide personal information, including address, career highlights, awards, honors, and biographical and critical sources as well as a chronological list of writings and work in progress. Also included is a guide to authors and a nationality index. This is an excellent source for anyone interested in Hispanic writers. Recommended for grade 5 and above.

Tenenbaum, Barbara A., ed. *The Encyclopedia of Latin American History and Culture*. New York: Charles Scribner's Sons, 1996. 5 vols. $485.00. ISBN 0-684-19253-5.

Nearly 5,300 alphabetically arranged articles cover persons, places, and things related to Latin American history and culture. Articles range from a paragraph to a page and are signed. However, certain topics are often given more coverage. There are several black-and-white photographs and illustrations. Cross-references are listed in an appendix. Other appendixes list biographies according to field of endeavor. There is also an index. Recommended for grade 6 and above.

Search for Hispanic Literature

Name_____ Class_____ Date_____

Use the Reference List for Hispanic Literature to find the answers to these questions. It is possible that you may find the correct answers for some questions in more than one source.

1. Use a reference that lists writers' addresses to find the address of Denise Chavez. Write her address in the space below.

_____

_____

_____

2. What is *Gauchesa* literature?

_____

_____

_____

3. Gabriel García Márquez, Nobel prize-winning author, credits his writing style to his grandmother. How did this come about?

_____

_____

_____

4. Name the author of the novel *Old Gringo*. Which famous American writer is one of the characters in the book?

_____

_____

_____

5. In 1989 Josefina Lopez, a 17-year-old Mexican immigrant, achieved a first for someone her age. What was it?

_____

_____

_____

6. In 1976 Gary Soto achieved a first as a Hispanic American writer. What was his achievement?

_____

_____

_____

7. Which work by John Chavez was nominated for a Pulitzer Prize in 1984?

_____

_____

_____

8. Who is Eugenio Florit? When and where was he born?

_____

_____

_____

9. What is *canloria*?

_____

_____

_____

10. Lucilla Godoy Alcayaga uses a pseudonym, or pen name. What is her pen name?

_____

_____

_____

Significant Latino People, Places, and Events

The questions in this search highlight individuals and groups of people important in history. A few historically significant places have been included as well. Events significant in family life and history complete this search.

Reference List for Significant Latino People, Places, and Events

Dresser, Norine. *Multicultural Manners: New Rules of Etiquette for a Changing Society*. New York: John Wiley & Sons, Inc., 1996. 286p. $14.95. ISBN 0-471-11819-2.

Dresser writes the Multicultural Manners column for the *Los Angeles Times*. Many items from her column have been collected here. Dresser is also a folklorist. As a result, her work is a delightful mix of information and folklore. It is also indicative of how America is changing. Part One of the work deals with communication, including body language, child-rearing practices, classroom behavior, gifts, and male and female relationships. Part Two deals with holidays and worship. Finally, Part Three deals with health practices. Included as well are a bibliography, an index, and an appendix of Southeast Asian refugees. Dresser supplies fascinating information on how different meanings are attached to the thumbs-up sign, offering food, gift taboos, and rules for worship. The book is a treasure. It is useful and appealing for all ages. Recommended for grade 5 and above.

Kanellos, Nicolás. *Hispanic Firsts: 500 Years of Extraordinary Achievements*. Detroit: Gale Research, 1997. 372p. $44.95. ISBN 0-7816-0517-4.

Kanellos, an award-winning expert in the field of Hispanic studies, has compiled another excellent reference. Contributions and achievements have been compiled chronologically according to fields of endeavor. Chapters include Art and Design, and Film, Labor, and Religion, as well as a Timeline, Calendar of Firsts, Bibliography, Index by Year, and General Index. There are several black-and-white photographs and illustrations. Kanellos has based his work on the premise that Hispanics have contributed greatly to U.S. civilization and that Hispanics are pioneers not only for their achievements but also for overcoming obstacles in American society that barred their success. Kanellos' work is informative and appealing; it is an excellent resource and fun to browse. Recommended for grade 5 and above.

Moss, Joyce, and George Wilson. *Peoples of the World: Latin Americans*. 1st ed. Detroit: Gale Research, 1991. 323p. $45.00. ISBN 0-8103-7445-5.

The series Peoples of the World profiles various ethnic groups. The authors have made the focus of their work the people of a country rather than the country itself. The premise of the work is that governments and other world events affect change in many countries, but culture and tradition do not change. Separate volumes have been devoted to North Americans and to Latin Americans as well as to other areas around the world. Each entry is introduced with phonetic spelling and definition. Information on population, location, language, and geographical setting is also included. Other sections for each culture include historical background and culture today. Special features include maps for each culture that indicate current location. While political and economic information may not be current, this work is a good source of cultural and historical information. Also included are black-and-white illustrations and photographs, a glossary, and an index. This set is written especially for students in junior high school, making it appropriate for students in grade 7 and above.

Nagel, Rob, and Sharon Rose. *Hispanic American Biography*. New York: UXL, 1995. 2 vols. $60.00. ISBN 0-8103-9808-1.

More than 90 prominent Hispanic Americans from all fields of endeavor are profiled in this set. Black-and-white photographs are provided for each entry as well as a list of sources for further reading. A quotation by or about the subject introduces each entry. Fields of endeavor, dates, and places of birth and death are listed. Entries provide personal and professional information, career highlights, achievements, and awards. Arranged alphabetically, the work lists subjects in a table of contents and has an index by field of endeavor. Published for students, this work is informative and appealing. Recommended for grade 5 and above.

Tenenbaum, Barbara A., ed. *The Encyclopedia of Latin American History and Culture*. New York: Charles Scribner's Sons, 1996. 5 vol. $485.00. ISBN 0-684-19253-5.

Nearly 5,300 alphabetically arranged articles cover persons, places, and things related to Latin American history and culture. Articles range from a paragraph to a page and are signed. However, certain topics are often given more coverage. There are several black-and-white photographs and illustrations. Cross-references are listed in an appendix. Other appendixes list biographies according to field of endeavor. There is also an index. Recommended for grade 6 and above.

Search for Significant Latino People, Places, and Events

Name_____ Class_____ Date_____

Use the Reference List for Significant Latino People, Places, and Events to find the answers to these questions.

1. What is significant about the Quito School of Sculpture?

   _____

   _____

   _____

2. The Day of the Dead is a Mexican holiday. What is the basis for this holiday?

   _____

   _____

   _____

3. Who was Jose Marti?

   _____

   _____

   _____

4. Who were the Maroons?

   _____

   _____

   _____

5. What did Ellen Ochoa achieve at age 33?

   _____

   _____

   _____

6. What is Casas Grandes?

_____

_____

_____

7. In 1512 the Dominicans built the first cathedral. What other firsts were built that year?

_____

_____

_____

8. Costa Rica lies between which two countries?

_____

_____

_____

9. Pancho Villa, a Mexican revolutionary, changed his name. What was his real name?

_____

_____

_____

10. The Louisiana Revolt of 1768 was fought against the Spanish Rule in New Orleans by merchants and planters. What was significant about the way it was fought?

_____

_____

_____

Answer Key for Latino Language and Culture

1. In Moss and Wilson. They are called New Yoricans or Neo-Ricans.
2. In Ayto. When the Spanish first saw alligators, they referred to them as *el lagarto*, which means lizard.
3. In Corbeil and Archamboult. It is called *mexcladora de ensaladas*.
4. In Kanellos. Made of a dried gourd or pumpkin shell, it is used to serve beverages.
5. In Kanellos. Made of finely carved wood, it is a chocolate beater.
6. In Tenenbaum. They are the largest group of Mexican Indians who are still intact. They live in the Sierra Madre Occidental.
7. In Ayto. It is a term derived from Anglo-Hispanic contact at the end of sixteenth century. The original form is *renagado*.
8. In Albyn and Webb. The original gazpacho was made of stale bread soaked in olive oil and tomato juice.
9. In Corbeil and Archamboult. Chain shot is *balas encedenadas*, and grape shot is *metralla*.
10. In Moss and Wilson. *Personalismo* is belief in trust and honor between people, but it also includes distrust of organizations and sensitivity to both praise and insult. *Machismo* refers to male dominance.

Answer Key for Hispanics in Arts and Entertainment

1. In *Grolier*. Dihigo was an all-around player. He consistently hit close to .400, his pitching record was 261–138, and his earned run average in 1938 was 0.92.
2. In Novas. Peña's parents named her after the New Jersey city where she was born.
3. In Telgen and Camp. Cruz wanted to be a wife, mother, and teacher.
4. In Kanellos. Luque became the first Hispanic American to play in the World Series.
5. In Nagel and Rose. Baca's mural is a half-mile long and is the largest mural in the world. It took her more than nine years to complete.
6. In Kanellos. Santana has nine platinum and 16 gold albums.
7. In Tenenbaum. Rivera's work shows Paul Cézanne.
8. In *Grolier*. Alou was named manager of the year in 1994.
9. In Telgen and Camp. Dolores Del Rio was an actress. Her real name was Lolita Dolores Asúnsolo y Lopéz.
10. In Kanellos. Galindo became the first Hispanic national figure-skating champion.

Answer Key for Hispanic Literature

1. In Ryan. The address for Denise Chavez is 1524 Sul Ross, Houston, TX 77006.
2. In Tenenbaum. Writers in Buenos Aires created this form of literature based on the speech of gauchos.
3. In Nagel and Rose. His grandmother invented fantasies as an escape from the bleak life they lived.
4. In Magill. Carlos Fuentes wrote *Old Gringo*. Ambrose Bierce is one of the characters.
5. In Kanellos. Lopez's play *Simplemento Maria or The American Dream* was broadcast on PBS.
6. In Kanellos. Soto won the United States Award of the International Poetry Forum for his work, *The Elements of San Joaquin*.
7. In Ryan. *The Lost Land: The Chicano Image of the Southwest*.
8. In Tenenbaum. Florit is a Cuban poet born in Madrid on October 15, 1903.
9. In Tenenbaum. *Canloria* is traditional poetry of northern Brazil. It is sung by *cantidores*, who accompany themselves on musical instruments.
10. In Ryan. Her pen name is Gabriela Mistral.

Answer Key for Significant Latino People, Places, and Events

1. In Tenenbaum. Begun in 1535, the Quito School of Sculpture was the first art school in America.
2. In Dresser. The Day of the Dead is based on the belief that the dead do not go immediately to their final resting place.
3. In Moss and Wilson. Marti, who has been called the Apostle of Cuban Liberty, led a revolution that resulted in Cuban independence.
4. In Moss and Wilson. The Maroons were Black slaves who escaped from their Spanish owners. They hampered British rule in Jamaica until they won a peace treaty in 1738.
5. In Nagel and Rose. Ochoa was the first female Hispanic astronaut.
6. In Tenenbaum. Casas Grandes is an archaeological site in Mexico.
7. In Kanellos. The first hospital and school were also built that year.
8. In Moss and Wilson. Costa Rica lies between Nicaragua and Panama.
9. In Nagel and Rose. Villa's real name was Doroteo Arango.
10. In Tenenbaum. The revolt was fought without bloodshed.

Chapter
Ten

Native Americans

The study of Native Americans is not the study of a culture. Rather, it is the study of many cultures. The following references and searches represent only a small sampling of the many aspects of these cultures. The history of Native American cultures is poignant, courageous, and often tragic. It is not possible to include every significant person, event, or facet of Native American cultures in these searches. However, the references and questions are designed to present a broad range of information. Your search for the answers should increase your desire to learn more about the first Americans.

Reference List for
Noteworthy Native Americans

Avery, Susan, and Linda Skinner. *Extraordinary American Indians*. Chicago: Children's Press, 1992. 252p. $15.95. ISBN 0-516-40583-7.

A collection of profiles of more than 60 individuals, this work consists of a wide range of individuals who have made contributions to American society. A few entries cover special topics, such as the American Indian Movement (AIM) and the Navajo Code Talkers, who used their language to create an undecipherable code used to send top-secret messages during World War II. The authors' intent is that the study of the extraordinary lives profiled here will inspire further research and lead readers to further achievement in their own lives. Also included are an index, a bibliography arranged by topic, and a videography. Most entries also have more than one black-and-white photograph or illustration. The forward provides a brief overview of Native Americans. Each page is decorated with a border that depicts elements from tribes in various areas of the country. Recommended for grade 6 and above.

Malinowski, Sharon, and George H. J. Abrams, eds. *Notable Native Americans*. Detroit: Gale Research, 1994. 492p. $80.00. ISBN 0-8103-9638-6.

More than 265 Native Americans from historical times to the present are featured in this biobibliography. Entrants from all fields of endeavor are listed alphabetically. Signed essays from one to three pages in length include tribal name, field of endeavor, dates of birth and death, and when possible, a black-and-white photograph. Sketches include details of family and early life, education, career highlights, honors and awards, a list of works when applicable, and a list of sources for further reading. Special features include a list of entries according to tribal group and a list according to occupation. Abrams provides an insightful introduction, Race, Culture, and Law: The Question of American Indian Identity. Written for students, teachers, librarians, and general readers, this book is appropriate for grade 5 and above.

Malinowski, Sharon, and Simon Glickman, eds. *Native North American Biography*. Detroit: Gale Research, 1996. 202p. $60.00. ISBN 0-8103-9821-4.

This two-volume set consists of alphabetically arranged biographical sketches of 112 famous Native Americans from the past and present and from all walks of life. Many sketches include a direct quotation by the subject as well as several black-and-white photographs and illustrations. Each sketch includes dates of birth and death, biographical information, and a Further Reading section, which is a short bibliography. Volume One begins with entries by tribal groups and a Reader's Guide. There is also an index by field of endeavor at the end of Volume Two. This set was written especially for students and is appropriate for grade 5 and above.

Swisher, Karen Gayton, and AnCita Benally. *Native North American Firsts*. Detroit: Gale Research, 1997. 263p. $48.55. ISBN 0-7876-0518-2.

Beginning with a month-by-month Calendar of Firsts and a Timeline, this work is arranged alphabetically by topic. Included are Education, Literature, Religious Life, Sciences, and many others. Under each topic there are also various subheadings. For example, under Military there are sections on the Civil War, World War I, and so on. Within each section, entries are listed chronologically. Also included are several black-and-white photographs, a bibliography, an index by year, and a general index. As a result, this work is very accessible. Overall, this is an excellent reference. Appropriate for grade 6 and above.

Search for Noteworthy
Native Americans

Name_____ Class_____ Date_____

Use the Reference List for Noteworthy Native Americans to find answers to the following questions. If you read carefully, you may find a clue in the question that will lead you to the source with the best answer.

1. Will Sampson, a Native American actor, channeled some of his movie earnings into an organization called Red Wind. What is the purpose of Red Wind?

   _____

   _____

   _____

2. Which first was achieved by Evelyn Yellow Robe in 1954?

   _____

   _____

   _____

3. What made Ira Hayes famous?

   _____

   _____

   _____

4. For which of his books did N. Scott Momaday win a Pulitzer prize in 1969?

   _____

   _____

   _____

5. Kiowa physician Edward Everett Rhoades was national director of the Indian Health Service. During his tenure, he was responsible for the health of how many Native Americans?

   _____

   _____

   _____

6. Native American runner Billy Mills set a record in distance running in the 1964 Olympic Games. Other than being an unknown with no chance of winning, what made his victory truly astounding?

_____

_____

_____

7. The Code Talkers of World War II were truly extraordinary. The Japanese were never able to decipher their codes during the war. Whose idea was it to use Native Americans (Navajo), and what were the requirements?

_____

_____

_____

8. Harold Cardinal is a Cree tribal leader born in Canada. In 1969 he wrote *The Unjust Society: The Tragedy of Canada's Indians*. For what reason did Cardinal write the book?

_____

_____

_____

9. Tecumseh, Shawnee warrior and tribal leader, was known by other names. What were they?

_____

_____

_____

10. Who is Maria Tallchief? List a first achieved by her.

_____

_____

_____

Native American Cultures

Completing this search should create an awareness of the closeness with nature that is part of many Native American cultures. Native Americans were the first ecologists and had great love and respect for nature. This search also highlights the cultural contributions of Native American individuals.

Reference List for Native American Cultures

Cayton, Mary Kupiec, Elliott J. Gorn, and Peter W. Williams, eds. *The Encyclopedia of American Social History*. New York: Charles Scribner's Sons, 1993. 2,653p. $350.00. ISBN 0-684-19246-2.

The Encyclopedia of American Social History, part of a larger Scribner's American Civilization Series, includes 180 essays on issues in daily American life from colonization through modern times. The work is arranged in 14 thematic sections, including Work and Labor, Ethnic and Racial Subcultures, Space and Place, and Patterns of Everyday Life. Essays are signed, and each is followed with a bibliography of related works. Several black-and-white maps and charts are included as well. Described as a work of scholarship that combines work in theology, gender study, geography, literature, religion, anthropology, and sociology, this work provides information not found in many other sources. Recommended for grade 7 and above.

Champagne, Duane, ed. *Chronology of Native North American History*. Detroit: Gale Research, 1994. 574p. $34.00. ISBN 0-8103-9195-3.

Champagne has compiled an impressive variety of entries, covering issues and events as well as people and places. Special features include Tribal Chronologies and Historical Timeline. Also included is an annotated bibliography. Champagne's introduction, written in chronological order, discusses Native North American creation stories, regional groups, and religious movements. Several black-and-white photographs, maps, and illustrations are provided. Of special interest are the Documents in History and Excerpts from Significant Legal Cases sections. There is also a general bibliography and an index. Recommended for grade 6 and above.

———. *Native North American Almanac*. Detroit: Gale Research, 1994. 1,200p. $60.00. ISBN 0-8103-8865-0.

In this four-volume work compiled by Champagne, topics covered include Activism, Environment, Education, Demography, Religion, Arts, and Media. He has compiled alphabetical and geographical lists of tribes, a multimedia bibliography, an occupational index, and a glossary. Several black-and-white photographs, illustrations, and maps have been included as well.

Champagne also provides information on Native Canadians, and lists museums, landmarks, and tribal collections. The glossary is informative, and the bibliography is excellent. Recommended for grade 6 and above.

Mail, Thomas E. *The Mystic Warriors of the Plains: The Culture, Arts, Craft, and Religion of the Plains Indians*. New York: Marlowe, 1995. 618p. $25.00. ISBN 1-56924-843-5.

Originally published in 1972, Mail's work is a comprehensive detailing of all aspects of life of the Plains Indians. It includes black-and-white and color illustrations, an index, notes on each chapter, a list of specific sources, and an extensive bibliography. It should be noted that the bibliography is not current. Mail, a Lutheran pastor, notes in his introduction that he includes religious references because he finds similarities between Christianity and the religion of the Plains Indians. Chapters cover such topics as social customs, government, personal qualities, religion, clothing, hairstyles, jewelry and headdresses. The book is especially appealing because of its many illustrations. Recommended for grade 5 and above.

Malinowski, Sharon, and Simon Glickman, eds. *Native North American Biography*. Detroit: Gale Research, 1996. 202p. $60.00. ISBN 0-8103-9821-4.

This two-volume set consists of alphabetically arranged biographical sketches of 112 famous Native Americans from the past and present and from all walks of life. Many sketches include a direct quotation by the subject as well as several black-and-white photographs and illustrations. Each sketch includes dates of birth and death, biographical information, and a Further Reading section, which is a short bibliography. Volume One begins with entries by tribal groups and a Reader's Guide. There is also an index by field of endeavor at the end of Volume Two. This set was written especially for students and is appropriate for grade 5 and above.

Moss, Joyce, and George Wilson. *Peoples of the World: North Americans*. 1st ed. Detroit: Gale Research, 1991. 441p. $45.00. ISBN 0-8103-7768-3.

The Peoples of the World series profiles various ethnic groups. The authors have made the focus of their work the people of a country rather than the country itself. The premise of the work is that governments and other world events affect change in many countries, but culture and tradition do not change. Separate volumes have been devoted to North Americans and to Latin Americans as well as to other areas around the world. Each entry is introduced with phonetic spelling and definition. Information on population, location, language, and geographical setting is also included. Other sections for each culture include historical background and culture today. Special features include maps for each culture that indicate current location. While political and economic information may not be current, this work is a good source of cultural and historical information. Also included are black-and-white illustrations and photographs, a glossary, and an index. This set is written especially for students in junior high school, making it appropriate for students in grade 7 and above.

Straub, Deborah Gillan, ed. *Native North American Voices*. Detroit: UXL, 1996. 235p. $34.00. ISBN 0-8103-9819-2.

Straub has collected speeches of 20 notable Native North Americans. The section Speech Topics at a Glance categorizes speeches. Topics include the American Indian Movement, Children, Education, Militancy, and Ethnic Stereotyping. Entries are arranged alphabetically by speaker. Each speech begins with a brief biographical sketch. Black-and-white illustrations are also included. Sidebars present vocabulary and quotations. Each excerpt is followed with a list of sources. Straub also provides a time line of important Native North American events, ranging from 1754 to 1995. Written especially for students, this work is appropriate for grade 5 and above.

Waldman, Carl. *The Encyclopedia of Native American Tribes*. New York: Facts on File, 1987. 293p. $45.00. ISBN 0-8160-1421-3.

Tribes are listed alphabetically along with general headings such as Mound Builders and Aztec and Maya Civilizations. In addition, Waldman supplies culture areas and maps for groups with different lifestyles. Color illustrations, a glossary, and a bibliography are included as well. The author limited his selection to approximately 150 entries, with choices based on historical or cultural significance. The book opens with a map and chart of culture areas. Content of entries varies. Larger entries provide information on ways of life, food, and religion. Shorter entries are more general. Recommended for grade 5 and above.

Search for Native American Cultures

Name_____ Class_____ Date_____

Use the Reference List for Native American Cultures to find answers to the following questions. If you look carefully, you may find a clue in the question that will indicate which source will provide the best answer to the question.

1. The Plains Indians wore a scalp lock. Describe it and explain its significance.

   _____

   _____

   _____

2. What was the primary lifestyle of the Apache?

   _____

   _____

   _____

3. Within the Southwest culture area, two tribes are part of the Athapascan language family. Name them.

   _____

   _____

   _____

4. The Hopi are fairly well-known people of North America. In the Hopi religion, there is a ceremonial calendar consisting of two seasons. Name the seasons and tell in which season the Women's Society dances are held.

   _____

   _____

   _____

5. Ben Nighthorse Campbell is a U.S. senator. For which artistic endeavor has he won awards?

   _____

   _____

   _____

 From *Multicultural Information Quests* by Marie E. Rodgers. © 2000 Libraries Unlimited. (800) 237-6124.

6. List four recreational activities enjoyed by Eskimos.

_____

_____

_____

7. Rock music is part of America's social history. Native American rights were brought to light in rock music of the 1970s. Identify the artist and the ethnicity of the person who recorded a Native American rights album based on Vine DeLoria's book, *Custer Died for Your Sins*.

_____

_____

_____

8. In 1899 the first novel written by a Native American was published. Name the novel and the author.

_____

_____

_____

9. Which plant is used in Native American medicine to treat aching muscles? How is it prepared and used?

_____

_____

_____

10. Which languages do the Aleuts speak?

_____

_____

_____

Significant Events in Native American History

This search focuses on events that have had great impact on Native Americans and on American history. Modern-day activists have poignantly drawn attention to the history of injustices toward Native Americans.

Reference List for Significant Events in Native American History

Champagne, Duane, ed. *Chronology of Native North American History*. Detroit: Gale Research, 1994. 574p. $34.00. ISBN 0-8103-9195-3.

Champagne has compiled an impressive variety of entries, covering issues and events as well as people and places. Special features include Tribal Chronologies and Historical Timeline. Also included is an annotated bibliography. Champagne's introduction, written in chronological order, discusses Native North American creation stories, regional groups, and religious movements. Several black-and-white photographs, maps, and illustrations are provided. Of special interest are the Documents in History and Excerpts from Significant Legal Cases sections. There is also a general bibliography and an index. Recommended for grade 6 and above.

———. *Native North American Almanac*. Detroit: Gale Research, 1994. 1,200p. $60.00. ISBN 0-8103-8865-0.

In this four-volume work compiled by Champagne, topics covered include Activism, Environment, Education, Demography, Religion, Arts, and Media. He has compiled alphabetical and geographical lists of tribes, a multimedia bibliography, an occupational index, and a glossary. Several black-and-white photographs, illustrations, and maps have been included as well. Champagne also provides information on Native Canadians, and lists museums, landmarks, and tribal collections. The glossary is informative, and the bibliography is excellent. Recommended for grade 6 and above.

Hazen-Hammond, Susan. *Timelines of Native American History: Through the Centuries with Mother Earth and Father Sky*. New York: Perigee, 1997. 332p. $16.00. ISBN 0-399-52307-3.

Arranged chronologically, Hazen-Hammond's work begins with a map and a key to symbols that identify regions where significant events occurred. The time period covered ranges from before 20,000 B.C. to 1997, with predictions for the year 2000 and beyond. The work contains more than 1,500 year-by-year entries. Sidebars of information and facts about customs and folklore, short bibliographical sketches, and questions are provided. Also included are an index and a bibliography. This is an authoritative and appealing work for grade 5 and above.

Historical Maps on File. New York: Facts on File, 1983. 313p. $155.00. ISBN 0-87196-708-1.

Arranged chronologically, this book consists of eight sections, each devoted to a specific period of time and place. Chapters include Ancient History, Medieval History, Asia, Australia, and Modern European History. The section on American History contains several maps related to Native Americans. The book may be accessed through the table of contents or through the subject index. Maps are printed on heavy stock and are easy to read. Recommended for grade 5 and above.

Langer, Howard J., comp. and ed. *American Indian Quotations*. Westport, CT: Greenwood Press, 1996. 260p. $49.95. ISBN 0-313-29121-7.

Arranged chronologically, Langer's work consists of more than 800 quotations, most of which were translated by white interpreters. The question of accuracy is resolved, Langer feels, by recurrent themes that emerge over time and throughout several regions. Included are several black-and-white photographs. Quotations are numbered, and the source of a quotation follows each item. Written for adults, Langer's work is appealing to students in grade 5 and above.

Malinowski, Sharon, and Simon Glickman, eds. *Native North American Biography*. Detroit: Gale Research, 1996. 202p. $60.00. ISBN 0-8103-9821-4.

This two-volume set consists of alphabetically arranged biographical sketches of 112 famous Native Americans from the past and present and from all walks of life. Many sketches include a direct quotation by the subject as well as several black-and-white photographs and illustrations. Each sketch includes dates of birth and death, biographical information, and a Further Reading section, which is a short bibliography. Volume One begins with entries by tribal groups and a Reader's Guide. There is also an index by field of endeavor at the end of Volume Two. This set was written especially for students and is appropriate for grade 5 and above.

Straub, Deborah Gillan, ed. *Voices of Multicultural America: Notable Speeches Delivered by African, Asian, Hispanic, and Native Americans, 1790–1995*. Detroit: Gale Research, 1996. 1,372p. $102.60. ISBN 0-8103-9378-6.

More than 130 orators are profiled in this work. Profiles include biographical information, education, career, and significant events. Selections were based on the entrant's recognition within his or her particular ethnic group as well as within American society as a whole. The introduction consists of four essays that provide an overview of oratory traditions for each group represented. In addition to profiles, more than 230 speeches are included. Information on selected speeches includes historical context and, where appropriate, philosophical outlook. Date and location of speeches are included. A brief summary and a list of relevant sources conclude each entry. Also included are a table of contents, ethnicity index, special category index, time line, black-and-white photographs, and a keyword index. This is a valuable source for students in grade 7 and above.

Search for Significant Events
in Native American History

Name_____ Class_____ Date_____

Use the Reference List for Significant Events in Native American History to find the answers to the following questions. If you read carefully, you may find a clue in some questions that will lead you to the best source for your answer.

1. What happened in September 1970 at Mt. Rushmore? Why did it happen?

    _____

    _____

    _____

2. In 1958 the Lumbee Indians of Robeson County, North Carolina, were harassed by the Ku Klux Klan. What was the outcome of the dispute?

    _____

    _____

    _____

3. On July 8, 1758, a major battle of the French and Indian War was fought. Find the state and name the place where this battle occurred by locating it on a historical map.

    _____

    _____

    _____

4. Who is Russell Means, and what did he do on Thanksgiving Day in 1970?

    _____

    _____

    _____

5. In 1977 Leonard Peltier was accused, tried, and convicted of murdering two FBI agents at Pine Ridge Reservation in South Dakota. At his sentencing, Peltier read a statement criticizing the trial and the treatment of Native American activists. In his statement, Peltier also said he felt no guilt. Why did he say this?

_____

_____

_____

6. On June 2, 1983, President Ronald Reagan was criticized by the National Indian Tribal Chairman's Association. Why?

_____

_____

_____

7. The Battle of Greasy Grass occurred on June 25 and 26, 1876. By what other name is this battle known?

_____

_____

_____

8. Native American activists occupied Alcatraz Island on November 9, 1969. What price did they offer to pay for the island?

_____

_____

_____

9. Who is Wilma Mankiller, and what did she say about the Alcatraz experience?

_____

_____

_____

10. On April 11, 1968, Congress passed the American Indian Civil Rights Act. However, the Pueblo did not support the act. Why?

_____

_____

_____

Native Americans
and the U.S. Government

This search focuses on the U.S. government's treatment of Native North Americans in past and present day. As with other minorities, the federal government has been harsh. There is a long history of legislation that serves as a permanent record.

Reference List for Native Americans and the U.S. Government

Champagne, Duane, ed. *Chronology of Native North American History*. Detroit: Gale Research, 1994. 574p. $34.00. ISBN 0-8103-9195-3.

Champagne has compiled an impressive variety of entries, covering issues and events as well as people and places. Special feature include Tribal Chronologies and Historical Timeline. Also included is an annotated bibliography. Champagne's introduction, written in chronological order, discusses Native North American creation stories, regional groups, and religious movements. Several black-and-white photographs, maps, and illustrations are provided. Of special interest are the Documents in History and Excerpts from Significant Legal Cases sections. There is also a general bibliography and an index. Recommended for grade 6 and above.

———. *Native North American Almanac*. Detroit: Gale Research, 1994. 1,200p. $60.00. ISBN 0-8103-8865-0.

In this four-volume work compiled by Champagne, topics covered include Activism, Environment, Education, Demography, Religion, Arts, and Media. He has compiled alphabetical and geographical lists of tribes, a multimedia bibliography, an occupational index, and a glossary. Several black-and-white photographs, illustrations, and maps have been included as well. Champagne also provides information about Native Canadians and lists museums, landmarks, and tribal collections. The glossary is informative, and the bibliography is excellent. Recommended for grade 6 and above.

Cusic, Don. *Cowboys and the Wild West: An A–Z Guide from the Chisolm Trail to the Silver Screen*. New York: Facts on File, 1994. 356p. $40.00. ISBN 0-8160-3030-8.

Organized alphabetically, Cusic's work focuses on cowboys. Cusic includes entries on folk heroes and places, television shows, films, and fictional characters such as the Lone Ranger (to whom the book is also dedicated). He does, however, provide information on Native Americans, including several entries on tribal groups and terms. This work is informative and fun to read. Entries range from one paragraph to several pages. Also included are an index and several black-and-white photographs. The author states he wrote the book because he wanted to own a book like it. This work is a delightful collection of American fact and folklore. Recommended for grade 5 and above.

Dinnerstein, Leonard, Roger L. Nichols, and David Reimers. *Natives and Strangers*. New York: Oxford University Press, 1996. 370p. $25.00. ISBN 0-19-509083-7.

Cultural and artistic contributions are not the focus of this work. Rather, it concentrates on the social and economic impact of ethnic groups on America and its impact on them. The work is arranged chronologically. Ethnic groups are represented for each time period, thus enabling the authors to intertwine the history of each ethnic group with the history of America. The time period covered ranges from 1600 through 1995. The authors wanted their study to provide an understanding of how American minority groups have experienced various forms of conflict and other social conditions. Included are an index and a bibliography for each chapter. This is especially useful for those whose research focuses on a specific period in American history. Also included are black-and-white photographs and tables. Although the work is arranged chronologically, some chapters cover the same time period but have a different focus. For example, there are several chapters covering the mid-1800s through the 1930s. The focus on these years may range from immigration to industrialism to development of the West. Events are described in an engaging narrative, making this an appealing source for grade 8 and above.

Hazen-Hammond, Susan. *Timelines of Native American History: Through the Centuries with Mother Earth and Father Sky*. New York: Perigee, 1997. 332p. $16.00. ISBN 0-399-52307-3.

Arranged chronologically, Hazen-Hammond's work begins with a map and a key to symbols that identify regions where significant events occurred. The time period covered ranges from before 20,000 B.C. to 1997, with predictions for the year 2000 and beyond. The work contains more than 1,500 year-by-year entries. Sidebars of information and facts about customs and folklore, short bibliographical sketches, and questions are provided. Also included are an index and a bibliography. This is an authoritative and appealing work for grade 5 and above.

Historical Maps on File. New York: Facts on File, 1983. 313p. $155.00. ISBN 0-87196-708-1.

Arranged chronologically, this book consists of eight sections, each devoted to a specific period of time and place. Chapters include Ancient History, Medieval History, Asia, Australia, and Modern European History. The section on American History contains several maps related to Native American. The book may be accessed through the table of contents or through the subject index. Maps are printed on heavy stock and are easy to read. Recommended for grade 5 and above.

Moss, Joyce, and George Wilson. *Peoples of the World: North Americans*. 1st ed. Detroit: Gale Research, 1991. 441p. $45.00. ISBN 0-8103-7768-3.

The Peoples of the World series profiles various ethnic groups. The authors have made the focus of their work the people of a country rather than the country itself. The premise of the work is that governments and other world events affect change in many countries, but culture and tradition do not change. Separate volumes have been devoted to North Americans and to Latin Americans as well as to other areas around the world. Each entry is introduced with phonetic spelling and definition. Information on population, location, language, and geographical setting is also included. Other sections for each culture include historical background and culture today. Special features include maps for each culture that indicate current location. While political and economic information may not be current, this work is a good source of cultural and historical information. Also included are black-and-white illustrations and photographs, a glossary, and an index. This set is written especially for students in junior high school, making it appropriate for students in grade 7 and above.

Search for Native Americans and the U.S. Government

Name_____ Class_____ Date_____

Use the Reference List for Native Americans and the U.S. Government to locate answers to the following questions. If you read carefully, you may find a clue in the question that will lead you to the best source for the answer to a particular question.

1. What is the Trail of Tears?

   _____

   _____

   _____

2. In the 1920s the Committee of 100 was formed to investigate and make recommendations regarding the treatment of Native Americans. Who created this committee, and what did it accomplish?

   _____

   _____

   _____

3. In 1919 there were approximately 10,000 Native American veterans of World War I. What was granted to them as a result of their service?

   _____

   _____

   _____

4. On August 9, 1888, the White Men and Indian Women Marriage Act was enacted. What benefits were provided to Native American women as a result of this act?

   _____

   _____

   _____

5. On which side did the Cherokee fight in the Civil War?

   _____

   _____

   _____

6. In 1886 a ruling was made regarding Kansas Native Americans. The ruling pertained to tribal organizations that remained intact and were recognized by the federal government. Who had jurisdiction over such groups?

_____

_____

_____

7. What are the address and phone number of the Bureau of Indian Affairs?

_____

_____

_____

8. Rain-in-the-Face, a Hunkpapa Sioux chief, who performed in Buffalo Bill's Wild West show, was arrested in 1875. Who arrested him and why?

_____

_____

_____

9. The Western Apache now have land for two reservations. Name them and the state where they are located.

_____

_____

_____

10. Use a historical map to locate major Indian wars and battles. In what state did the Battle of Wyoming Valley occur? In what year did the battle take place?

_____

_____

_____

Native American Leaders

This search focuses on Native American leaders past and present. How many names do you recognize?

Reference List for Native American Leaders

Champagne, Duane, ed. *Chronology of Native North American History*. Detroit: Gale Research, 1994. 574p. $34.00. ISBN 0-8103-9195-3.

Champagne has compiled an impressive variety of entries, covering issues and events as well as people and places. Special features include Tribal Chronologies and Historical Timeline. Also included is an annotated bibliography. Champagne's introduction, written in chronological order, discusses Native North American creation stories, regional groups, and religious movements. Several black-and-white photographs, maps, and illustrations are provided. Of special interest are the Documents in History and Excerpts from Significant Legal Cases sections. There is also a general bibliography and an index. Recommended for grade 6 and above.

Cusic, Don. *Cowboys and the Wild West: An A–Z Guide from the Chisolm Trail to the Silver Screen*. New York: Facts on File, 1994. 356p. $40.00. ISBN 0-8160-3030-8.

Organized alphabetically, Cusic's work focuses on cowboys. Cusic includes entries on folk heroes and places, television shows, films, and fictional characters such as the Lone Ranger (to whom the book is also dedicated). He does, however, provide information on Native Americans, including several entries on tribal groups and terms. This work is informative and fun to read. Entries range from one paragraph to several pages. Also included are an index and several black-and-white photographs. The author states he wrote the book because he wanted to own a book like it. This work is a delightful collection of American fact and folklore. Recommended for grade 5 and above.

Dinnerstein, Leonard, Roger L. Nichols, and David Reimers. *Natives and Strangers*. New York: Oxford University Press, 1996. 370p. $25.00. ISBN 0-19-509083-7.

Cultural and artistic contributions are not the focus of this work. Rather, it concentrates on the social and economic impact of ethnic groups on America and its impact on them. The work is arranged chronologically. Ethnic groups are represented for each time period, thus enabling the authors to intertwine the history of each ethnic group with the history of America. The time period covered ranges from 1600 through 1995. The authors wanted their study to provide an understanding of how American minority groups have experienced various forms of conflict and other social conditions. Included are an index and a bibliography for each chapter. This is especially useful for those whose research focuses on a specific period in American history. Also included are black-and-white photographs and tables. Although the work is arranged chronologically, some chapters cover the same time period but have a different focus. For example, there are several chapters covering the mid-1800s through the 1930s. The focus on these years may range from immigration to industrialism to development of the West. Events are described in an engaging narrative, making this an appealing source for grade 8 and above.

Langer, Howard J., comp. and ed. *American Indian Quotations*. Westport, CT: Greenwood, 1996. 260p. $49.95. ISBN 0-313-29121-7.

Arranged chronologically, Langer's work consists of more than 800 quotations, most of which were translated by white interpreters. The question of accuracy is resolved, Langer feels, by recurrent themes that emerge over time and throughout several regions. Included are several black-and-white photographs. Quotations are numbered, and the source of a quotation follows each item. Written for adults, Langer's work is appealing to students in grade 5 and above.

Malinowski, Sharon, and Simon Glickman, eds. *Native North American Biography*. Detroit: Gale Research, 1996. 202p. $60.00. ISBN 0-8103-9821-4.

This two-volume set consists of alphabetically arranged biographical sketches of 112 famous Native Americans from the past and present and from all walks of life. Many sketches include a direct quotation by the subject as well as several black-and-white photographs and illustrations. Each sketch includes dates of birth and death, biographical information, and a Further Reading section, which is a short bibliography. Volume One begins with entries by tribal groups and a Reader's Guide. There is also an index by field of endeavor at the end of Volume Two. This set was written especially for students and is appropriate for grade 5 and above.

Straub, Deborah Gillan, ed. *Native North American Voices*. Detroit: UXL, 1996. 235p. $34.00. ISBN 0-8103-9819-2.

Straub has collected speeches of 20 notable Native North Americans. The section Speech Topics at a Glance categorizes speeches. Topics include the American Indian Movement, Children, Education, Militancy, and Ethnic Stereotyping. Entries are arranged alphabetically by speaker. Each speech begins with a brief biographical sketch. Black-and-white illustrations are also included. Sidebars present vocabulary and quotations. Each excerpt is followed with a list of sources. Straub also provides a time line of important Native North American events, ranging from 1754 to 1995. Written especially for students, this work is appropriate for grade 5 and above.

Swisher, Karen Gayton, and AnCita Benally. *Native North American Firsts*. Detroit: Gale Research, 1997. 263p. $48.55. ISBN 0-7876-0518-2.

Beginning with a month-by-month Calendar of Firsts and a Timeline, this work is arranged alphabetically by topic. Included are Education, Literature, Religious Life, Sciences, and many others. Under each topic there are also various subheadings. For example, under Military there are sections on the Civil War, World War I, and so on. Within each section, entries are listed chronologically. Also included are several black-and-white photographs, a bibliography, an index by year, and a general index. As a result, this work is very accessible. Overall, this is an excellent reference. Appropriate for grade 6 and above.

Waldman, Carl. *The Encyclopedia of Native American Tribes*. New York: Facts on File, 1987. 293p. $45.00. ISBN 0-8160-1421-3.

Tribes are listed alphabetically along with general headings such as Mound Builders and Aztec and Maya Civilizations. In addition, Waldman supplies culture areas and maps for groups with different lifestyles. Color illustrations, a glossary, and a bibliography are included as well. The author limited his selection to approximately 150 entries, with choices based on historical or cultural significance. The book opens with a map and chart of culture areas. Content of entries varies. Larger entries provide information on ways of life, food, and religion. Shorter entries are more general. Recommended for grade 5 and above.

Search for Native American Leaders

Name_____ Class_____ Date_____

Use the Reference List for Native American Leaders to locate answers to the questions below. If you read each question carefully, you may find a clue to the best source for your answer.

1. Mickey Free was a young boy captured by the Apache. Which famous Native American leader was wrongly arrested as a result of this incident?

   _____

   _____

   _____

2. What words did Baptiste Goode, a Sioux chief, use to describe the white man and General George A. Custer in particular?

   _____

   _____

   _____

3. A significant first in the U.S. military occurred in August 1864 for U.S. Army scout Coruxtechodish. What was it?

   _____

   _____

   _____

4. Cochise, a Chiricahua Apache tribal leader, killed 14 mail carriers who worked for a man named Thomas J. Jeffords. How did Jeffords resolve the situation?

   _____

   _____

   _____

5. On December 12, 1958, the leaders of the Federated Indian Tribes organized in Los Angeles and reached a decision regarding urban Native Americans. What was the objective of this decision?

   _____

   _____

   _____

6. Crazy Horse led the attack at Little Big Horn. How many of his men were killed there? How many U.S. soldiers were killed there?

_____

_____

_____

7. Sitting Bull, a Hunkpapa Sioux tribal leader and warrior, was born in South Dakota. What name did the Sioux give to the year of his birth, and according to historians, what year was it?

_____

_____

_____

8. Red Jacket, chief of the Seneca tribe, was considered by himself and others to be an orator rather than a warrior. What did he say about the difference between the white man's and the red man's religion?

_____

_____

_____

9. Smohalla, spiritual leader of the Wanapam tribe, also founded a religion. What was the name of his religion?

_____

_____

_____

10. Which national organization did Charles Eastman help create? Of which tribal group was he a member?

_____

_____

_____

Answer Key for Noteworthy Native Americans

1. In Avery and Skinner. Red Wind provides assistance to Native American substance abusers.
2. In Swisher and Benally. Yellow Robe was the first Native American to be awarded a Fulbright scholarship.
3. In Malinowski and Glickman. Hayes was one of the U.S. Marines who helped raise the American flag on Mt. Suribachi during the Battle of Iwo Jima. The event was memorialized in a monument in Washington, D.C.
4. In Swisher and Benally. *House Made of Dawn* won the Pulitzer prize in 1969.
5. In Malinowski and Abrams. Rhoades was responsible for the health of 1.5 million Native Americans.
6. In Malinowski and Abrams. Mills was pushed and stumbled. He lost 20 yards but still won the race and broke the record.
7. In Avery and Skinner. Philip Johnston, son of a missionary, is credited with the idea of using Navajo as Code Talkers. Requirements were to be fluent in both English and Navajo, to memorize a specialized list of military terms, and to learn radio communications.
8. In Malinowski and Glickman. Cardinal wrote his book to protest a plan by the Canadian government that would have wiped out Indian culture in Canada.
9. In Malinowski and Glickman. He was also called Panther Passing Across, Moves from One Place to Another, and Shooting Star.
10. In Malinowski and Glickman. Maria Tallchief is an Osage ballerina who was the first American dancer to perform at the Paris Opera.

Answer Key for Native American Cultures

1. In Mail. Strands of hair on the crown of a man's head were braided to about 12 inches in length. It could be worn as a bun, hang free, or even be pulled forward. It symbolized challenge to enemies. Cutting it would have been a sign of cowardice.
2. In Waldman. They were nomadic hunters and gatherers.
3. In Malinowski and Glickman. They are the Apache and Navajo.
4. In Moss and Wilson. Two seasons are Kachina and Non kachina. Women's Society dances are held in Non-kachina season.
5. In Straub. Campbell has won awards for creating jewelry.
6. In Waldman. Eskimos enjoy kickball, gymnastics, nugluk tag, and telling stories.
7. In Cayton, Gorn, and Williams. The album was recorded by Floyd Westerman, a Sioux.
8. In Champagne, *Chronology*. The first Native American novel was *Queen of the Woods* by Chief Simon Pokagon.
9. In Champagne, *Native North American Almanac*. Devil's Club is boiled and drunk as a tea to cure aching muscles.
10. In Moss and Wilson. The Aleuts speak Aleut, English, and Russian.

Answer Key for Significant Events in Native American History

1. In Champagne, *Chronology*. Approximately 50 Native Americans from different tribes climbed the monument and planned to occupy it until 123,000 acres unjustly taken from them were returned.
2. In Hazen-Hammond. The Lumbee broke up the KKK rally and drove the Klan out of the county.
3. In *Historical Maps on File*. The battle was at Ticonderoga.
4. In Malinowski and Glickman. A group of whites dressed up as pilgrims to celebrate the arrival of the English in America were confronted by Russell Means, a Lakota activist in Plymouth, Massachusetts.
5. In Straub. As an innocent man, Peltier could feel no guilt.
6. In Champagne, *Chronology*. Reagan was criticized because he did not follow through on his promise to remove federal regulations imposed on Native Americans.
7. In Hazen-Hammond. The Battle of Greasy Grass is also known as the Battle of Little Big Horn.
8. In Champagne, *Chronology*. The price offered was $24 worth of glass beads and red cloth.
9. In Langer. Mankiller was the first female to become principal chief of the Cherokee Nation of Oklahoma. Her hope was that the Alcatraz experience would bring justice for her people.
10. In Champagne, *Native North American Almanac*. The Pueblo did not wish to change their traditions or their culture.

Answer Key for Native Americans and the U.S. Government

1. In Champagne, *Native North American Almanac* in the glossary. During the 1830s the Removal Act caused the forced relocation of groups of Cherokee, Creek, Seminole, and some Choctaw. It became known as the Trail of Tears.
2. In Dinnerstein, Nichols, and Reimers. The Committee of 100 was formed by the government. It documented unjust treatment and questioned the effort of forced assimilation of Native Americans.
3. In Hazen-Hammond. They received U.S. citizenship.
4. In Champagne, *Chronology*. They received U.S. citizenship.
5. In Moss and Wilson. The Cherokee were divided during the Civil War.
6. In Champagne, *Chronology*. The federal government had jurisdiction.
7. In Champagne, *Native North American Almanac*. Bureau of Indian Affairs, 1849 C Street, N.W., Washington, DC 20245. The phone number is 202-208-3711.
8. In Cusic. Rain-in-the-Face was arrested by Tom Custer for killing his brother George A. Custer.
9. In Moss and Wilson. They are San Carlos and Fort Apache in Arizona.
10. In *Historical Maps on File*. The Battle of Wyoming Valley occurred in Pennsylvania in 1778.

Answer Key for Native American Leaders

1. In Cusic. Cochise was wrongly arrested.
2. In Langer. White men were called maggots. Custer was called Chief of All Thieves.
3. In Swisher and Benally. He was the first Native American to be awarded the Medal of Honor.
4. In Malinowski and Glickman. Jeffords entered Cochise's camp alone and offered to exchange his weapons for a meeting. As a result, Jeffords' mail carriers were able to pass through Cochise's territory unharmed.
5. In Champagne. The objective was to allow urban Native Americans to live as traditionally as possible—even in the city.
6. In Malinowski and Glickman. Twenty Native Americans were killed. Custer and all of his men died—a total of 225.
7. In Malinowski and Glickman. Sitting Bull was born in Winter-When-Yellow-Eyes-Played-in-the-Snow, 1831.
8. In Straub. Red Jacket questioned the fact that whites quarreled about religion. His people never quarreled about religion.
9. In Straub. Smohalla founded the Dreamer religion.
10. In Waldman. Eastman, a Sioux, helped to create Boy Scouts of America.

Chapter
Eleven

African
Americans

African Americans have given so much to American culture. From the tragic beginnings of slavery to the present day, America is indebted to African Americans for the sacrifices and contributions they have made in spite of tremendous obstacles and injustices. These searches are designed to illustrate not only African American contributions to our society but also to illuminate the dignity, pride, and incredible spirit of African Americans that are part of America.

African American Culture

This search focuses on various aspects of African American culture. It is impossible to touch on every aspect of a culture in 10 questions. The references for this search, however, provide a great deal of information on African American culture. Hopefully, the search for answers to these 10 questions will also provide an opportunity for the searcher to learn even more.

Reference List for African American Culture

Anyike, James C. *African American Holidays*. Chicago: Popular Truth, 1991. 102p. $7.95. ISBN 0-9631547-0-2.

Anyike's work devotes each chapter to a specific celebration with one exception—Chapter One presents a historical perspective on several holidays that came about during slavery. Chapters Two through Eight focus on celebrations for Black History Month, Malcolm X Day, and Juneteenth National Freedom Day, to name a few. Biographic and historical information are presented for each holiday, and suggestions for celebrating them are offered. Appendixes include Important Dates in African American History, the Historic Origin of Popular American Holidays, a Bibliography, and Organizations. As the author points out, many of these celebrations are unknown to mainstream Americans. Anyike's work presents insightful information about these holidays. Recommended for grade 5 and above.

Asante, Molefi K., and Mark T. Mattson. *Historical and Cultural Atlas of African Americans*. New York: Macmillan, 1992. 198p. $120.00. ISBN 0-02-897021-7.

Organized into 13 chapters beginning with African origins, this work traces the African American experience in America. More than 130 maps, tables, and diagrams illustrate historically significant events in African American history. Maps illustrate aspects of lives of notable African Americans such as Sojourner Truth and Nat Turner. One map shows birthplaces of major African American writers; another illustrates centers of influence in African American music. Several black-and-white photographs and biographical sketches accompany text and maps. Among other areas covered are population, marriage, countries involved in the slave trade, and education. There is also a chronology of dates to remember in African American history and culture, a selected bibliography, and an index. Asante and Mattson's highly visual representation of important material should appeal to readers of all ages. Recommended for grade 5 and above.

Cowan, Tom, Ph.D., and Jack Maguire. *Timelines of African American History: 500 Years of Black Achievement*. New York: Roundtable Press/Perigee, 1994. 368p. $15.00. ISBN 0-399-52127-5.

A year-by-year arrangement of more than 1,500 entries chronicles major events and details the lives of both famous and lesser-known people important in African American history. All fields of endeavor and all aspects of culture and history are represented. Entries for each year are arranged by topic, some of which include Politics and Civil Rights, Business and Employment, Religion and Education, Performing Arts, and Sports. Several sidebars highlight significant people and events in a particular year or era. The arrangement and an index provide easy access to this comprehensive source. Recommended for grade 6 and above.

Galens, Judy, Anna Sheets, and Robin V. Young, eds. *Gale Encyclopedia of Multicultural America*. Detroit: Gale Research, 1995. 1,477p. $125.00. ISBN 0-8103-9163-5.

More than 100 alphabetically arranged signed essays have been compiled in this work. Articles, ranging from 5,000 to 20,000 words, have been written by experts in their field. Essays focus on the experiences of each ethnic group discussed. Entries begin with an overview and a history and provide information on each group's individual contributions to American society. Also discussed are language, religion, politics, organizations, and achievers from each group. There are several black-and-white photographs and illustrations, a general bibliography, and an index. Recommended for grade 5 and above.

Mabunda, L. Mpho. *Reference Library of Black America*. Philadelphia: Afro-American Press, 1997. 5 vols. $305.00. ISBN 188-0208-008-8.

The five volumes in this set cover various aspects of African American culture. Volume One consists of a substantial Chronology, Firsts, Significant Documents, and Landmarks significant to African American history and culture. Volume Two focuses on historical and geographic aspects and provides country profiles. Volume Three provides information on politics, population, employment, education, religion, and family life. Volume Four focuses on literature, music, media, and the arts. Volume Five presents information on popular music, science, sports, and the military. In all there are 27 subject chapters, many of which begin with an overview. Several chapters also provide biographical sketches. There are three appendixes that list award winners, Olympic medal winners, and other achievements. There is an extensive bibliography that is arranged according to topic. Finally, there are name and keyword indexes. Recommended for grade 5 and above.

Moss, Joyce, and George Wilson. *Peoples of the World: North Americans*. 1st ed. Detroit: Gale Research, 1991. 441p. $45.00. ISBN 0-8103-7768-3.

The Peoples of the World series profiles various ethnic groups. The authors have made the focus of their work the people of a country rather than the country itself. The premise of the work is that governments and other world events affect change in many countries, but culture and tradition do not change. Separate volumes have been devoted to North Americans and to Latin Americans as well as to other areas around the world. Each entry is introduced with phonetic spelling and definition. Information on population, location, language, and geographical setting is also included. Other sections for each culture include historical background and culture today. Special features include maps for each culture that indicate current location. While political and economic information may not be current, this work is a good source of cultural and historical information. Also included are black-and-white illustrations and photographs, a glossary, and an index. This set is written especially for students in junior high school, making it appropriate for students in grade 7 and above.

Smith, Jessie Carney, ed. *Epic Lives: 100 Black Women Who Made a Difference*. Detroit: Visible Ink, 1993. 632p. $18.95. ISBN 0-8103-9426-X.

Arranged alphabetically, this work profiles African American women achievers in all fields of endeavor. Each profile includes a black-and-white photograph, dates of birth and death, and field of endeavor. Profiles trace early life and highlight achievements, but the real focus is on how each subject made a difference in her field of endeavor and her impact on the world. Profiles are signed. A bibliography lists sources for each subject profiled. Recommended for grade 5 and above.

Stewart, Jeffrey E. *1001 Things Everyone Should Know About African American History*. New York: Doubleday, 1996. 406p. $24.95. ISBN 0-385-47309-5.

The 1,001 things in this book, which Stewart has numbered, refer to people, events, movements, ideas, terms, and places significant in history. Six sections—including Great Migrations, Civil Rights and Politics, Culture and Religion, and Sports—cover every aspect of African American culture. A brief introduction is provided for each section. Entries range from a paragraph to half a page in length and are arranged chronologically within each section. Also included are more than 150 black-and-white photographs and illustrations, a bibliography, and an index. Stewart's work is an excellent resource for teachers, students, and general readers. His writing is clear, engaging, and insightful. Recommended for grade 5 and above.

Valade, III, Roger M., ed. With Denise Kasinec. *The Schomburg Center Guide to Black Literature: From the 18th Century to the Present*. Detroit: Gale Research, 1996. 545p. $75.00. ISBN 0-78760289-2.

All aspects of African American literature—including authors, works, characters, themes, and theories—are presented in this guide. Designed to be used as a ready reference, the guide includes biographical essays; synopses of works; and discussion of themes, topics, and literary movements. There are also nearly 100 black-and-white photographs and illustrations. Essays on themes, genres, and movements define, explain, and offer examples. Biographical essays focus on professional rather than personal aspects of subjects' lives. Special features include a Master Chronology and an essay that traces the history of the Schomburg Center. The work is arranged alphabetically, and a list of sources for further reading follows many entries. Recommended for grade 5 and above.

Search for African American Culture

Name_____ Class_____ Date_____

Use the Reference List for African American Culture to find the answers to these questions. Answers to many of the questions may be found in more than one of the listed sources.

1. In a wedding ceremony, many modern African American couples adopt an African custom in which the groom wears an item belonging to the bride. What is this item?

   _____

   _____

   _____

2. Among African American landmarks is the Henry Ossawa Tanner House, a home where the painter once lived in Philadelphia. What is the exact address?

   _____

   _____

   _____

3. When is Malcolm X Day?

   _____

   _____

   _____

4. When and where did the Black Muslim movement begin?

   _____

   _____

   _____

5. Use a map to locate the university that offered the only Ph.D. in African American studies in 1989 (year of publication of the source).

   _____

   _____

   _____

6. In 1934 Aaron Douglas completed his group of murals titled *Aspects of Negro Life*. Where were they located?

_____

_____

_____

7. What tribute to Shakespearean actor Ira Aldridge is found at the Shakespeare Memorial Theatre at Stratford-upon-Avon?

_____

_____

_____

8. If you had been involved in the Black Arts Movement, would you tend to lean toward the philosophy of Malcolm X or Martin Luther King, Jr.? The music of John Coltrane or Screamin' Jay Hawkins? The writing of Lucille Clifton or Sonia Sanchez?

_____

_____

_____

9. When Jackie Torrance was a child, she had a speech impediment that greatly affected her ability to speak clearly. By what title is she now known, and how does she contribute to African American culture?

_____

_____

_____

10. Who was Sissieretta Jones? By what other name was she known?

_____

_____

_____

African American Achievers

Many African American achievers are highlighted in these searches. Their names are recognizable to most people. This search, however, focuses on those who may not be widely known in the mainstream.

Reference List for African American Achievers

Asante, Molefi K., and Mark T. Mattson. *Historical and Cultural Atlas of African Americans*. New York: Macmillan, 1992. 198p. $120.00. ISBN 0-02-897021-7.

Organized into 13 chapters beginning with African origins, this work traces the African American experience in America. More than 130 maps, tables, and diagrams illustrate historically significant events in African American history. Maps illustrate aspects of lives of notable African Americans such as Sojourner Truth and Nat Turner. One map shows birthplaces of major African American writers; another illustrates centers of influence in African American music. Several black-and-white photographs and biographical sketches accompany text and maps. Among other areas covered are population, marriage, countries involved in the slave trade, and education. There is also a chronology of dates to remember in African American history and culture, a selected bibliography, and an index. Asante and Mattson's highly visual representation of important material should appeal to readers of all ages. Recommended for grade 5 and above.

Hirsch, Jr., E. D., Joseph Kett, and James Trefil. *The Dictionary of Cultural Literacy*. 2nd ed. Revised and updated. Boston: Houghton Mifflin, 1993. 619p. $24.95. ISBN 0-395-65597-8.

Hirsch and his colleagues compiled what they have identified as shared common knowledge of literate Americans. This information is categorized into 23 subject sections. Sections include The Bible, World History, Mythology and Folklore, American Geography, Medicine and Health, and Technology. Entries within these sections are arranged alphabetically. Included are more than 250 illustrations, maps, and charts. Entries offer definitions as well as current cultural connotations. Cross-references and a pronunciation key are provided. Hirsch also presents an essay, "The Theory Behind the Dictionary." Written for general readers and students, this work is appropriate for grade 5 and above.

Hoobler, Dorothy, and Thomas Hoobler. *The African American Family Album*. (American Family Album Series). New York: Oxford University Press, 1995. 128p. $19.95. ISBN 0-19-508128-5.

Arranged chronologically, the book begins with life in Africa and concludes in the present day. Many black-and-white photographs enhance the text. Sections of each chapter discuss pertinent issues of a particular era. For example, the Great Migration is discussed in the early part of this century. Other topics include family, religion, schools, sports, and entertainment. A unique feature in this book is that excerpts from firsthand accounts are presented throughout. For example, in the chapter Neighborhoods, Langston Hughes' account of Chicago is presented, Daisy Lee Bates describes her hometown, and Jackie Robinson describes his family's move to Pasadena, California. Also included are an African American time line, a bibliography, and an index. Recommended for grade 5 and above.

Nagel, Carol DeKane, ed. *African American Biography*. Detroit: UXL, 1994. 4 vols. $120.00. ISBN 0-8103-9234-8.

Consisting of four volumes, this set profiles 300 African Americans in all fields of endeavor. Arranged alphabetically, most profiles are one to three pages in length. Each profile is accompanied by a black-and-white photograph, dates of birth and death, and field of endeavor. Most profiles begin with a quotation by the subject. Details of personal life and career achievements as well as honors and awards are provided. Also included is an index by field of endeavor. Written especially for students, this work is recommended for grade 5 and above.

Page, James A. *Black Olympian Medalists*. Englewood, CO: Libraries Unlimited, 1991. 190p. $27.50. ISBN 0-87287-618-7.

A biographical dictionary of African American Olympians, this work chronicles medal winners from 1904, when George Poage became the first Black Olympian, to 1988. Biographical sketches, arranged alphabetically, list places and dates of birth and death (if known), medals won, and a brief biographical sketch. Sources for information in each sketch are also provided. Sketches include information on schools attended, career highlights, and other achievements in sports. Sketches range from a few sentences to a paragraph. Special features include group profiles, Black Management in U.S. Professional Sports, statistics by place and year, and lists of sponsoring countries. A bibliography and an index are provided as well. This is an excellent source for students in grade 6 and above.

Rust, Edna, and Art Rust, Jr. *Art Rust's Illustrated History of the Black Athlete*. Garden City, NY: Doubleday, 1985. 435p. $15.95. ISBN 0-385-15140-3.

Arranged by sport, this volume traces the history of African American athletes in nine sports. The Rusts present a historical overview of each sport and then profile African Americans who excelled in the sport. Profiles include black-and-white photographs and quotations by or about each subject.

Many profiles are one to one-and-a-half pages in length, although such true greats as Joe Louis, Jackie Robinson, and Jesse Owens receive lengthier coverage. Several black-and-white photographs enhance the Rusts' clearly written and appealing narrative. There are sections on the Harlem Globetrotters and Olympic Gold Medalists. More than a series of profiles or a list of facts, dates, and statistics, this work is a social history rich in detail. It provides insight into the history of sports in the United States and chronicles obstacles overcome, injustices, and the impact of African Americans on American sports. Written for general readers, this work is also recommended for grade 5 and above.

Sammons, Vivian Ovelton. *Blacks in Science and Medicine*. New York: Hemisphere, 1990. 293p. $63.00. ISBN 0-89116-665-3.

Listed in alphabetical order, more than 1,500 African Americans who have made contributions to science are briefly profiled. Fields of endeavor from all areas of science, such as biology, chemistry, medicine, invention, psychology, and mathematics are included. Profiles provide details of birth, death, field of endeavor, contribution, and career highlights. Awards, honors, and affiliations are provided as well. Dissertation titles and publications are also listed at the end of each entry. There are lists by field of endeavor and subject heading; however, there is no index. A list of firsts allows the reader to look at the achievement and then read the profile. Recommended for grade 6 and above.

Search for African American Achievers

Name_____ Class_____ Date_____

Use the Reference List for African American Achievers to find the answers to these questions. It is possible that more than one of the sources on the list has the correct answer.

1. Several firsts were achieved by Juanita Kidd Stout in the field of law, but law was not her first field of endeavor. What was?

   _____

   _____

   _____

   _____

2. By what name was Harriet Tubman known to slaves on plantations?

   _____

   _____

   _____

3. Patrick Ewing won an Olympic Medal in 1984, the year before he graduated from Georgetown University. What was his major in college?

   _____

   _____

   _____

4. What did Benjamin Banneker teach himself so that he could make astronomical calculations?

   _____

   _____

   _____

5. In what years did Jesse Jackson run in primary elections for President of the United States?

   _____

   _____

   _____

6. Robert Smalls was one of the first African American Navy heroes. He distinguished himself by sailing a Confederate steamboat, the *Planter*, out of Charleston harbor. Why was this heroic?

_____

_____

_____

7. In 1970, President Richard Nixon gave Pearl Bailey a special appointment. What title was she given as the result of that appointment?

_____

_____

_____

8. What is significant about mathematician Thomas Fuller?

_____

_____

_____

9. James "Cool Papa" Bell was known as the fastest runner in baseball. In 1933, a 200-game season, how many bases were stolen by Bell?

_____

_____

_____

10. Percy Julian distinguished himself in medical research by formulating drugs to treat which two ailments?

_____

_____

_____

Martin Luther King, Jr.

As a civil rights leader, Martin Luther King, Jr., is unparalleled in the minds of many Americans. His words live on as inspiration to all. It is difficult to select only one notable American from any ethnic group. However, this book is in part devoted to events in the school year. This search is included for possible use in conjunction with Dr. Martin Luther King, Jr.'s, birthday, January 15, which is a federal holiday as well.

Reference List for Martin Luther King, Jr.

Cowan, Tom, Ph.D., and Jack Maguire. *Timelines of African American History: 500 Years of Black Achievement.* New York: Roundtable Press/Perigee, 1994. 368p. $15.00. ISBN 0-399-52127-5.

A year-by-year arrangement of more than 1,500 entries chronicles major events and details the lives of both famous and lesser-known people important in African American history. All fields of endeavor and all aspects of culture and history are represented. Entries for each year are arranged by topic, some of which include Politics and Civil Rights, Business and Employment, Religion and Education, Performing Arts, and Sports. Several sidebars highlight significant people and events in a particular year or era. The arrangement and an index provide easy access to this comprehensive source. Recommended for grade 6 and above.

Galens, Judy, Anna Sheets, and Robin V. Young, eds. *Gale Encyclopedia of Multicultural America.* Detroit: Gale Research, 1995. 1,477p. $125.00. ISBN 0-8103-9163-5.

More than 100 alphabetically arranged signed essays have been compiled in this work. Articles, ranging from 5,000 to 20,000 words, have been written by experts in their field. Essays focus on the experiences of each ethnic group discussed. Entries begin with an overview and a history and provide information on each group's individual contributions to American society. Also discussed are language, religion, politics, organizations, and achievers from each group. There are several black-and-white photographs and illustrations, a general bibliography, and an index. Recommended for grade 5 and above.

Hoobler, Dorothy, and Thomas Hoobler. *The African American Family Album*. (American Family Album Series). New York: Oxford University Press, 1995. 128p. $19.95. ISBN 0-19-508128-5.

Arranged chronologically, the book begins with life in Africa and concludes in the present day. Many black-and-white photographs enhance the text. Sections of each chapter discuss pertinent issues of a particular era. For example, the Great Migration is discussed in the early part of this century. Other topics include family, religion, schools, sports, and entertainment. A unique feature in this book is that excerpts from firsthand accounts are presented throughout. For example, in the chapter Neighborhoods, Langston Hughes' account of Chicago is presented, Daisy Lee Bates describes her hometown, and Jackie Robinson describes his family's move to Pasadena, California. Also included are an African American time line, a bibliography, and an index. Recommended for grade 5 and above.

Kranz, Rachel. *The Biographical Dictionary of Black America*. New York: Facts on File, 1992. 190p. $24.95. ISBN 0-8160-2324-7.

African Americans distinguished in all fields of endeavor, past and present, are profiled in this volume. Each of more than 180 entries includes biographical information as well as dates of birth and death, achievements, honors, and awards. There are also several black-and-white photographs, and many of the sketches list sources for further reading. Most sketches range from one-half to one-and-a-half pages. There is a list of notable African Americans by field of endeavor and a general bibliography. The work is arranged alphabetically. Recommended for grade 5 and above.

Mabunda, L. Mpho. *Reference Library of Black America*. Philadelphia: Afro-American Press, 1997. 5 vols. $305.00. ISBN 188-0208-008-8.

The five volumes in this set cover various aspects of African American culture. Volume One consists of a substantial Chronology, Firsts, Significant Documents, and Landmarks significant to African American history and culture. Volume Two focuses on historical and geographical aspects and provides country profiles. Volume Three provides information on politics, population, employment, education, religion, and family life. Volume Four focuses on literature, music, media, and the arts. Volume Five presents information on popular music, science, sports, and the military. In all there are 27 subject chapters, many of which begin with an overview. Several chapters also provide biographical sketches. There are three appendixes that list award winners, Olympic medal winners, and other achievements. There is an extensive bibliography that is arranged according to topic. Finally, there are name and keyword indexes. Recommended for grade 5 and above.

Nagel, Carol DeKane, ed. *African American Biography*. Detroit: UXL, 1994. 4 vols. $120.00. ISBN 0-8103-9234-8.

Consisting of four volumes, this set profiles 300 African Americans in all fields of endeavor. Arranged alphabetically, most profiles are one to three pages in length. Each profile is accompanied by a black-and-white photograph, dates of birth and death, and field of endeavor. Most profiles begin with a quotation by the subject. Details of personal life and career achievements as well as honors and awards are provided. Also included is an index by field of endeavor. Written especially for students, this work is recommended for grade 5 and above.

Stewart, Jeffrey E. *1001 Things Everyone Should Know About African American History*. New York: Doubleday, 1996. 406p. $24.95. ISBN 0-385-47309-5.

The 1,001 things in this book, which Stewart has numbered, refer to people, events, movements, ideas, terms, and places significant in history. Six sections—including Great Migrations, Civil Rights and Politics, Culture and Religion, and Sports—cover every aspect of African American culture. A brief introduction is provided for each section. Entries range from a paragraph to half a page in length and are arranged chronologically within each section. Also included are more than 150 black-and-white photographs and illustrations, a bibliography, and an index. Stewart's work is an excellent resource for teachers, students, and general readers. His writing is clear, engaging, and insightful. Recommended for grade 5 and above.

Search for Martin Luther King, Jr.

Name_____ Class_____ Date_____

Use the Reference List for Martin Luther King, Jr., to find the answers to the following questions. It is likely that you will find correct answers to some questions in more than one of the sources listed.

1. What significant event in Dr. King's life occurred on December 10, 1964?

    _____

    _____

    _____

2. Where did Dr. King attend college?

    _____

    _____

    _____

3. What was established in 1981 by Coretta Scott King?

    _____

    _____

    _____

4. What role did A. Philip Randolph play in the 1963 march on Washington?

    _____

    _____

    _____

5. Who are the president and chief executive officer of the Martin Luther King, Jr., Center for Nonviolent Social Change?

    _____

    _____

    _____

6. Why was Martin Luther King, Jr., arrested in Albany, Georgia, in 1961?

_____

_____

_____

7. Howard Thurman, a noted theologian, was a major influence on Dr. Martin Luther King, Jr. In what way did he influence Dr. King?

_____

_____

_____

8. What role did Yolanda King play in *King*, the television movie about her father's life?

_____

_____

_____

9. Martin Luther King, Jr., was pastor of which church when he led the Montgomery bus boycott?

_____

_____

_____

10. What first occurred on January 20, 1986?

_____

_____

_____

African Americans and Civil Rights

African Americans have implemented several changes to civil-rights legislation. Many people are aware of the Civil Rights Movement of the 1960s; however, African Americans became involved in civil rights at the moment they became enslaved. This search will deal with the African American struggle for freedom and their ongoing involvement in civil-rights legislation from early times to the modern day.

Reference List for African Americans and Civil Rights

Asante, Molefi K., and Mark T. Mattson. *Historical and Cultural Atlas of African Americans*. New York: Macmillan, 1992. 198p. $120.00. ISBN 0-02-897021-7.

Organized into 13 chapters beginning with African origins, this work traces the African American experience in America. More than 130 maps, tables, and diagrams illustrate historically significant events in African American history. Maps illustrate aspects of lives of notable African Americans such as Sojourner Truth and Nat Turner. One map shows birthplaces of major African American writers; another illustrates centers of influence in African American music. Several black-and-white photographs and biographical sketches accompany text and maps. Among other areas covered are population, marriage, countries involved in the slave trade, and education. There is also a chronology of dates to remember in African American history and culture, a selected bibliography, and an index. Asante and Mattson's highly visual representation of important material should appeal to readers of all ages. Recommended for grade 5 and above.

Hornsby, Jr., Alton. *Chronology of African American History*. Detroit: Gale Research, 1991. 526p. $60.00. ISBN 0-8103-7093-X.

Chronologically arranged by year, then by month and day, this work traces significant events in African American history and culture. Hornsby's work spans the years 1619 to 1990. Although the arrangement is chronological, there are 17 chapters, each of which deals with specific periods in American history. For example, Chapter Four, The Age of Booker T. Washington, focuses on 1901 through 1917; Chapter Seven, War Again, focuses on events significant during World War II. Entries include significant births and deaths, brief biographies, awards, legal milestones, and cultural, social, and economic events. Hornsby's substantial introduction provides a historical overview of the African American experience. Included as well are black-and-white photographs, an appendix of legislation and court decisions that includes excerpts of slave laws, and tables related to economic and political rankings. There is a selected bibliography for each chapter and an index. The arrangement makes this book easily accessible and fun to browse. Recommended for grade 5 and above.

Kranz, Rachel. *The Biographical Dictionary of Black America*. New York: Facts on File, 1992. 190p. $24.95. ISBN 0-8160-2324-7.

African Americans distinguished in all fields of endeavor, past and present, are profiled in this volume. Each of more than 180 entries includes biographical information as well as dates of birth and death, achievements, honors, and awards. There are also several black-and-white photographs, and many of the sketches list sources for further reading. Most sketches range from one-half to one-and-a-half pages. There is a list of notable African Americans by field of endeavor and a general bibliography. The work is arranged alphabetically. Recommended for grade 5 and above.

Moss, Joyce, and George Wilson. *Peoples of the World: North Americans*. 1st ed. Detroit: Gale Research, 1991. 441p. $45.00. ISBN 0-8103-7768-3.

The Peoples of the World series profiles various ethnic groups. The authors have made the focus of their work the people of a country rather than the country itself. The premise of the work is that governments and other world events affect change in many countries, but culture and tradition do not change. Separate volumes have been devoted to North Americans and to Latin Americans as well as to other areas around the world. Each entry is introduced with phonetic spelling and definition. Information on population, location, language, and geographical setting is also included. Other sections for each culture include historical background and culture today. Special features include maps for each culture that indicate current location. While political and economic information may not be current, this work is a good source of cultural and historical information. Also included are black-and-white illustrations and photographs, a glossary, and an index. This set is written especially for students in junior high school, making it appropriate for students in grade 7 and above.

Nagel, Carol DeKane, ed. *African American Biography*. Detroit: UXL, 1994. 4 vols. $120.00. ISBN 0-8103-9234-8.

Consisting of four volumes, this set profiles 300 African Americans in all fields of endeavor. Arranged alphabetically, most profiles are one to three pages in length. Each profile is accompanied by a black-and-white photograph, dates of birth and death, and field of endeavor. Most profiles begin with a quotation by the subject. Details of personal life and career achievements as well as honors and awards are provided. Also included is an index by field of endeavor. Written especially for students, this work is recommended for grade 5 and above.

Smith, Jessie Carney. *Black Firsts: 2,000 Years of Extraordinary Achievement.* Detroit: Visible Ink, 1994. 529p. $16.95. ISBN 0-8103-9490-1.

Smith's work is well respected, and this volume is an outstanding example. The work is arranged by topic; there are 15 in all, including civil rights and protest, religion, sports, and writers. Categories within a subject topic are used as well. For example, under Arts and Entertainment there are categories for film, music, and theater. Firsts are arranged chronologically by year in each category. Sources are listed for each entry. Included as well are several black-and-white photographs and tables. Dates of birth and death of achievers are also listed. Special features include a foldout time line, a month-by-month calendar of firsts, and an index by year. There are cross-references and a keyword index. This is an excellent resource for research and fun to browse. Recommended for grade 5 and above.

Stewart, Jeffrey E. *1001 Things Everyone Should Know About African American History.* New York: Doubleday, 1996. 406p. $24.95. ISBN 0-385-47309-5.

The 1,001 things in this book, which Stewart has numbered, refer to people, events, movements, ideas, terms, and places significant in history. Six sections—including Great Migrations, Civil Rights and Politics, Culture and Religion, and Sports—cover every aspect of African American culture. A brief introduction is provided for each section. Entries range from a paragraph to half a page in length and are arranged chronologically within each section. Also included are more than 150 black-and-white photographs and illustrations, a bibliography, and an index. Stewart's work is an excellent resource for teachers, students, and general readers. His writing is clear, engaging, and insightful. Recommended for grade 5 and above.

Valade, III, Roger M., ed. With Denise Kasinec. *The Schomburg Center Guide to Black Literature: From the 18th Century to the Present.* Detroit: Gale Research, 1996. 545p. $75.00. ISBN 0-78760289-2.

All aspects of African American literature—including authors, works, characters, themes, and theories—are presented in this guide. Designed to be used as a ready reference, the guide includes biographical essays; synopses of works; and discussion of themes, topics, and literary movements. There are also nearly 100 black-and-white photographs and illustrations. Essays on themes, genres, and movements define, explain, and offer examples. Biographical essays focus on professional rather than personal aspects of subjects' lives. Special features include a Master Chronology and an essay that traces the history of the Schomburg Center. The work is arranged alphabetically, and a list of sources for further reading follows many entries. Recommended for grade 5 and above.

Search for African Americans and Civil Rights

Name_____ Class_____ Date_____

Use the Reference List for African Americans and Civil Rights to find the answers to the following questions. It is possible that you will find correct answers for some questions in more than one source.

1. Even though the 13th Amendment abolished slavery, what were some rights still denied to African Americans?

_____

_____

_____

2. Walter White was a powerful force in the civil rights movement. Early in his career, White was a field investigator for the N.A.A.C.P. Why was he so successful?

_____

_____

_____

3. Martin Robinson Delaney, ethnologist and abolitionist, worked as an editor and as a doctor. His entrance to Harvard University Medical School was protested by his white classmates. He was finally expelled by the head of the medical faculty. Name the man who expelled him.

_____

_____

_____

4. How did Motown Records make an impact on the Civil Rights Movement?

_____

_____

_____

5. A map of the Underground Railroad shows a route that originated in Charleston. Which two cities were the final destination?

_____

_____

_____

6. Early in his career as a lawyer, Thurgood Marshall took on the University of Maryland and won the case. In what way was this a personal victory for Marshall?

_____

_____

_____

7. Which state was the first to abolish slavery?

_____

_____

_____

8. On December 8, 1936, the N.A.A.C.P. filed a case, *Gibbs v. Board of Education*. What precedent was set by the case?

_____

_____

_____

9. Use a map depicting John Brown's Raid on Harper's Ferry to identify the bridges on either side of the location where the raid took place. Write the names of the bridges in the space below.

_____

_____

_____

10. On October 6, 1989, two former employees (one white and one black) of Shoney's restaurant filed a lawsuit against the chain's Atlanta restaurants. The African American filed because of discrimination and limited promotion opportunity. Why did the white person file the lawsuit?

_____

_____

_____

African American Firsts

Finding out who did something first can be both fun and educational. In this search, all firsts were achieved by African Americans. Searchers will quickly discover that African Americans have been first to achieve something in virtually every field of endeavor.

Reference List for African American Firsts

Hoobler, Dorothy, and Thomas Hoobler. *The African American Family Album.* (American Family Album Series). New York: Oxford University Press, 1995. 128p. $19.95. ISBN 0-19-508128-5.

Arranged chronologically, the book begins with life in Africa and concludes in the present day. Many black-and-white photographs enhance the text. Sections of each chapter discuss pertinent issues of a particular era. For example, the Great Migration is discussed in the early part of this century. Other topics include family, religion, schools, sports, and entertainment. A unique feature in this book is that excerpts from firsthand accounts are presented throughout. For example, in the chapter Neighborhoods, Langston Hughes' account of Chicago is presented, Daisy Lee Bates describes her hometown, and Jackie Robinson describes his family's move to Pasadena, California. Also included are an African American time line, a bibliography, and an index. Recommended for grade 5 and above.

Kane, Joseph Nathan. *Famous First Facts.* 5th ed. Revised and expanded. New York: H. W. Wilson, 1997. 1,350p. $80.00. ISBN 0-8242-0930-3.

A popular ready reference book, *Famous First Facts* consists of more than 9,000 entries of what is listed as happenings, discoveries, and inventions in American history. Entries—arranged alphabetically by subject—are brief. One of the special features of this work is its indexes. Not only do they make the book easily accessible but they allow readers to find information by year, days of the month, geographical locations, and personal name. The work is also cross-referenced. Recommended for grade 5 and above.

Kranz, Rachel. *The Biographical Dictionary of Black America.* New York: Facts on File, 1992. 190p. $24.95. ISBN 0-8160-2324-7.

African Americans distinguished in all fields of endeavor, past and present, are profiled in this volume. Each of more than 180 entries includes biographical information as well as dates of birth and death, achievements, honors, and awards. There are also several black-and-white photographs, and many of the sketches list sources for further reading. Most sketches range from one-half to one-and-a-half pages. There is a list of notable African Americans by field of endeavor and a general bibliography. The work is arranged alphabetically. Recommended for grade 5 and above.

Mabunda, L. Mpho. *Reference Library of Black America*. Philadelphia: Afro-American Press, 1997. 5 vols. $305.00. ISBN 188-0208-008-8.

The five volumes in this set cover various aspects of African American culture. Volume One consists of a substantial Chronology, Firsts, Significant Documents, and Landmarks significant to African American history and culture. Volume Two focuses on historical and geographical aspects and provides country profiles. Volume Three provides information on politics, population, employment, education, religion, and family life. Volume Four focuses on literature, music, media, and the arts. Volume Five presents information on popular music, science, sports, and the military. In all there are 27 subject chapters, many of which begin with an overview. Several chapters also provide biographical sketches. There are three appendixes that list award winners, Olympic medal winners, and other achievements. There is an extensive bibliography that is arranged according to topic. Finally, there are name and keyword indexes. Recommended for grade 5 and above.

Moss, Joyce, and George Wilson. *Peoples of the World: North Americans*. 1st ed. Detroit: Gale Research, 1991. 441p. $45.00. ISBN 0-8103-7768-3.

The Peoples of the World series profiles various ethnic groups. The authors have made the focus of their work the people of a country rather than the country itself. The premise of the work is that governments and other world events affect change in many countries, but culture and tradition do not change. Separate volumes have been devoted to North Americans and to Latin Americans as well as to other areas around the world. Each entry is introduced with phonetic spelling and definition. Information on population, location, language, and geographical setting is also included. Other sections for each culture include historical background and culture today. Special features include maps for each culture that indicate current location. While political and economic information may not be current, this work is a good source of cultural and historical information. Also included are black-and-white illustrations and photographs, a glossary, and an index. This set is written especially for students in junior high school, making it appropriate for students in grade 7 and above.

Smith, Jessie Carney. *Black Firsts: 2,000 Years of Extraordinary Achievement*. Detroit: Visible Ink, 1994. 529p. $16.95. ISBN 0-8103-9490-1.

Smith's work is well respected, and this volume is an outstanding example. The work is arranged by topic; there are 15 in all, including civil rights and protest, religion, sports, and writers. Categories within a subject topic are used as well. For example, under Arts and Entertainment there are categories for film, music, and theater. Firsts are arranged chronologically by year in each category. Sources are listed for each entry. Included as well are several black-and-white photographs and tables. Dates of birth and death of achievers are also listed. Special features include a foldout time line, a month-by-month calendar of firsts, and an index by year. There are cross-references and a keyword index. This is an excellent resource for research and fun to browse. Recommended for grade 5 and above.

Stewart, Jeffrey E. *1001 Things Everyone Should Know About African American History*. New York: Doubleday, 1996. 406p. $24.95. ISBN 0-385-47309-5.

The 1,001 things in this book, which Stewart has numbered, refer to people, events, movements, ideas, terms, and places significant in history. Six sections—including Great Migrations, Civil Rights and Politics, Culture and Religion, and Sports—cover every aspect of African American culture. A brief introduction is provided for each section. Entries range from a paragraph to half a page in length and are arranged chronologically within each section. Also included are more than 150 black-and-white photographs and illustrations, a bibliography, and an index. Stewart's work is an excellent resource for teachers, students, and general readers. His writing is clear, engaging, and insightful. Recommended for grade 5 and above.

World Almanac and Book of Facts, 1998. Mahwah, NJ: World Almanac Books, 1999. 1,008p. $10.95. ISBN 0-8868-7832-2.

A ready reference most students should be familiar with, the *World Almanac* presents timely information on people, places, current events, awards, entertainment, prizes, facts and dates, and geographical information. Statistics, maps, flags of countries, and the year in pictures are other features. Written for general readers, but recommended for grade 5 and above.

Search for African American Firsts

Name_____ Class_____ Date_____

Use the Reference List for African American Firsts to find the answers to the questions in this search. Not all the answers will be found in Smith's *Black Firsts*.

1. What is recognized as the first African American novel? List title, author, and date of publication.

   _____

   _____

   _____

2. Which first was achieved by Bernice Collins?

   _____

   _____

   _____

3. Moses Fleetwood Walker, who achieved two firsts in baseball, had a unique way of playing his position. List his firsts, and describe what was unique about the way he played.

   _____

   _____

   _____

4. Who won the first Springarn Medal?

   _____

   _____

   _____

5. Singer Lena Horne achieved three firsts in film. What were they?

   _____

   _____

   _____

6. Which first is attributed to Eatonsville, Florida, birthplace of Zora Neale Hurston?

    _____

    _____

    _____

7. Which first was achieved by Thomas Jennings on March 3, 1821?

    _____

    _____

    _____

8. John Hope Franklin was the first black president of three major U.S. historical associations. Name them.

    _____

    _____

    _____

9. Explorer and adventurer Jean Baptiste Pointe Du Sable was the first settler and built a prosperous trading post on what is now a large American city. Name the city.

    _____

    _____

    _____

10. When was a march on Washington first proposed?

    _____

    _____

    _____

African Americans in the Arts

African Americans have had to overcome many obstacles and injustices to achieve anything in the arts. However, many have excelled in spite of the odds. This search will highlight some notable African Americans in fine and performing arts.

Reference List for African Americans in the Arts

Cowan, Tom, Ph.D., and Jack Maguire. *Timelines of African American History: 500 Years of Black Achievement*. New York: Roundtable Press/Perigee, 1994. 368p. $15.00. ISBN 0-399-52127-5.

A year-by-year arrangement of more than 1,500 entries chronicles major events and details the lives of famous and lesser-known people important in African American history. All fields of endeavor and all aspects of culture and history are represented. Entries for each year are arranged by topic, some of which include Politics and Civil Rights, Business and Employment, Religion and Education, Performing Arts, and Sports. Several sidebars highlight significant people and events in a particular year or era. The arrangement and an index provide easy access to this comprehensive source. Recommended for grade 6 and above.

Haskins, James. *Black Dance in America: A History Through Its People*. New York: HarperCollins, 1990. 240p. $15.00. ISBN 0-690-04657-X.

Haskins traces the origins of African American dance, discusses dance crazes, and highlights dancers such as Bill Robinson, Alvin Ailey, and Gregory Hines. The work is arranged chronologically, beginning in Chapter One with a discussion of various dances done by slaves. Other chapters provide information on dances during the 1930s through the 1980s. There are several black-and-white photographs. Also included are a bibliography and a videography. Haskins' work is an excellent social history rich in detail and skillfully written. Recommended for grade 5 and above.

———. *Black Music in America: A History Through Its People*. New York: HarperTrophy, 1987. 198p. $6.95. ISBN 0-06-446136-X.

Haskins, a prolific writer, presents a chronological survey of various forms of African American music beginning with slavery and ending in the 1980s. Each chapter represents an era in U.S. history. Haskins provides social history, explains types of music, and presents profiles of significant African American musicians of each era. There are several black-and-white illustrations, a selected bibliography, and an index. Individual chapters discuss Ragtime, the Harlem Renaissance, Rhythm and Blues, and Soul Music. Haskins' clear and straightforward style is appealing to students and adults. Recommended for grade 5 and above.

Hoobler, Dorothy, and Thomas Hoobler. *The African American Family Album*. (American Family Album Series). New York: Oxford University Press, 1995. 128p. $19.95. ISBN 0-19-508128-5.

Arranged chronologically, the book begins with life in Africa and concludes in the present day. Many black-and-white photographs enhance the text. Sections of each chapter discuss pertinent issues of a particular era. For example, the Great Migration is discussed in the early part of this century. Other topics include family, religion, schools, sports, and entertainment. A unique feature in this book is that excerpts from firsthand accounts are presented throughout. For example, in the chapter Neighborhoods, Langston Hughes' account of Chicago is presented, Daisy Lee Bates describes her hometown, and Jackie Robinson describes his family's move to Pasadena, California. Also included are an African American time line, a bibliography, and an index. Recommended for grade 5 and above.

Kranz, Rachel. *The Biographical Dictionary of Black America*. New York: Facts on File, 1992. 190p. $24.95. ISBN 0-8160-2324-7.

African Americans distinguished in all fields of endeavor, past and present, are profiled in this volume. Each of more than 180 entries includes biographical information as well as dates of birth and death, achievements, honors, and awards. There are also several black-and-white photographs, and many of the sketches list sources for further reading. Most sketches range from one-half to one-and-a-half pages. There is a list of notable African Americans by field of endeavor and a general bibliography. The work is arranged alphabetically. Recommended for grade 5 and above.

Mabunda, L. Mpho. *Reference Library of Black America*. Philadelphia: Afro-American Press, 1997. 5 vols. $305.00. ISBN 188-0208-008-8.

The five volumes in this set cover various aspects of African American culture. Volume One consists of a substantial Chronology, Firsts, Significant Documents, and Landmarks significant to African American history and culture. Volume Two focuses on historical and geographic aspects and provides country profiles. Volume Three provides information on politics, population, employment, education, religion, and family life. Volume Four focuses on literature, music, media, and the arts. Volume Five presents information on popular music, science, sports, and the military. In all there are 27 subject chapters, many of which begin with an overview. Several chapters also provide biographical sketches. There are three appendixes that list award winners, Olympic medal winners, and other achievements. There is an extensive bibliography that is arranged according to topic. Finally, there are name and keyword indexes. Recommended for grade 5 and above.

Malinowski, Sharon, ed. *Black Writers: A Selection of Sketches from Contemporary Authors*. 2nd ed. Detroit: Gale Research, 1994. 721p. $95.00. ISBN 0-8103-7788-8.

Metzger, Linda. *Black Writers: A Selection of Sketches from Contemporary Authors*. Detroit: Gale Research, 1989. 619p. $89.00. ISBN 0-8103-7772-4.

Each volume contains more than 400 profiles. Entries provide biographical as well as bibliographical material. Writers from artistic, journalistic, political, and scholarly backgrounds have been included. Information provided includes dates and places of birth and death, parents' names and occupations, names and dates pertaining to spouse and children, colleges and degrees, affiliations, address, career highlights, honors and awards, and chronological bibliography. Volume Two has a cumulative index to both editions as well as nationality and gender indexes. Special features include Sidelights, a section containing further biographical information, career and critical commentary, and in many cases comments by the author. Finally, biographical and critical sources list books, articles, and reviews of the author's work. Recommended for grade 5 and above.

Nagel, Carol DeKane, ed. *African American Biography*. Detroit: UXL, 1994. 4 vols. $120.00. ISBN 0-8103-9234-8.

Consisting of four volumes, this set profiles 300 African Americans in all fields of endeavor. Arranged alphabetically, most profiles are one to three pages in length. Each profile is accompanied by a black-and-white photograph, dates of birth and death, and field of endeavor. Most profiles begin with a quotation by the subject. Details of personal life and career achievements as well as honors and awards are provided. Also included is an index by field of endeavor. Written especially for students, this work is recommended for grade 5 and above.

Valade, III, Roger M., ed. With Denise Kasinec. *The Schomburg Center Guide to Black Literature: From the 18th Century to the Present*. Detroit: Gale Research, 1996. 545p. $75.00. ISBN 0-78760289-2.

All aspects of African American literature—including authors, works, characters, themes, and theories—are presented in this guide. Designed to be used as a ready reference, the guide includes biographical essays; synopses of works; and discussion of themes, topics, and literary movements. There are also nearly 100 black-and-white photographs and illustrations. Essays on themes, genres, and movements define, explain, and offer examples. Biographical essays focus on professional rather than personal aspects of subjects' lives. Special features include a Master Chronology and an essay that traces the history of the Schomburg Center. The work is arranged alphabetically, and a list of sources for further reading follows many entries. Recommended for grade 5 and above.

Search for African Americans
in the Arts

Name_____ Class_____ Date_____

Use the Reference List for African Americans in the Arts to find the answers to these questions.

1. Which two works of Chester Himes have been produced as films?

    _____

    _____

    _____

2. Which of Toni Morrison's novels deals with characters who move north because of the Great Migration?

    _____

    _____

    _____

3. Entertainer Florence Mills died November 1, 1927. Two other singers were born that same year. Name them.

    _____

    _____

    _____

4. In what year did Jessye Norman win an award as Outstanding Musician of the Year?

    _____

    _____

    _____

5. Who is Nigeria Greene?

    _____

    _____

    _____

From *Multicultural Information Quests* by Marie E. Rodgers. © 2000 Libraries Unlimited. (800) 237-6124.

6. According to one source, the word soul was first used to describe which recording artist's music?

_____

_____

_____

7. Gregory Hines starred in the film *The Cotton Club*. How was that film significant in his family's history?

_____

_____

_____

8. Roland Hayes, noted concert singer, wanted his music to be heard by everyone—rich or poor. How did he make this possible?

_____

_____

_____

9. For which relief sculpture is artist Selma Burke best known?

_____

_____

_____

10. Which African American has won the most Tony (Antoinette Perry) Awards for Supporting or Featured Actor in a musical?

_____

_____

_____

Answer Key for African American Culture

1. In Galens, Sheets, and Young. The groom wears one of the bride's earrings.
2. In Mabunda. It is located at 2903 West Diamond Street.
3. In Anyike. Malcolm X day is May 19.
4. In Moss and Wilson. It began in 1913 in Newark, New Jersey.
5. In Asante and Mattson. It was Temple University.
6. In Cowan and Maguire. They were at the 135th Street branch of the New York Public Library.
7. In Stewart. Aldridge, the first African American to play Othello, has a chair in the fourth row of the theater dedicated to him.
8. In Valade. You would prefer Malcolm X, John Coltrane, and both Lucille Clifton and Sonia Sanchez.
9. In Smith. Torrance is a nationally known storyteller. She is called the Story Lady and keeps the oral tradition alive.
10. In Stewart. Jones, also known as Black Patti, was a well-known nineteenth-century concert singer.

Answer Key for African American Achievers

1. In Nagel. Stout first studied music in college.
2. In Hoobler and Hoobler. Tubman was known as Moses by slaves.
3. In Page. Ewing majored in fine arts.
4. In Hirsch, Kett, and Trefil. Banneker taught himself calculus and trigonometry.
5. In Hirsch, Kett, and Trefil. Jackson ran in 1984 and 1988.
6. In Asante and Mattson. Smalls, a slave, was left on board with five other slaves. He sailed the ship on an intricate course out of a Confederate harbor and surrendered the ship to Union forces.
7. In Nagel. Nixon named Bailey Ambassador of Love.
8. In Sammons. As a slave, Fuller could not read or write, but he could perform mathematical calculations faster in his head than many who could read and write.
9. In Rust and Rust. Bell stole 133 bases that year.
10. In Asante and Mattson. Julian formulated treatments for arthritis and glaucoma.

Answer Key for Martin Luther King, Jr.

1. In Mabunda. King won the Nobel Peace Prize.
2. In Mabunda. King attended Morehouse, Crozier Theological Seminary, and Boston University.
3. In Cowan and Maguire. She established the Martin Luther King, Jr., Library.
4. In Stewart. Randolph organized the march.
5. In Galens, Sheets, and Young. Coretta Scott King is president, and Dexter Scott King is chairman and CEO.
6. In Cowan and Maguire. King and several others were arrested in a civil rights march on the local city hall.
7. In Kranz. It was Thurman who introduced King to the teachings of Gandhi, which led to King's philosophy of nonviolence.
8. In Nagel. Yolanda King played Rosa Parks.
9. In Hoobler and Hoobler. King was pastor of the Dexter Avenue Baptist Church.
10. In Mabunda. King's birthday was celebrated as a federal holiday for the first time.

Answer Key for African Americans and Civil Rights

1. In Moss and Wilson. It was still illegal for blacks to serve on a jury, marry whites, and own land.
2. In Valade. White's appearance—blue eyes and blond hair—made it easy for him to "pass" as a white so that he could infiltrate hate groups.
3. In Kranz. Delaney was expelled by Oliver Wendell Holmes, future Chief Justice of the U.S. Supreme Court.
4. In Stewart. Motown recorded political speeches, including Martin Luther King, Jr.'s, "Why I Oppose the War in Vietnam," which won a Grammy Award.
5. In Asante and Mattson. The route originating in Charleston ended in either Providence or New York City.
6. In Nagel. The university had refused to admit Marshall because he was black. After Marshall won his case, the university had to admit black students.
7. In Smith. Vermont abolished slavery on July 2, 1777.
8. In Hornsby. The precedent set was that equal salaries be paid to both black and white teachers.
9. In Asante and Mattson. The raid took place between the Shenandoah Bridge and the Potomac Bridge.
10. In Hornsby. The white person sued because of the chain's policy of retaliation against nonblacks who did not support the company's racist policies.

Answer Key for African American Firsts

1. In Moss and Wilson. *Clotel, The President's Daughter*, by William Wells Brown, was published in 1853.
2. In Smith. Collins was the first black woman clown with Ringling Brothers Circus.
3. In Kane. Walker was the first black college varsity baseball player and the first black in minor league baseball. He was a catcher and caught bare-handed.
4. In *World Almanac*. Ernest Everett Just won the first Springarn Medal in 1915.
5. In Kranz. Horne was the first black actress presented as a glamourous woman, the first to receive publicity from a studio, and the first black to be given a long-term contract by Metro-Goldwyn-Mayer.
6. In Hoobler and Hoobler. Eatonsville was the first formally incorporated black town in the United States.
7. In Stewart. He was the first African American to receive a U.S. patent.
8. In Kranz. Franklin was president of the American Historical Association, the Organization of American Historians, and the Southern Historical Association.
9. In Kranz. Du Sable's trading post was built on what is now known as Chicago.
10. In Stewart. A. Philip Randolph proposed the first march on Washington in 1941.

Answer Key for African Americans in the Arts

1. In Malinowski. Himes' works made into film are *Cotton Comes to Harlem* and *The Heat's On*, which was produced as *Come Back Charleston Blue*.
2. In Hoobler and Hoobler. *Jazz* is the novel with characters who were part of the Great Migration.
3. In Cowan and Maguire. Leontine Price and Harry Belafonte, Jr., were born the year Mills died.
4. In Nagel. Norman won the award in 1982.
5. In Valade. Nigeria Greene is a character in *A Hero Ain't Nothin' But a Sandwich*, by Alice Childress.
6. In Haskins, *Black Music*. The word soul was first used to describe Ray Charles' music.
7. In Haskins, *Black Dance*. Hines' grandmother was a dancer in the real Cotton Club.
8. In Kranz. Hayes insisted on low prices for admission to his concerts.
9. In Mabunda. Burke designed the sculpture of Franklin Delano Roosevelt used on the American dime.
10. In Mabunda. Hinton Battle won in 1981, 1984, and 1991.

Chapter
Twelve

Women

Women have made many contributions to America and to the world in general. These searches will demonstrate that women from various fields of endeavor have made contributions that affect all areas of our lives today. Art, literature, and science are only a few of the fields of endeavor in which women have excelled. Most questions in these searches pertain to women who were born in or immigrated to America. A few questions focus on other notable women.

Reference List for Women Who Write

Several great works of literature have been written by women. This search will demonstrate their talent in literature as well as in other areas of writing.

Bernikow, Louise, in association with the National Women's History Project. *The American Women's Almanac: An Inspiring and Irreverent Women's History*. New York: Berkley Books, 1997. 388p. $29.95. ISBN 0-425-15686-9.
This work is devoted to women who made contributions to American history. It is arranged in nine sections, some of which include Politics, The Female Mind, Entertainers, Domestic Life, and Work. A chapter called Last Word lists 25 things women have done for one another. There are several black-and-white photographs and illustrations, a bibliography, and an index. Another feature includes sidebar articles on related topics in each section. Very lively and fun to read, this work contains a history of women in America. It is written for general readers and those interested in women's studies, but it should also appeal to students in grade 6 and above.

Felder, Deborah G. *The 100 Most Influential Women of All Time: A Ranking Past and Present.* New York: Citadel Press, 1996. 374p. $24.95. ISBN 0-8065-1726-3.

Felder has ranked her subjects according to importance. This alone makes her work interesting and provocative. Readers are likely to debate the rankings. Whether or not they agree with the ranking order, readers will recognize that the women here have all made great contributions to the world. Among those listed are Rosa Parks, Freda Kahlo, Bessie Smith, Joan of Arc, and Lucille Ball. The list was compiled by means of a survey sent to Women's Studies departments of American colleges and universities. Using the surveys, Felder devised her list based on whom she felt had the greatest impact on the world. Profiles of the 100 subjects begin with dates of birth and death, a quotation by or about the subject, and a black-and-white photograph or illustration. Most profiles are two to three pages in length. Also included are career highlights, achievements, and personal information. There is an index and a bibliography as well. Recommended for grade 7 and above.

Grolier Library of International Biographies. Danbury, CT: Grolier Education Corp., 1996. 10 vols. $299.00. ISBN 0-7172-7527-2.

Twentieth-century achievers from various fields of endeavor are profiled in this 10-volume set. Each entry provides personal information ranging from childhood events to career highlights to values and beliefs. Achievements are detailed as well. Written for students, this work is written in clear, straightforward language. Each volume is devoted to a particular field of endeavor, covering areas such as scientists, performing artists, writers, and explorers. Boldface is used to indicate that the word and its definition will be found in a glossary specific to each volume's subject area. Black-and-white photographs, bibliographies, and indexes for each volume and a general index by subject, country, and name are included. Recommended for grade 5 and above.

McElroy, Lorie Jenkins, ed. *Women's Voices: A Documentary History of Women in America.* Detroit: UXL, 1996. 2 vols. $55.00. ISBN 0-7876-0663-4.

Speeches, diary entries, and other documents are compiled in this set. The purpose of this set is to trace the development of women's rights in America. Familiar names such as Sojourner Truth and Susan B. Anthony are featured along with less-familiar figures such as Lucy Stone and Alice Paul. Each volume consists of three chapters that focus on themes such as education, abolition, and suffrage in Volume One, and property, equality, and reproduction in Volume Two. The format for each of these sections consists of an introduction, Things to Remember, Excerpt, What Happened Next, Did You Know?, and Further Reading. Other features include biographical boxes and boxes that examine related events and time lines. Sidebars contain a glossary for each reproduced document. This work was written specifically for students. Recommended for grade 6 and above.

Smith, Jessie Carney, ed. *Notable Black American Women*, Book 2. Detroit: Gale Research, 1996. 775p. $105.75. ISBN 0-8103-9177-5.

———. *Notable Black American Women*. Detroit: Gale Research, 1991. 1,333p. $80.00. ISBN 0-8103-4749-0.

Smith, a well-respected author, has compiled a series of sketches on African American women from all walks of life. Criteria for selection can be found in the introduction. Many of the essays contain personal quotations. In addition, there are black-and-white photographs for most entrants. When possible, addresses have been included as well. Arranged alphabetically, the sketches provide personal and professional information, awards, career highlights, and a list of references. There is also a List of Entrants, Occupation, and an index. Thoroughly researched and well-written, this work is recommended for grade 6 and above.

Zia, Helen, and Susan B. Gall, eds. *Asian American Biography*. Detroit: UXL, 1995. 2 vols. $63.00. ISBN 0-8103-9687-4.

More than 130 Americans of Asian descent are profiled in this alphabetically arranged two-volume set. Most entries include field of endeavor, dates of birth and death, and an overview. Information on childhood, family, and education is also provided. Career highlights, awards, achievements, and Sources for Further Reading are included as well. Most entries also include a black-and-white photograph. Access is by a table of contents or a Field of Endeavor Index. Written especially for students, this work is recommended for grade 5 and above.

Zilboorg, Caroline, ed. *Women's Firsts*. Detroit: Gale Research, 1996. 564p. $48.55. ISBN 0-7876-0151-9.

A reference work designed to highlight women's achievements from ancient times to the present, this work is arranged by field of endeavor. Included are activism, literature, military service, science, and religion. Coverage is international, and more than 2,000 achievements are detailed here. Within each field of endeavor, achievements are listed chronologically with a citation for the source. Special features of this work include a Time Line of Events in Women's History and a bibliography. An index by day and month, an index by year, and a general index provide easy access. Recommended for grade 5 and above.

Search for Women Who Write

Name_____ Class_____ Date_____

Use the Reference List for Women Who Write to find the answers to these questions. It is likely that you will find the answers to a particular question in more than one source.

1. As a result of Ida Tarbell's study of the Standard Oil Company, what happened to the company?

   _____

   _____

   _____

2. English writer Daphne du Maurier is best known for her novel *Rebecca*, which was filmed by Alfred Hitchcock. Name two other films made by Hitchcock based on du Maurier's writing.

   _____

   _____

   _____

3. Who wrote the introduction to Ida Wells Barnet's book, *The Red Record*?

   _____

   _____

   _____

4. Dalia Messick changed her first name to Dale and mailed her work into her publisher. Name her work and tell why she mailed her work in.

   _____

   _____

   _____

5. Laura Esquivel, a Mexican author, wrote a best-selling novel and turned it into a screenplay. Name the work.

   _____

   _____

   _____

From *Multicultural Information Quests* by Marie E. Rodgers. © 2000 Libraries Unlimited. (800) 237-6124.

6. If you wanted to write a letter to author Gloria Naylor, where would you send it?

_____

_____

_____

7. A women's first occurred on December 7, 1993. Name the woman and her achievement.

_____

_____

_____

8. Cathy Song, noted American poet, wrote a collection called *Picture Bride*. What is a picture bride?

_____

_____

_____

9. Why did Beatrix Potter originally write her stories of Peter Rabbit?

_____

_____

_____

10. Bette Bao Lord wrote *Eighth Moon: The True Story of a Young Girl's Life in Communist China*. Who was the young girl written about in the book?

_____

_____

_____

Women in the Arts

In this section, women who have made contributions to fine and performing arts will be highlighted. Choosing which women to include in this search was difficult, for so many women have excelled in the arts. The references in this list provide profiles and information on several outstanding women in the arts.

Reference List for Women in the Arts

Bernikow, Louise, in association with the National Women's History Project. *The American Women's Almanac: An Inspiring and Irreverent Women's History*. New York: Berkley Books, 1997. 388p. $29.95. ISBN 0-425-15686-9.

This work is devoted to women who made contributions to American history. It is arranged in nine sections, some of which include Politics, The Female Mind, Entertainers, Domestic Life, and Work. A chapter called Last Word lists 25 things women have done for one another. There are several black-and-white photographs and illustrations, a bibliography, and an index. Another feature includes sidebar articles on related topics in each section. Very lively and fun to read, this work contains a history of women in America. It is written for general readers and those interested in women's studies, but it should also appeal to students in grade 6 and above.

Felder, Deborah G. *The 100 Most Influential Women of All Time: A Ranking Past and Present*. New York: Citadel Press, 1996. 374p. $24.95. ISBN 0-8065-1726-3.

Felder has ranked her subjects according to importance. This alone makes her work interesting and provocative. Readers are likely to debate the rankings. Whether or not they agree with the ranking order, readers will recognize that the women here have all made great contributions to the world. Among those listed are Rosa Parks, Freda Kahlo, Bessie Smith, Joan of Arc, and Lucille Ball. The list was compiled by means of a survey sent to Women's Studies departments of American colleges and universities. Using the surveys, Felder devised her list based on whom she felt had the greatest impact on the world. Profiles of the 100 subjects begin with dates of birth and death, a quotation by or about the subject, and a black-and-white photograph or illustration. Most profiles are two to three pages in length. Also included are career highlights, achievements, and personal information. There is an index and a bibliography as well. Recommended for grade 7 and above.

Hirsch, Jr., E. D., Joseph Kett, and James Trefil. *The Dictionary of Cultural Literacy.* 2nd ed. Revised and updated. Boston: Houghton Mifflin, 1993. 619p. $24.95. ISBN 0-395-65597-8.

Hirsch and his colleagues compiled what they have identified as shared common knowledge of literate Americans. This information is categorized into 23 subject sections. Sections include The Bible, World History, Mythology and Folklore, American Geography, Medicine and Health, and Technology. Entries within these sections are arranged alphabetically. Included are more than 250 illustrations, maps, and charts. Entries offer definitions as well as current cultural connotations. Cross-references and a pronunciation key are provided. Hirsch also presents an essay, "The Theory Behind the Dictionary." Written for general readers and students, this work is appropriate for grade 5 and above.

Read, Phyllis J., and Bernard Witlieb. *The Book of Women's Firsts: Breakthrough Achievements of Almost 1,000 American Women.* New York: Random House, 1992. 511p. $16.00. ISBN 0-679-74280-8.

Arranged alphabetically by subject, this work presents nearly 1,000 firsts achieved by women in the United States. The authors explain that the scarcity of early achievements by Native American women is due to the absence of written languages. Similarly, early achievements of African American women are scarce due to laws forbidding slaves to read or write. This work is intended as a reference. Sketches include name, achievement, and date of achievement in boldface, dates and places of birth and death when available, and a brief biographical sketch. Also included are black-and-white photographs and an index. Recommended for grade 6 and above.

Smith, Jessie Carney, ed. *Notable Black American Women*, Book 2. Detroit: Gale Research, 1996. 775p. $105.75. ISBN 0-8103-9177-5.

———. *Notable Black American Women.* Detroit: Gale Research, 1991. 1,333p. $80.00. ISBN 0-8103-4749-0.

Smith, a well-respected author, has compiled a series of sketches on African American women from all walks of life. Criteria for selection can be found in the introduction. Many of the essays contain personal quotations. In addition there are black-and-white photographs for most entrants. When possible, addresses have been included as well. Arranged alphabetically, the sketches provide personal and professional information, awards, career highlights, and a list of references. There is also a List of Entrants, Occupation, and an index. Thoroughly researched and well-written, this work is recommended for grade 6 and above.

Telgen, Diane, and Jim Camp, eds. *Notable Hispanic Women*. Detroit: Gale Research, 1993. 448p. $59.95. ISBN 0-8103-7578-8.

Nearly 300 alphabetically arranged entries comprise this work. Entrants were chosen by an advisory board of experts. After evaluation and selection, many subjects were interviewed by telephone. Entries range from 500 to 2,500 words and include personal, family, and career highlights. Longer entries also provide a black-and-white photograph. The work is cross-referenced for locating compound surnames. In addition to alphabetical listings of the subjects, there are listings by ethnicity and field of endeavor. This is an excellent resource for students in grade 5 and above.

Zia, Helen, and Susan B. Gall, eds. *Asian American Biography*. Detroit: UXL, 1995. 2 vols. $63.00. ISBN 0-8103-9687-4.

More than 130 Americans of Asian descent are profiled in this alphabetically arranged two-volume set. Most entries include field of endeavor, dates of birth and death, and an overview. Information on childhood, family, and education is also provided. Career highlights, awards, achievements, and Sources for Further Reading are included as well. Most entries also include a black-and-white photograph. Access is by a table of contents or a Field of Endeavor Index. Written especially for students, this work is recommended for grade 5 and above.

Search for Women in the Arts

Name_____ Class_____ Date_____

Use the Reference List for Women in the Arts to find the answers to these questions. It is possible that you will find answers in more than one source.

1. Vicki Carr won a Grammy in 1992. Name the album and the category for which she won her award.

   _____

   _____

   _____

2. Which first was achieved by Dyan Cannon?

   _____

   _____

   _____

3. Steve Martin's movie *Dead Men Don't Wear Plaid* was dedicated to Academy Award winner Edith Head. In what field did she excel, and how many Academy Award nominations did she receive throughout her career?

   _____

   _____

   _____

4. What beauty contest did Oprah Winfrey win in 1972?

   _____

   _____

   _____

5. What made Grandma Moses famous?

   _____

   _____

   _____

6. Name the well-known work of art located in Washington, D.C., designed by Chinese American architect-sculptor Maya Lin.

_____

_____

_____

7. Ivie Anderson, singer with the Duke Ellington orchestra, retired in 1941. What business did she successfully run after her retirement?

_____

_____

_____

8. Linda Ronstadt recorded an album of songs in memory of her father. What style of music was it?

_____

_____

_____

9. According to one reference on this list, every American needs to know about artist Mary Cassatt. With which group of French painters is she often associated? For what subjects is she best known?

_____

_____

_____

10. Ann Hobson-Pilot is an African American musician. Which instrument does she play?

_____

_____

_____

Phenomenal Women

Women have had many obstacles to overcome throughout history. This search presents only a minute sampling of women who have made breakthroughs, whether they made great scientific discoveries, lived nontraditional lifestyles, or trod new ground professionally and personally.

Reference List for Phenomenal Women

Bernikow, Louise, in association with the National Women's History Project. *The American Women's Almanac: An Inspiring and Irreverent Women's History*. New York: Berkley Books, 1997. 388p. $29.95. ISBN 0-425-15686-9.

This work is devoted to women who made contributions to American history. It is arranged in nine sections, some of which include Politics, The Female Mind, Entertainers, Domestic Life, and Work. A chapter called Last Word lists 25 things women have done for one another. There are several black-and-white photographs and illustrations, a bibliography, and an index. Another feature includes sidebar articles on related topics in each section. Very lively and fun to read, this work contains a history of women in America. It is written for general readers and those interested in women's studies, but it should also appeal to students in grade 6 and above.

Cooney, Miriam P., ed. *Celebrating Women in Mathematics and Science*. Reston, VA: National Council of Teachers of Mathematics, 1996. 223p. $22.50. ISBN 0-87353-425-5.

Written especially for middle- and high-school students, this collection of 20 profiles was compiled by a group of mathematics teachers. Each profile was researched and written by a different math teacher. The profiles focus on both the personal and professional lives of the subjects. A black-and-white illustration has been provided for each subject. Profiles demonstrate obstacles these great women faced in their chosen professions. Clearly written and engaging, this work provides information and inspiration. Recommended for grade 5 and above.

Grolier Library of International Biographies. Danbury, CT: Grolier Education Corp., 1996. 10 vols. $299.00. ISBN 0-7172-7527-2.

Twentieth-century achievers from various fields of endeavor are profiled in this 10-volume set. Each entry provides personal information ranging from childhood events to career highlights to values and beliefs. Achievements are detailed as well. Written for students, this work is written in clear, straightforward language. Each volume is devoted to a particular field of endeavor, covering areas such as scientists, performing artists, writers, and explorers. Boldface is used to indicate that the word and its definition will be found in a glossary specific to each volume's subject area. Black-and-white photographs, bibliographies, and indexes for each volume and a general index by subject, country, and name are included. Recommended for grade 5 and above.

Mahoney, M. H. *Women in Espionage: A Biographical Dictionary*. Santa Barbara, CA: ABC-CLIO, 1993. 253p. $65.00. ISBN 0-87436-743-3.

Arranged alphabetically, this volume lists biographical sketches of more than 150 women involved in espionage. Most entries range from half a page to two pages. Entries list given name, other names used, and places and dates of birth and death. Sketches provide details of the subject's early life, family life, and circumstances that led to her activities in espionage. Mahoney's narrative is straightforward and lively. Sources and related publications are listed at the end of each sketch. Several black-and-white photographs, a bibliography, a list of acronyms and abbreviations, and an index are provided as well. Written for general readers, this book is recommended for grade 7 and above.

McElroy, Lorie Jenkins, ed. *Women's Voices: A Documentary History of Women in America*. Detroit: UXL, 1996. 2 vols. $55.00. ISBN 0-7876-0663-4.

Speeches, diary entries, and other documents are compiled in this set. The purpose of this set is to trace the development of women's rights in America. Familiar names such as Sojourner Truth and Susan B. Anthony are featured along with less-familiar figures such as Lucy Stone and Alice Paul. Each volume consists of three chapters that focus on themes such as education, abolition, and suffrage in Volume One, and property, equality, and reproduction in Volume Two. The format for each of these sections consists of an introduction, Things to Remember, Excerpt, What Happened Next, Did You Know?, and Further Reading. Other features include biographical boxes and boxes that examine related events and time lines. Sidebars contain a glossary for each reproduced document. This work was written specifically for students. Recommended for grade 6 and above.

Platt, Richard. Photographed by Tina Chambers. *Pirate*. (Eyewitness Books). New York: Alfred A. Knopf, 1995. 64p. $19.00. ISBN 0-679-87255-8.

Eyewitness Books are popular with readers because of the numerous illustrations. This one is no exception. There are many excellent illustrations in color and black-and-white of authentic memorabilia related to piracy. The book is arranged so that one or two pages are devoted to an aspect of the subject. Text and illustrations are used to present an accurate representation of each aspect chosen. Among topics discussed in this book are "Pirates in Film and Theatre," "Food on Board," "Women Pirates," and "Pirates in Literature." The quality and quantity of the illustrations make this series fascinating for readers of all ages. Recommended for grade 5 and above.

Telgen, Diane, and Jim Camp, eds. *Notable Hispanic Women*. Detroit: Gale Research, 1993. 448p. $59.95. ISBN 0-8103-7578-8.

Nearly 300 alphabetically arranged entries comprise this work. Entrants were chosen by an advisory board of experts. After evaluation and selection, many subjects were interviewed by telephone. Entries range from 500 to 2,500 words and include personal, family, and career highlights. Longer entries also provide a black-and-white photograph. The work is cross-referenced for locating compound surnames. In addition to alphabetical listings of the subjects, there are listings by ethnicity and field of endeavor. This is an excellent resource for students in grade 5 and above.

Yount, Lisa. *Twentieth-Century Women Scientists*. (Global Profiles). New York: Facts on File, 1996. 123p. $19.95. ISBN 0-8160-3173-8.

Ten women are profiled in this work. Profiles detail the subject's life and work; however, the focus is on work and contributions to the chosen field. Following each essay is a chronology of the subject's achievements and a list of sources for further reading. There are black-and-white photographs of each subject as well as photographs related to the subject's work. Another special feature is the sidebars, which provide quotations by each subject. Yount also writes a notable introduction on women in the field of science. Yount's writing is clear, lively, and engaging. Even those who may not have an inclination toward science will be drawn to Yount's profiles on the lives of these women. Written for students and general readers. Recommended for grade 6 and above.

Search for Phenomenal Women

Name_____ Class_____ Date_____

Use the Reference List for Phenomenal Women to find the answers to these questions. It is likely that you will find answers to particular questions in more than one source on the list.

1. Which fabric is the trademark of fashion designer Isabel Toledo?

    _____

    _____

    _____

2. Why was Katsuko Saruhashi awarded the Avon Special Prize for Women in 1981?

    _____

    _____

    _____

3. Agnes Pockels was a chemist. What is significant about her education?

    _____

    _____

    _____

4. What is unusual about the clock in computer expert Grace Murray Hopper's office? By what maternal title is she known?

    _____

    _____

    _____

5. Lucy Stone pioneered the idea that married women should keep something after marriage. What was it?

    _____

    _____

    _____

From *Multicultural Information Quests* by Marie E. Rodgers. © 2000 Libraries Unlimited. (800) 237-6124.

6. Scientist Rosalyn Yalow has won many awards, including the Nobel prize. But to her, something else is even more gratifying and exciting. What is it?

_____

_____

_____

7. Name the city where Frances Garcia has served two terms as mayor. At the time of her election, what percentage of the population was Hispanic?

_____

_____

_____

8. Where did Louise Blanchard Bethune, the first professional woman architect in America, receive her education?

_____

_____

_____

9. Among a number of female pirates was Alvilda. Why did she go to sea?

_____

_____

_____

10. Angela Calomiris was recruited by the FBI to spy on Communists. She did this as a member of a special interest group. Name the group.

_____

_____

_____

Women Achievers

Comprehensive lists of women who changed the world can be found in the pages of the references listed in this chapter. Even a quick browse through any of these works would present the reader with an exhaustive list of women achievers in many fields of endeavor. The bulk of this search, however, focuses on strides made by women who are lesser known. The names of many of these women may not be recognized, but their contributions have had enormous and far-reaching effects on our lives.

Reference List for Women Achievers

Cooney, Miriam P., ed. *Celebrating Women in Mathematics and Science.* Reston, VA: National Council of Teachers of Mathematics, 1996. 223p. $22.50. ISBN 0-87353-425-5.
    Written especially for middle- and high-school students, this collection of 20 profiles was compiled by a group of mathematics teachers. Each profile was researched and written by a different math teacher. The profiles focus on both the personal and professional lives of the subjects. A black-and-white illustration has been provided for each subject. Profiles demonstrate obstacles these great women faced in their chosen professions. Clearly written and engaging, this work provides information and inspiration. Recommended for grade 5 and above.

Felder, Deborah G. *The 100 Most Influential Women of All Time: A Ranking Past and Present.* New York: Citadel Press, 1996. 374p. $24.95. ISBN 0-8065-1726-3.
    Felder has ranked her subjects according to importance. This alone makes her work interesting and provocative. Readers are likely to debate the rankings. Whether or not they agree with the ranking order, readers will recognize that the women here have all made great contributions to the world. Among those listed are Rosa Parks, Freda Kahlo, Bessie Smith, Joan of Arc, and Lucille Ball. The list was compiled by means of a survey sent to Women's Studies departments of American colleges and universities. Using the surveys, Felder devised her list based on whom she felt had the greatest impact on the world. Profiles of the 100 subjects begin with dates of birth and death, a quotation by or about the subject, and a black-and-white photograph or illustration. Most profiles are two to three pages in length. Also included are career highlights, achievements, and personal information. There is an index and bibliography as well. Recommended for grade 7 and above.

Mahoney, M. H. *Women in Espionage: A Biographical Dictionary.* Santa Barbara, CA: ABC-CLIO, 1993. 253p. $65.00. ISBN 0-87436-743-3.

Arranged alphabetically, this volume lists biographical sketches of more than 150 women involved in espionage. Most entries range from half a page to two pages. Entries list given name, other names used, and places and dates of birth and death. Sketches provide details of the subject's early life, family life, and circumstances that led to her activities in espionage. Mahoney's narrative is straightforward and lively. Sources and related publications are listed at the end of each sketch. Several black-and-white photographs, a bibliography, a list of acronyms and abbreviations, and an index are provided as well. Written for general readers, this book is recommended for grade 7 and above.

McElroy, Lorie Jenkins, ed. *Women's Voices: A Documentary History of Women in America.* Detroit: UXL, 1996. 2 vols. $55.00. ISBN 0-7876-0663-4.

Speeches, diary entries, and other documents are compiled in this set. The purpose of this set is to trace the development of women's rights in America. Familiar names such as Sojourner Truth and Susan B. Anthony are featured along with less-familiar figures such as Lucy Stone and Alice Paul. Each volume consists of three chapters that focus on themes such as education, abolition, and suffrage in Volume One, and property, equality, and reproduction in Volume Two. The format for each of these sections consists of an introduction, Things to Remember, Excerpt, What Happened Next, Did You Know?, and Further Reading. Other features include biographical boxes and boxes that examine related events and time lines. Sidebars contain a glossary for each reproduced document. This work was written specifically for students. Recommended for grade 6 and above.

Saari, Peggy, and Stephen Allison, eds. *Scientists: The Lives and Works of 150 Scientists.* Detroit: Gale Research, 1996. 3 vols. $105.00. ISBN 0-7876-0960-9.

Biographical information in this work focuses on personal life as well as scientific contribution. Each sketch includes black-and-white photographs or illustrations of the scientist, dates of birth and death, early life, contribution, and an Impact box that details the scientific discovery and its impact on the world. There are also bibliographies on each subject and biographical boxes of major influences on a particular scientist's life. The scope of the work is from the Industrial Revolution to the present day. Each volume begins with a complete list of Scientists by Field of Specialization, a Time Line of Scientific Breakthroughs, and Words to Know. There is also a general index. Written for students, this is an excellent reference for grade 5 and above.

Smith, Jessie Carney, ed. *Notable Black American Women*, Book 2. Detroit: Gale Research, 1996. 775p. $105.75. ISBN 0-8103-9177-5.

————. *Notable Black American Women*. Detroit: Gale Research, 1991. 1,333p. $80.00. ISBN 0-8103-4749-0.

Smith, a well-respected author, has compiled a series of sketches on African American women from all walks of life. Criteria for selection can be found in the introduction. Many of the essays contain personal quotations. In addition, there are black-and-white photographs for most entrants. When possible, addresses have been included as well. Arranged alphabetically, the sketches provide personal and professional information, awards, career highlights, and a list of references. There is also a List of Entrants, Occupation, and an index. Thoroughly researched and well-written, this work is recommended for grade 6 and above.

Yount, Lisa. *Twentieth-Century Women Scientists*. (Global Profiles). New York: Facts on File, 1996. 123p. $19.95. ISBN 0-8160-3173-8.

Ten women are profiled in this work. Profiles detail the subject's life and work; however, the focus is on work and contributions to the chosen field. Following each essay is a chronology of the subject's achievements and a list of sources for further reading. There are black-and-white photographs of each subject as well as photographs related to the subject's work. Another special feature is the sidebars, which provide quotations by each subject. Yount also writes a notable introduction on women in the field of science. Yount's writing is clear, lively, and engaging. Even those who may not have an inclination toward science will be drawn to Yount's profiles on the lives of these women. Written for students and general readers. Recommended for grade 6 and above.

Zia, Helen, and Susan B. Gall, eds. *Asian American Biography*. Detroit: UXL, 1995. 2 vols. $63.00. ISBN 0-8103-9687-4.

More than 130 Americans of Asian descent are profiled in this alphabetically arranged two-volume set. Most entries include field of endeavor, dates of birth and death, and an overview. Information on childhood, family, and education is also provided. Career highlights, awards, achievements, and Sources for Further Reading are included as well. Most entries also include a black-and-white photograph. Access is by a table of contents or a Field of Endeavor Index. Written especially for students, this work is recommended for grade 5 and above.

Search for Women Achievers

Name_____ Class_____ Date_____

Use the Reference List for Women Achievers to find the answers to these questions. It is likely that more than one source will have the correct answer.

1. Carrie Chapman Catt was involved in the suffrage movement at an international level. She was a strong force in the women's movement, and her efforts led to ratification of the 19th Amendment. However, she and her husband also had a prenuptial agreement. What stipulation was made regarding her suffrage activities?

   _____

   _____

   _____

2. Ilene Natividad, a political activist, was the first Asian American woman to chair a national women's group. Name the group and state its purpose.

   _____

   _____

   _____

3. Sybil Ludington was a spy during which war?

   _____

   _____

   _____

4. For what scientific development is scientist Lynn Conway known?

   _____

   _____

   _____

5. Maxine Waters, a politician, has been concerned with women's rights. Name the national organization she helped found.

   _____

   _____

   _____

6. Elizabeth Cady Stanton wrote and delivered a speech in 1848. It contains many similarities to another document. Name Stanton's document and the document after which it was modeled.

_____

_____

_____

7. Which first was achieved by physicist Shirley Ann Jackson? Another person involved with her college education also achieved a first. Who is it? What was the first achieved by that person?

_____

_____

_____

8. What technique of therapy was developed by Melanie Klein?

_____

_____

_____

9. Rita Levi-Montalcini discovered a natural substance that makes nerves grow. Name the substance.

_____

_____

_____

10. In what field of mathematics did German-born Emmy Noether excel?

_____

_____

_____

From *Multicultural Information Quests* by Marie E. Rodgers. © 2000 Libraries Unlimited. (800) 237-6124.

Women's Firsts

This search focuses on firsts involving women. Some are groundbreaking, some are historically significant, and others fall into the category of trivia. The reference list, however, is an indicator of the many valuable firsts that women have achieved.

Reference List for Women's Firsts

Bernikow, Louise, in association with the National Women's History Project. *The American Women's Almanac: An Inspiring and Irreverent Women's History.* New York: Berkley Books, 1997. 388p. $29.95. ISBN 0-425-15686-9.

This work is devoted to women who made contributions to American history. It is arranged in nine sections, some of which include Politics, The Female Mind, Entertainers, Domestic Life, and Work. A chapter called Last Word lists 25 things women have done for one another. There are several black-and-white photographs and illustrations, a bibliography, and an index. Another feature includes sidebar articles on related topics in each section. Very lively and fun to read, this work contains a history of women in America. It is written for general readers and those interested in women's studies, but it should also appeal to students in grade 6 and above.

Cooney, Miriam P., ed. *Celebrating Women in Mathematics and Science.* Reston, VA: National Council of Teachers of Mathematics, 1996. 223p. $22.50. ISBN 0-87353-425-5.

Written especially for middle- and high-school students, this collection of 20 profiles was compiled by a group of mathematics teachers. Each profile was researched and written by a different math teacher. The profiles focus on both the personal and professional lives of the subjects. A black-and-white illustration has been provided for each subject. Profiles demonstrate obstacles these great women faced in their chosen professions. Clearly written and engaging, this work provides information and inspiration. Recommended for grade 5 and above.

Kane, Joseph Nathan. *Famous First Facts.* 5th ed. Revised and expanded. New York: H. W. Wilson, 1997. 1,350p. $80.00. ISBN 0-8242-0930-3.

A popular ready reference book, *Famous First Facts* consists of more than 9,000 entries of what is listed as happenings, discoveries, and inventions in American history. Entries—arranged alphabetically by subject—are brief. One of the special features of this work is its indexes. Not only do they make the book easily accessible but they allow readers to find information by year, days of the month, geographical locations, and personal name. The work is also cross-referenced. Recommended for grade 5 and above.

Malinowski, Sharon, and Simon Glickman, eds. *Native North American Biography*. Detroit: Gale Research, 1996. 202p. $60.00. ISBN 0-8103-9821-4.

This two-volume set consists of alphabetically arranged biographical sketches of 112 famous Native Americans from the past and present and from all walks of life. Many sketches include a direct quotation by the subject as well as several black-and-white photographs and illustrations. Each sketch includes dates of birth and death, biographical information, and a Further Reading section, which is a short bibliography. Volume One begins with entries by tribal groups and a Reader's Guide. There is also an index by field of endeavor at the end of Volume Two. This set was written especially for students and is appropriate for grade 5 and above.

Olsen, Kirsten. *Chronology of Women's History*. Westport, CT: Greenwood Publishing Group, 1994. 506p. $39.95. ISBN 0-313-28803-8.

Olsen's work presents achievements on women's history from 20,000 B.C. to 1993. It is arranged year by year, and most chapters have categories. In addition to Literature and Visual Arts, Religion, Activism and Government, and the Law, Olsen presents information on General Status and Daily Life, Education and Scholarship, and Science and Medicine. There is a select bibliography and a general index. Recommended for grade 7 and above.

Read, Phyllis J., and Bernard Witlieb. *The Book of Women's Firsts: Breakthrough Achievements of Almost 1,000 American Women*. New York: Random House, 1992. 511p. $16.00. ISBN 0-679-74280-8.

Arranged alphabetically by subject, this work presents nearly 1,000 firsts achieved by women in the United States. The authors explain that the scarcity of early achievements by Native American women is due to the absence of written languages. Similarly, early achievements of African American women are scarce due to laws forbidding slaves to read or write. This work is intended as a reference. Sketches include name, achievement, and date of achievement in boldface, dates and places of birth and death when available, and a brief biographical sketch. Also included are black-and-white photographs and an index. Recommended for grade 6 and above.

Telgen, Diane, and Jim Camp, eds. *Notable Hispanic Women*. Detroit: Gale Research, 1993. 448p. $59.95. ISBN 0-8103-7578-8.

Nearly 300 alphabetically arranged entries comprise this work. Entrants were chosen by an advisory board of experts. After evaluation and selection, many subjects were interviewed by telephone. Entries range from 500 to 2,500 words and include personal, family, and career highlights. Longer entries also provide a black-and-white photograph. The work is cross-referenced for locating compound surnames. In addition to alphabetical listings of the subjects, there are listings by ethnicity and field of endeavor. This is an excellent resource for students in grade 5 and above.

Zia, Helen, and Susan B. Gall, eds. *Asian American Biography*. Detroit: UXL, 1995. 2 vols. $63.00. ISBN 0-8103-9687-4.

More than 130 Americans of Asian descent are profiled in this alphabetically arranged two-volume set. Most entries include field of endeavor, dates of birth and death, and an overview. Information on childhood, family, and education is also provided. Career highlights, awards, achievements, and Sources for Further Reading are included as well. Most entries also include a black-and-white photograph. Access is by a table of contents or a Field of Endeavor Index. Written especially for students, this work is recommended for grade 5 and above.

Zilboorg, Caroline, ed. *Women's Firsts*. Detroit: Gale Research, 1996. 564p. $48.55. ISBN 0-7876-0151-9.

A reference work designed to highlight women's achievements from ancient times to the present, this work is arranged by field of endeavor. Included are activism, literature, military service, science, and religion. Coverage is international, and more than 2,000 achievements are detailed here. Within each field of endeavor, achievements are listed chronologically with a citation for the source. Special features of this work include a Time Line of Events in Women's History and a bibliography. An index by day and month, an index by year, and a general index provide easy access. Recommended for grade 5 and above.

Search for Women's Firsts

Name_____ Class_____ Date_____

Use the Reference List for Women's Firsts to find the answers to these questions. It is possible that you will find answers in more than one source.

1. Which women's first occurred on January 12, 1909?

   _____

   _____

   _____

2. Betty Mae Tiger Jumper is a Native North American woman of firsts. Name her tribal group and list three firsts she achieved.

   _____

   _____

   _____

3. For which Broadway show did Willa Kim win her first Tony Award?

   _____

   _____

   _____

4. Which first was achieved by Margaret Chung?

   _____

   _____

   _____

5. In what way was Evelyn Thomas involved in the first automobile accident? Explain what happened, and tell where it happened.

   _____

   _____

   _____

6. Which first in the field of math was achieved in the same year by African Americans Evelyn Boyd Granville and Marjorie Lee Browne?

_____

_____

_____

7. Ellen Church was the first flight attendant. What other skill was required of Church and other flight attendants of the time?

_____

_____

_____

8. What first was achieved by Estela Portillo Trambley?

_____

_____

_____

9. Which famous first occurred on March 12, 1912, in Savannah, Georgia?

_____

_____

_____

10. In November 1876, Juliet Corson opened a specialized school. It was the first of its kind in the United States. What kind of school was it?

_____

_____

_____

Answer Key for Women Who Write

1. In Felder. Tarbell's writing led to a federal investigation and eventually to the breakup of the company.
2. In *Grolier*. *Jamaica Inn* and *The Birds* were both made into films by Hitchcock.
3. In McElroy. Frederick Douglass wrote the introduction.
4. In Bernikow. Messick, who created the comic strip *Brenda Starr*, didn't want anyone to know she was female.
5. In *Grolier*. Esquirel's work was called *Like Water for Chocolate*.
6. In Smith, Vol. 2. Gloria Nayor, c/o Viking Penguin, 375 Hudson Street, New York, NY 10014-3657.
7. In Zilboorg. Toni Morrison was the first African American woman to win the Nobel prize for literature.
8. In Zia and Gall. Asian men living in America chose brides from their hometowns by looking at pictures. The women then joined their prospective husbands in the United States.
9. In *Grolier*. Potter originally wrote the stories in her correspondence with Noel Moore to cheer him up.
10. In Zia and Gall. Lord wrote the book about her younger sister, who was unable to leave China with the rest of the family.

Answer Key for Women in the Arts

1. In Telgen and Camp. Carr won her award for *Cosas del Amor*, Best Latin Pop Album.
2. In Read and Witlieb. Cannon was the first woman nominated for an Academy Award as director (1977) and actress (1979).
3. In Felder. Martin's film was dedicated to Head because it was the last film she completed before her death. She was nominated 35 times for Academy Awards for costume design.
4. In Bernikow. Winfrey was Miss Black Nashville.
5. In Hirsch, Kett, and Trefil. Moses, who was known for painting in a style called Primitivism, started painting when she was in her late 70s.
6. In Zia and Gall. Lin designed the Vietnam Veterans Memorial.
7. In Smith, Vol. 2. Anderson ran Ivie's Chicken Shack, a successful restaurant in Los Angeles.
8. In Telgen and Camp. Ronstadt's album dedicated to her father was mariachi music.
9. In Hirsch, Kett, and Trefil. Associated with French Impressionists, Cassatt's paintings of mothers and children were her best-known works.
10. In Smith, Vol. 2. Hobson-Pilot is a harpist.

Answer Key for Phenomenal Women

1. In Telgen and Camp. Toledo's trademark fabric is denim.
2. In Yount. Saruhashi received the award for pursuing the peaceful use of nuclear energy and working to give recognition to women scientists.
3. In *Grolier*. Pockels was self-taught.

4. In Cooney. Murray Hopper's office clock runs backwards, and the numbers are reversed. It is indicative of her habit of always looking for a new way of seeing things. She has been called the Grandmother of the Computer Age.
5. In McElroy. Stone felt women should keep their birth names after marriage.
6. In Cooney. Yalow's greatest joy is working in the lab.
7. In Telgen and Camp. Garcia is mayor of Hutchinson, Kansas. At the time of her election only 2% of the population was Hispanic.
8. In Bernikow. Blanchard Bethune received her education at home.
9. In Platt. Alvilda went to sea to avoid a forced marriage to Danish Prince Alf.
10. In Mahoney. Calomiris was a member of the Photo League.

Answer Key for Women Achievers

1. In McElroy. The agreement stipulated that Catt could devote four months of each year to the movement.
2. In Zia and Gall. The National Women's Political Caucus was formed to put women in public office.
3. In Mahoney. Ludington was a spy in the American Revolution.
4. In Saari and Allison. Conway simplified the design of the computer chip.
5. In Smith, Vol 2. Waters founded the National Political Congress of Black Women.
6. In McElroy. Stanton used the Declaration of Independence as the model for her speech "A Declaration of Sentiments."
7. In Saari and Allison. Jackson, the first African American woman to receive a Ph.D. from M.I.T., studied under James Young, the first African American full-tenured professor of physics at M.I.T.
8. In Felder. Klein developed a therapy used with children called play therapy.
9. In Yount. Levi-Montalcini named her discovery NGF, nerve growth factor.
10. In Cooney. Noether excelled in algebra.

Answer Key for Women's Firsts

1. In Zilboorg. The first all-female auto race took place.
2. In Malinowski and Glickman. Tiger Jumper was the first Seminole woman to graduate high school, the first to become a nurse, and the first to be elected to tribal council and lead it.
3. In Zia and Gall. Kim won a Tony for *Sophisticated Ladies*.
4. In Bernikow. Chung was the first Chinese American woman physician.
5. In Kane. Thomas was riding her bicycle when a car driven by Henry Wells of Springfield, Massachusetts, collided with her in New York City.
6. In Cooney. Both received a doctorate degree in math.
7. In Read and Witlieb. They were also required to be nurses.
8. In Telgen and Camp. She was the first Chicano to publish a short-story collection and the first to write a musical comedy.
9. In Kane. The Girl Scouts were formed.
10. In Olsen. It was a culinary school.

Chapter
Thirteen

Asian Americans

Asian Americans have made many contributions to America, but their story is both tragic and triumphant. Many Asians helped build the transcontinental railroad more than 100 years ago. In more recent history, the bombing of Pearl Harbor caused anti-Japanese sentiments in America for the duration of World War II. The searches in this section will examine contributions and achievements, injustices and issues, and Asian customs and traditions.

Reference List for Asian American Achievers

There are many Asian American success stories. This search focuses on 10 Asian American achievers. How many names are familiar to you?

Baron, Deborah G., and Susan B. Gall, eds. *Asian American Chronology*. New York: UXL, 1996. 173p. $39.00. ISBN 0-8103-9692-0.

Milestones in Asian American history are recorded here using a calendar arrangement. Spanning time from prehistory to 1995, entries range from a few lines to one page. Coverage includes topics such as immigration, world wars, and contributions made by Asian Americans from more than 20 countries of origin. There are more than 90 black-and-white illustrations and maps. In addition, boxes highlight important, relevant information. Cross-references, boxes with related charts and statistics, and an index provide easy access. The section Further Reading lists sources on Asian Americans in general as well as sources for specific groups. Recommended for grade 5 and above.

Gall, Susan, and Irene Natividad, eds. *The Asian American Almanac*. Detroit: Gale Research, 1995. 834p. $99.00. ISBN 0-8103-9193-7.

More than 40 chapters discuss various groups of Asian Americans, their culture, their history, and aspects of their life in America. Chapter One discusses Asian Americans as a whole. Chapters Two through Fifteen discuss individual groups by ethnicity. Among groups discussed are Asian Indians, Cambodians, Hmong, Pakistani, Thai, and Nepali. Chapters Sixteen and Seventeen present a chronology of Asian American history. The remaining chapters focus on specific topics and issues, such as education, civil rights, the arts, culture, history, and the workplace. Notable Asian Americans are profiled as well. Black-and-white photographs, illustrations, and charts are included. There is also an index. Written for general readers, this is also an excellent source for students in grade 5 and above.

Grolier Library of International Biographies. Danbury CT: Grolier Education Corp., 1996. 10 vols. $299.00. ISBN 0-7172-7527-2.

Twentieth-century achievers from various fields of endeavor are profiled in this 10-volume set. Each entry provides personal information ranging from childhood events to career highlights to values and beliefs. Achievements are detailed as well. Written for students, this work is written in clear, straightforward language. Each volume is devoted to a particular field of endeavor, covering areas such as scientists, performing artists, writers, and explorers. Boldface is used to indicate that the word and its definition will be found in a glossary specific to each volume's subject area. Black-and-white photographs, bibliographies, and indexes for each volume and a general index by subject, country, and name are included. Recommended for grade 5 and above.

Niiya, Brian, ed. *Japanese American History: An A to Z Reference from 1868 to the Present*. New York: Facts on File, 1993. 386p. $50.00. ISBN 0-8160-2680-7.

This well-written volume consists of three sections: a narrative historical overview, a chronology of Japanese history, and dictionary entries that focus on various aspects of Japanese American history. Among topics discussed are Picture Brides, Immigration, Japanese Internment Camps, and the Revolution of 1954. Dictionary entries range from a few lines to a page. Sources for further reading follow each entry. Cross-references, a pronunciation guide, an index, and black-and-white photographs are included as well. A special feature of this work is a bibliography entitled 100 Titles: A Basic Library on Japanese Americans. Written for general readers, this work is appropriate for grade 6 and above.

Saari, Peggy, and Stephen Allison, eds. *Scientists: The Lives and Works of 150 Scientists*. Detroit: Gale Research, 1996. 3 vols. $105.00. ISBN 0-7876-0960-9.

Biographical information in this work focuses on personal life as well as on scientific contribution. Each sketch includes black-and-white photographs or illustrations of the scientist, dates of birth and death, early life, contributions, and an Impact box that details the scientific discovery and its impact on the world. There are also bibliographies on each subject and biographical boxes of major influences on a particular scientist's life. The scope of the work is from the Industrial Revolution to the present day. Each volume begins with a complete list of Scientists by Field of Specialization, a Timeline of Scientific Breakthroughs, and Words to Know. There is also a general index. Written for students, this is an excellent reference for grade 5 and above.

Zia, Helen, and Susan B. Gall, eds. *Asian American Biography*. New York: UXL, 1995. 2 vols. $63.00. ISBN 0-8103-9687-4.

More than 130 Americans of Asian descent are profiled in this alphabetically arranged two-volume set. Most entries include field of endeavor, dates of birth and death, and an overview. Information on childhood, family, and education is provided. Career highlights, awards, achievements, and Sources for Further Reading are included as well. Most entries also include a black-and-white photograph. Access is by a table of contents or a Field of Endeavor Index. Written especially for students, this work is recommended for grade 5 and above.

Note: *Asian American Biography* is a condensed version of the following text. Both are listed here for those who may have access to only one of the two sources. A note that directs the reader to "see also" an additional reference will be used in any future reference lists.

Zia, Helen, and Susan B. Gall, eds. *Notable Asian Americans*. Detroit: Gale Research, 1995. 468p. $75.00. ISBN 0-8103-9623-8.

Biographical sketches of 250 Asian Americans from various fields of endeavor—many of which have been taken from personal interviews—are listed alphabetically in this volume. Most entries are accompanied by black-and-white photographs. Sketches include field of endeavor, personal and professional information, and honors and awards. Sources are listed at the end of each signed sketch. Also included are Occupational Index, Ethnicity Index, and Subject Index. Recommended for grade 5 and above.

Search for Asian American Achievers

Name_____ Class_____ Date_____

Use the Reference List for Asian American Achievers to locate answers to the following questions. Correct answers may be found in more than one source.

1. Tomia "Tommy" T. Kono, Olympic weight lifter, distinguished himself by winning a body-building title three times. Name the title and the years in which he won.

    _____

    _____

    _____

2. Which Asian American actor received a star on the Hollywood Walk of Fame in 1994?

    _____

    _____

    _____

3. What is notable about Kotaro Suto?

    _____

    _____

    _____

4. Heiiti Aki made a notable contribution to the measurement of earthquakes. What is it called?

    _____

    _____

    _____

5. Automotive designer Tom Matano worked on the design of a classic two-seat auto. Name the car.

    _____

    _____

    _____

6. Jade Snow Wong gained recognition with a memoir of her childhood in San Francisco. What is the name of the book?

_____

_____

_____

7. Hanae Mori is an internationally known fashion designer. Describe her trademark dress design.

_____

_____

_____

8. Why is film producer Ismail Merchant in the *Guinness Book of World Records*?

_____

_____

_____

9. Toshiro Mifune, a Japanese actor and producer, made a Japanese version of *Macbeth* with director Akira Kurosawa. Name the film.

_____

_____

_____

10. Safi U. Qureshy, one of the founders of AST Research, a computer-manufacturing company, was and still is president of the company. How did he achieve his position?

_____

_____

_____

Asian Americans
and the U.S. Government

Although Asian Americans have made great contributions to America, their civil rights were frequently violated by the U.S. government. This search focuses on that aspect of Asian American life in America.

Reference List for Asian Americans and the U.S. Government

Baron, Deborah G., and Susan B. Gall, eds. *Asian American Chronology*. New York: UXL, 1996. 173p. $39.00. ISBN 0-8103-9692-0.

Milestones in Asian American history are recorded here using a calendar arrangement. Spanning time from prehistory to 1995, entries range from a few lines to one page. Coverage includes topics such as immigration, world wars, and contributions made by Asian Americans from more than 20 countries of origin. There are approximately 90 black-and-white illustrations and maps. In addition, boxes highlight important, relevant information. Cross-references, boxes with related charts and statistics, and an index provide easy access. The section Further Reading lists sources on Asian Americans in general as well as sources for specific groups. Recommended for grade 5 and above.

Cao, Lan, and Himilce Novas. *Everything You Need to Know About Asian American History*. New York: Plume, 1996. 366p. $12.95. ISBN 0-452-27315-3.

Written in a question-and-answer format, this book devotes one chapter to each of seven groups: Chinese, Japanese, Filipino, Southeast Asian, Korean, Asian Indians, and Pacific Islanders. The introduction is in part also written in a question-and-answer format. Information boxes are placed in relevant areas throughout the book. Examples include Asian American Heartthrobs, Thirteen Asian American Women Who Made a Difference, and Some Popular Asian American Dishes. There is a recommended reading list for each ethnic group and an index. Although the question-and-answer format makes this book fun to browse, it is also an excellent source of information. Recommended for grade 5 and above.

Gall, Susan, and Irene Natividad, eds. *The Asian American Almanac*. Detroit: Gale Research, 1995. 834p. $99.00. ISBN 0-8103-9193-7.

More than 40 chapters discuss various groups of Asian Americans, their culture, their history, and aspects of their life in America. Chapter One discusses Asian Americans as a whole. Chapters Two through Fifteen discuss individual groups by ethnicity. Among groups discussed are Asian Indians,

Cambodians, Hmong, Pakistani, Thai, and Nepali. Chapters Sixteen and Seventeen present a chronology of Asian American history. The remaining chapters focus on specific topics and issues, such as education, civil rights, the arts, culture, history, and the workplace. Notable Asian Americans are profiled as well. Black-and-white photographs, illustrations, and charts are included. There is also an index. Written for general readers, this is also an excellent source for students in grade 5 and above.

Hoobler, Dorothy, and Thomas Hoobler. *The Chinese American Family Album*. (American Family Album Series). New York: Oxford University Press, 1994. 128p. $19.95. ISBN 0-19-508130-7.

Described as a scrapbook of family letters and diary entries, excerpts from literature, documents, and newspaper articles, this work details the history of the Chinese in America. Black-and-white photographs enhance the text to create a moving historical testament. Topics discussed are the transcontinental railroad, Chinatowns, laundries, immigration, and noteworthy Chinese Americans. Illustrations, sidebars, and a time line are included. This is part of a wonderful series on ethnic groups in America. An excellent resource for students in grade 5 and above, this work should appeal to adults as well.

Kim, Hyung-Chan, ed. *The Dictionary of Asian American History*. New York: Greenwood Press, 1986. 628p. $89.50. ISBN 0-313-23760-3.

This valuable resource provides information on people, places, concepts, and significant events. It opens with a series of essays, each of which focuses on a specific Asian ethnic group. Essays present a historical perspective on the group discussed. Another group of essays, focusing on Asian Americans in general, discuss literature, popular culture, immigration, law, mental health, and American justice. The essays are followed by the dictionary, which comprises the bulk of the book. In all, the dictionary contains more than 800 entries, which range from a paragraph to one-and-a-half pages. There are see and see-also references as well. Appendixes provide a bibliography, census data, and a chronology. Written for general readers, the essays may be difficult for younger students. However, the dictionary is appropriate for grade 6 and above.

Zia, Helen, and Susan B. Gall, eds. *Asian American Biography*. Detroit: UXL, 1995. 2 vols. $63.00. ISBN 0-8103-9687-4.

More than 130 Americans of Asian descent are profiled in this alphabetically arranged two-volume set. Most entries include field of endeavor, dates of birth and death, and an overview. Information on childhood, family, and education is provided. Career highlights, awards, achievements, and Sources for Further Reading are included as well. Most entries also include a black-and-white photograph. Access is by a table of contents or a Field of Endeavor Index. Written especially for students, this work is recommended for grade 5 and above.

See also: Zia, Helen, and Susan B. Gall, eds. *Notable Asian Americans*. Detroit: Gale Research, 1995. 468 p. $75.00. ISBN 0-8103-9623-8.

This is a more comprehensive version of *Asian American Biography*.

Search for Asian Americans and the U.S. Government

Name_____ Class_____ Date_____

Use the Reference List for Asian Americans and the U.S. Government to find the answers to the following questions. It is likely that you may find answers in more than one of the sources listed.

1. What was Executive Order 9066?

   _____

   _____

   _____

2. On October 6, 1948, the Supreme Court made a ruling regarding Asian American marriage. What was it?

   _____

   _____

   _____

3. What was prohibited by the Chinese Exclusion Act of 1882?

   _____

   _____

   _____

4. Who is Fred Korematsu?

   _____

   _____

   _____

5. How did the Irwin Convention of 1885 impact on Asian Americans?

   _____

   _____

   _____

6. How did the Cable Act of 1922 affect American women?

_____

_____

_____

7. Internment camps were created to incarcerate Japanese Americans during World War II. Name the first camp to be opened.

_____

_____

_____

8. Salvador Roldan wanted to marry Marjorie Rogers in 1931. Because Roldan was a Filipino, the couple had to petition the court for permission to marry. In 1933, the court ruled in favor of the couple, but their victory was short-lived. Why?

_____

_____

_____

9. What was Angel Island?

_____

_____

_____

10. On January 5, 1942, the government made a ruling regarding Japanese men of draft age. What was it?

_____

_____

_____

Asian American Firsts

We have all benefited as a result of the discoveries and firsts contributed to this country by Asian Americans. This search presents only a sampling of the many discoveries that have made our lives easier, better, and happier.

Reference List for Asian American Firsts

Baron, Deborah G., and Susan B. Gall, eds. *Asian American Chronology*. New York: UXL, 1996. 173p. $39.00. ISBN 0-8103-9692-0.

Milestones in Asian American history are recorded here using a calendar arrangement. Spanning time from prehistory to 1995, entries range from a few lines to one page. Coverage includes topics such as immigration, world wars, and contributions made by Asian Americans from more than 20 countries of origin. There are more than 90 black-and-white illustrations and maps. In addition, boxes highlight important, relevant information. Cross-references, boxes with related charts and statistics, and an index provide easy access. The section Further Reading lists sources on Asian Americans in general as well as sources for specific groups. Recommended for grade 5 and above.

Cao, Lan, and Himilce Novas. *Everything You Need to Know About Asian American History*. New York: Plume, 1996. 366p. $12.95. ISBN 0-452-27315-3.

Written in a question-and-answer format, this book devotes one chapter to each of seven groups: Chinese, Japanese, Filipino, Southeast Asian, Korean, Asian Indians, and Pacific Islanders. The introduction is in part also written in a question-and-answer format. Information boxes are placed in relevant areas throughout the book. Examples include Asian American Heartthrobs, Thirteen Asian American Women Who Made a Difference, and Some Popular Asian American Dishes. There is a recommended reading list for each ethnic group and an index. Although the question-and-answer format makes this book fun to browse, it is also an excellent source of information. Recommended for grade 5 and above.

Gall, Susan, and Irene Natividad, eds. *The Asian American Almanac*. Detroit: Gale Research, 1995. 834p. $99.00. ISBN 0-8103-9193-7.

More than 40 chapters discuss various groups of Asian Americans, their culture, their history, and aspects of their life in America. Chapter One discusses Asian Americans as a whole. Chapters Two through Fifteen discuss individual groups by ethnicity. Among groups discussed are Asian Indians, Cambodians, Hmong, Pakistani, Thai, and Nepali. Chapters Sixteen and Seventeen present a chronology of Asian American history. The remaining chapters focus on specific topics and issues, such as education, civil rights, the arts, culture, history, and the workplace. Notable Asian Americans are profiled as well. Black-and-white photographs, illustrations, and charts are included. There is also an index. Written for general readers, this is also an excellent source for students in grade 5 and above.

Hoobler, Dorothy, and Thomas Hoobler. *The Chinese American Family Album.* (American Family Album Series). New York: Oxford University Press, 1994. 128p. $19.95. ISBN 0-19-508130-7.

Described as a scrapbook of family letters and diary entries, excerpts from literature, documents, and newspaper articles, this work details the history of the Chinese in America. Black-and-white photographs enhance the text to create a moving historical testament. Topics discussed are the transcontinental railroad, Chinatowns, laundries, immigration, and noteworthy Chinese Americans. Illustrations, sidebars, and a time line are included. This is part of a wonderful series on ethnic groups in America. An excellent resource for students in grade 5 and above, this work should appeal to adults as well.

Moss, Joyce, and George Wilson. *Peoples of the World: North Americans.* 1st ed. Detroit: Gale Research, 1991. 441p. $45.00. ISBN 0-8103-7768-3.

The Peoples of the World series profiles various ethnic groups. The authors have made the focus of their work the people of a country rather than the country itself. The premise of the work is that governments and other world events affect change in many countries, but culture and tradition do not change. Separate volumes have been devoted to North Americans and to Latin Americans as well as to other areas around the world. Each entry is introduced with phonetic spelling and definition. Information on population, location, language, and geographical setting is also included. Other sections for each culture include historical background and culture today. Special features include maps for each culture that indicate current location. While political and economic information may not be current, this work is a good source of cultural and historical information. Also included are black-and-white illustrations and photographs, a glossary, and an index. This set is written especially for students in junior high school, making it appropriate for students in grade 7 and above.

Niiya, Brian, ed. *Japanese American History: An A-to-Z Reference from 1868 to the Present.* New York: Facts on File, 1993. 386p. $50.00. ISBN 0-8160-2680-7.

This well-written volume consists of three sections: a narrative historical overview, a chronology of Japanese history, and dictionary entries that focus on various aspects of Japanese American history. Among topics discussed are Picture Brides, Immigration, Japanese Internment Camps, and the Revolution of 1954. Dictionary entries range from a few lines to a page.

Sources for further reading follow each entry. Cross-references, a pronunciation guide, an index, and black-and-white photographs are included as well. A special feature of this work is a bibliography entitled 100 Titles: A Basic Library on Japanese Americans. Written for general readers, this work is appropriate for grade 6 and above.

Saari, Peggy, and Stephen Allison, eds. *Scientists: The Lives and Works of 150 Scientists*. Detroit: Gale Research, 1996. 3 vols. $105.00. ISBN 0-7876-0960-9.

Biographical information in this work focuses on personal life as well as on scientific contribution. Each sketch includes black-and-white photographs or illustrations of the scientist, dates of birth and death, early life, contributions, and an Impact box that details the scientific discovery and its impact on the world. There are also bibliographies on each subject and biographical boxes of major influences on a particular scientist's life. The scope of the work is from the Industrial Revolution to the present day. Each volume begins with a complete list of Scientists by Field of Specialization, a Timeline of Scientific Breakthroughs, and Words to Know. There is also a general index. Written for students, this is an excellent reference for grade 5 and above.

Zia, Helen, and Susan B. Gall, eds. *Notable Asian Americans*. Detroit: Gale Research, 1995. 468p. $75.00. ISBN 0-8103-9623-8.

Biographical sketches of 250 Asian Americans from various fields of endeavor—many of which have been taken from personal interviews—are listed alphabetically in this volume. Most entries are accompanied by black-and-white photographs. Sketches include field of endeavor, personal and professional information, and honors and awards. Sources are listed at the end of each signed sketch. Also included are Occupational Index, Ethnicity Index, and Subject Index. Recommended for grade 5 and above.

Note: See also: Zia, Helen, and Susan B. Gall, eds. *Asian American Biography*. Detroit: UXL, 1995. 2 vols. $63.00. ISBN 0-8103-9687-4.
This is a condensed version of *Notable Asian Americans*.

Search for Asian American Firsts

Name_____ Class_____ Date_____

Use the Reference List for Asian American Firsts to find the answers to these questions. You may find the answers in more than one of the sources listed below.

1. In 1903, the first group of Filipino students, called *pensionados*, came to America under sponsorship of the U.S. government. Why did they come to America, and why were they given this name?

_____

_____

_____

2. Who was Okei?

_____

_____

_____

3. Which first was achieved by Myoshi Umeki on March 26, 1958?

_____

_____

_____

4. Which first was achieved by Hizoko Hamada in 1850?

_____

_____

_____

5. Sammy Lee achieved an Olympic first. What was it?

_____

_____

_____

 From *Multicultural Information Quests* by Marie E. Rodgers. © 2000 Libraries Unlimited. (800) 237-6124.

6. On November 28, 1910, Sara Choe arrived in the United States. Why is that significant?

_____

_____

_____

7. According to a time line, in what year did Chinese sailors first arrive in New York City?

_____

_____

_____

8. Chien-Shiung Wu is the first living scientist to have something named for her. What is it, and where is it?

_____

_____

_____

9. Which first was achieved by Herbert Choy?

_____

_____

_____

10. The year 1790 marks a first on a time line of Asian American history. What is it?

_____

_____

_____

Significant Asian American
People, Places, and Events

This search focuses on various aspects of Asian American history. Many of these questions refer to people, places, or events of historical importance. A few others, however, present little-known or unusual pieces of information. The facts presented here are both informative and fun.

Reference List for Significant Asian American People, Places, and Events

Baron, Deborah G., and Susan B. Gall, eds. *Asian American Chronology*. New York: UXL, 1996. 173p. $39.00. ISBN 0-8103-9692-0.

Milestones in Asian American history are recorded here using a calendar arrangement. Spanning time from prehistory to 1995, entries range from a few lines to one page. Coverage includes topics such as immigration, world wars, and contributions made by Asian Americans from more than 20 countries of origin. There are more than 90 black-and-white illustrations and maps. In addition, boxes highlight important, relevant information. Cross-references, boxes with related charts and statistics, and an index provide easy access. The section Further Reading lists sources on Asian Americans in general as well as sources for specific groups. Recommended for grade 5 and above.

Galens, Judy, Anna Sheets, and Robin V. Young, eds. *Gale Encyclopedia of Multicultural America*. Detroit: Gale Research, 1995. 1,477p. $125.00. ISBN 0-8103-9163-5.

More than 100 alphabetically arranged signed essays have been compiled in this work. Articles, ranging from 5,000 to 20,000 words, have been written by experts in their field. Essays focus on the experiences of each ethnic group discussed. Entries begin with an overview and a history and provide information on each group's individual contributions to American society. Also discussed are language, religion, politics, organizations, and achievers from each group. There are several black-and-white photographs and illustrations, a general bibliography, and an index. Recommended for grade 5 and above.

Gall, Susan, and Irene Natividad, eds. *The Asian American Almanac*. Detroit: Gale Research, 1995. 834p. $99.00. ISBN 0-8103-9193-7.

More than 40 chapters discuss various groups of Asian Americans, their culture, their history, and aspects of their life in America. Chapter One discusses Asian Americans as a whole. Chapters Two through Fifteen discuss individual groups by ethnicity. Among groups discussed are Asian Indians, Cambodians, Hmong, Pakistani, Thai, and Nepali. Chapters Sixteen and Seventeen present a chronology of Asian American history. The remaining chapters focus on specific topics and issues, such as education, civil rights, the arts, culture, history, and the workplace. Notable Asian Americans are profiled as well. Black-and-white photographs, illustrations, and charts are included. There is also an index. Written for general readers, this is also an excellent source for students in grade 5 and above.

Hoobler, Dorothy, and Thomas Hoobler. *The Chinese American Family Album*. (American Family Album Series). New York: Oxford University Press, 1994. 128p. $19.95. ISBN 0-19-508130-7.

Described as a scrapbook of family letters and diary entries, excerpts from literature, documents, and newspaper articles, this work details the history of the Chinese in America. Black-and-white photographs enhance the text to create a moving historical testament. Topics discussed are the transcontinental railroad, Chinatowns, laundries, immigration, and noteworthy Chinese Americans. Illustrations, sidebars, and a time line are included. This is part of a wonderful series on ethnic groups in America. An excellent resource for students in grade 5 and above, this work should appeal to adults as well.

Kim, Hyung-Chan, ed. *The Dictionary of Asian American History*. New York: Greenwood Press, 1986. 628p. $89.50. ISBN 0-313-23760-3.

This valuable resource provides information on people, places, concepts, and significant events. It opens with a series of essays, each of which focuses on a specific Asian ethnic group. Essays present a historical perspective on the group discussed. Another group of essays, focusing on Asian Americans in general, discuss literature, popular culture, immigration, law, mental health, and American justice. The essays are followed by the dictionary, which comprises the bulk of the book. In all, the dictionary contains more than 800 entries, which range from a paragraph to one-and-a-half pages. There are see and see-also references as well. Appendixes provide a bibliography, census data, and a chronology. Written for general readers, the essays may be difficult for younger students. However, the dictionary is appropriate for grade 6 and above.

Moss, Joyce, and George Wilson. *Peoples of the World: North Americans*. 1st ed. Detroit: Gale Research, 1991. 441p. $45.00. ISBN 0-8103-7768-3.

The Peoples of the World series profiles various ethnic groups. The authors have made the focus of their work the people of a country rather than the country itself. The premise of the work is that governments and other world events affect change in many countries, but culture and tradition do not change. Separate volumes have been devoted to North Americans and to Latin Americans as well as to other areas around the world. Each entry is introduced with phonetic spelling and definition. Information on population, location, language, and geographical setting is also included. Other sections for each culture include historical background and culture today. Special features include maps for each culture that indicate current location. While political and economic information may not be current, this work is a good source of cultural and historical information. Also included are black-and-white illustrations and photographs, a glossary, and an index. This set is written especially for students in junior high school, making it appropriate for students in grade 7 and above.

Search for Significant Asian American People, Places, and Events

Name_____ Class_____ Date_____

Use the Reference List for Significant Asian American People, Places, and Events to find the answers to these questions. It is possible that the answers may be found in more than one of the sources listed.

1. What is the Lost Colony of Wakamatsu?

   _____

   _____

   _____

2. On September 23, 1950, the McCarran Internal Security Act was passed over presidential veto. What authority did this act give the President of the United States?

   _____

   _____

   _____

3. What is the name and address of the leading Chinese civil-rights organization in the United States?

   _____

   _____

   _____

4. Why is Goleta, California, significant in U.S. history?

   _____

   _____

   _____

5. What part did a Chinese laundry play in the capture of the notorious bank robber Black Bart?

   _____

   _____

   _____

6. How did the San Francisco earthquake benefit Chinese living there at that time?

_____

_____

_____

7. What is significant about the Buddhist Church of Bakersfield in Bakersfield, California?

_____

_____

_____

8. What is significant about the men of the 100th Infantry Battalion?

_____

_____

_____

9. What is significant about the affect on Filipinos of the Tydings-McDuffie Act of 1934?

_____

_____

_____

10. Why were Camp Pendleton, California; Fort Chaffee, Arkansas; Fort Indiantown Gap, Pennsylvania; and Elgin Air Force Base, Florida; significant to Vietnamese refugees in the 1970s?

_____

_____

_____

Asian American Culture

This search focuses on the various cultures of Asian Americans. Questions relate to food, dress, customs, and traditions.

Reference List for Asian American Culture

Cao, Lan, and Himilce Novas. *Everything You Need to Know About Asian American History*. New York: Plume, 1996. 366p. $12.95. ISBN 0-452-27315-3.

Written in a question-and-answer format, this book devotes one chapter to each of seven groups: Chinese, Japanese, Filipino, Southeast Asian, Korean, Asian Indians, and Pacific Islanders. The introduction is in part also written in a question-and-answer format. Information boxes are placed in relevant areas throughout the book. Examples include Asian American Heartthrobs, Thirteen Asian American Women Who Made a Difference, and Some Popular Asian American Dishes. There is a recommended reading list for each ethnic group and an index. Although the question-and-answer format makes this book fun to browse, it is also an excellent source of information. Recommended for grade 5 and above.

Dresser, Norine. *Multicultural Manners: New Rules of Etiquette for a Changing Society*. New York: John Wiley & Sons, Inc., 1996. 286p. $14.95. ISBN 0-471-11819-2.

Dresser writes the Multicultural Manners column for the *Los Angeles Times*. Many items from her column have been collected here. Dresser is also a folklorist. As a result, her work is a delightful mix of information and folklore. It is also indicative of how America is changing. Part One of the work deals with communication, including body language, child-rearing practices, classroom behavior, gifts, and male and female relationships. Part Two deals with holidays and worship. Finally, Part Three deals with health practices. Included as well are a bibliography, an index, and an appendix of Southeast Asian refugees. Dresser supplies fascinating information on how different meanings are attached to the thumbs-up sign, offering food, gift taboos, and rules for worship. The book is a treasure. It is useful and appealing for all ages. Recommended for grade 5 and above.

Galens, Judy, Anna Sheets, and Robin Young, eds. *Gale Encyclopedia of Multicultural America*. Detroit: Gale Research, 1995. 1,477p. $125.00. ISBN 0-8103-9163-5.

More than 100 alphabetically arranged signed essays have been compiled in this work. Articles, ranging from 5,000 to 20,000 words, have been written by experts in their field. Essays focus on the experiences of each ethnic group discussed. Entries begin with an overview and a history and provide information on each group's individual contributions to American society. Also discussed are language, religion, politics, organizations, and achievers from each group. There are several black-and-white photographs and illustrations, a general bibliography, and an index. Recommended for grade 5 and above.

Gall, Susan, and Irene Natividad, eds. *The Asian American Almanac*. Detroit: Gale Research, 1995. 834p. $99.00. ISBN 0-8103-9193-7.

More than 40 chapters discuss various groups of Asian Americans, their culture, their history, and aspects of their life in America. Chapter One discusses Asian Americans as a whole. Chapters Two through Fifteen discuss individual groups by ethnicity. Among groups discussed are Asian Indians, Cambodians, Hmong, Pakistani, Thai, and Nepali. Chapters Sixteen and Seventeen present a chronology of Asian American history. The remaining chapters focus on specific topics and issues, such as education, civil rights, the arts, culture, history, and the workplace. Notable Asian Americans are profiled as well. Black-and-white photographs, illustrations, and charts are included. There is also an index. Written for general readers, this is also an excellent source for students in grade 5 and above.

Hoobler, Dorothy, and Thomas Hoobler. *The Chinese American Family Album*. (American Family Album Series). New York: Oxford University Press, 1994. 128p. $19.95. ISBN 0-19-508130-7.

Described as a scrapbook of family letters and diary entries, excerpts from literature, documents, and newspaper articles, this work details the history of the Chinese in America. Black-and-white photographs enhance the text to create a moving historical testament. Topics discussed are the transcontinental railroad, Chinatowns, laundries, immigration, and noteworthy Chinese Americans. Illustrations, sidebars, and a time line are included. This is part of a wonderful series on ethnic groups in America. An excellent resource for students in grade 5 and above, this work should appeal to adults as well.

Moss, Joyce, and George Wilson. *Peoples of the World: North Americans*. 1st ed. Detroit: Gale Research, 1991. 441p. $45.00. ISBN 0-8103-7768-3.

The Peoples of the World series profiles various ethnic groups.The authors have made the focus of their work the people of a country rather than the country itself. The premise of the work is that governments and other world events affect change in many countries, but culture and tradition do not change. Separate volumes have been devoted to North Americans and to Latin Americans as well as to other areas around the world. Each entry is introduced with phonetic spelling and definition. Information on population, location, language, and geographical setting is also included. Other sections for each culture include historical background and culture today. Special features include maps for each culture that indicate current location. While political and economic information may not be current, this work is a good source of cultural and historical information. Also included are black-and-white illustrations and photographs, a glossary, and an index. This set is written especially for students in junior high school, making it appropriate for students in grade 7 and above.

Search for Asian American Culture

Name_____ Class_____ Date_____

Use the Reference List for Asian American Culture to find the answers to these questions. It is likely that more than one of the sources will have the answers you need.

1. Why would it be in poor taste to bring white flowers as a gift when having dinner in a Chinese home?

   _____

   _____

   _____

2. What is the difference between Hindi and Hindu?

   _____

   _____

   _____

3. *Halo-halo* is popular in Filipino cuisine. What is it?

   _____

   _____

   _____

4. What is the purpose of the U.S. Japan Culture Center?

   _____

   _____

   _____

5. Workers on the transcontinental railroad suffered hardships and disease. What staple of the Chinese diet probably protected Chinese workers from many of the diseases?

   _____

   _____

   _____

6. What dialects of the Hmong language are spoken by Hmong in the United States?

_____

_____

_____

7. Traditionally, Chinese parents expect high achievement in school from their children. Why is this important to the entire family?

_____

_____

_____

8. Koreans and Japanese people have a different concept of being on time than most Americans. If you invited a Korean or Japanese friend to your home at 3 P.M., what time would they probably arrive?

_____

_____

_____

9. To Spaniards, a *fandango* is a dance. What is a *fandango* to someone from Guam?

_____

_____

_____

10. Why is there so much yelling in karate?

_____

_____

_____

Answer Key for Asian American Achievers

1. In Zia and Gall, *Notable*. Kono was Mr. Universe in 1955, 1957, and 1961.
2. In Baron and Gall. Mako received a star in 1994.
3. In Niiya. Suto has been credited for being one of the builders of Miami Beach.
4. In Saari and Allison. Aki's contribution is called the seismic moment.
5. In Zia and Gall, *Notable*. Matano designed the Mazda Miata.
6. In Zia and Gall, *Notable*. Wong's work is titled *The Fifth Chinese Daughter*.
7. In *Grolier*. Mori combined a Japanese kimono and the Western-style evening gown to create the butterfly dress.
8. In Gall and Natividad. Merchant, James Ivory, and Ruth Prawer Jhabvala have the longest creative partnership in film history.
9. In *Grolier*. The film is *Throne of Blood*.
10. In Zia and Gall, *Asian American Biography*. Qureshey, who founded his company with two friends, drew straws for his position.

Answer Key for Asian Americans and the U.S. Government

1. In Cao and Novas. It authorized the evacuation and internment of 120,000 people of Japanese descent.
2. In Baron and Gall. The court declared that the ban on interracial marriages was unconstitutional.
3. In Baron and Gall. It prohibited the entrance of Chinese laborers to America and also prohibited courts from granting citizenship to Chinese.
4. In Zia and Gall. Korematsu is an American citizen of Japanese descent who resisted internment, resulting in his arrest. Forty years later, he and others were vindicated.
5. In Gall and Natividad. The Irwin Convention made it illegal to help aliens hired as laborers to immigrate to the U.S.
6. In Gall and Natividad. According to the Cable Act, American women who were citizens of the United States lost their citizenship by marrying men considered not eligible for citizenship.
7. In Baron and Gall. Manzanar was the first camp.
8. In Kim. In 1933, Bill 175 was passed, making marriages between whites and nonwhites illegal. Roldan was considered nonwhite.
9. In Hoobler and Hoobler. Angel Island was a detention center in San Francisco Bay. Chinese trying to enter the United States were held there for a period of six weeks to as long as two years.
10. In Baron and Gall. Japanese Americans of draft age were considered 4C, enemy aliens.

Answer Key for Asian American Firsts

1. In Moss and Wilson. They came to study at American colleges and were called *pensionados* because they received a stipend.
2. In Niiya. Okei was the first Japanese woman to die in America.
3. In Niiya. Umeki was the first person of Japanese descent to win an Academy Award.
4. In Baron and Gall. He was the first Japanese naturalized as an American citizen.
5. In Cao and Novas. Lee was the first male diver to win two gold medals in high diving in two Olympics in a row, 1948 and 1952.
6. In Gall and Natividad. Choe was the first picture bride.
7. In Hoobler and Hoobler. They arrived in 1830.
8. In Saari and Allison. An asteroid is named for her, and it is orbiting between Mars and Jupiter.
9. In Zia and Gall. Choy was the first Asian Pacific American to be named to a federal court.
10. In Baron and Gall. The first Asian Indians arrived in Salem, Massachusetts.

Answer Key for Significant Asian American People, Places, and Events

1. In Moss and Wilson. The Lost Colony was made up of a small group who came to America to escape political persecution. Unfortunately, they did not survive.
2. In Baron and Gall. As a result of this act, anyone could be incarcerated solely on suspicion.
3. In Galens, Sheets, and Young. Chinese for Affirmative Action is located at 17 Walter U. Lum Place, San Francisco, CA 98108.
4. In Kim. Goleta was the site of the only Japanese attack on the U.S. mainland. The attack occurred on February 23, 1942.
5. In Hoobler and Hoobler. Black Bart dropped a handkerchief with a Chinese laundry mark that led authorities to Black Bart's real identity. He was Chester Boles, a mining engineer.
6. In Hoobler and Hoobler. All records were destroyed, enabling Chinese immigrants to say they were born in America.
7. In Gall and Natividad. It is the oldest Buddhist church built by its congregation still in use.
8. In Gall and Natividad. It was made up entirely of men who had been interned.
9. In Moss and Wilson. The act limited the number of immigrants from the Philippines to 50 a year.
10. In Moss and Wilson. Each of these places served as a temporary resettlement camp.

Answer Key for Asian American Culture

1. In Dresser. White is a color of death. Bringing white flowers into a Chinese home would be interpreted as bringing death to the home.
2. In Cao and Novas. Hindi is the official language of India. A Hindu is a person who follows the Hindu religion.
3. In Cao and Novas. It is a milk shake made from coconut, egg custard, sweet red beans, and other ingredients.
4. In Galens, Sheets, and Young. The purpose of the center is to promote understanding between Japan and the United States.
5. In Hoobler and Hoobler. Boiled tea was a staple in the diet of Chinese railroad workers. Boiling the water probably saved them from illness.
6. In Gall and Natividad. Hmong in America speak Blue Hmong and White Hmong.
7. In Moss and Wilson. High achievement is a reflection of family honor.
8. In Dresser. Your guests would probably show up 30 minutes early.
9. In Cao and Novas. In Guam a *fandango* is a wedding reception held the night before (usually a Friday) the wedding ceremony.
10. In Cao and Novas. The yell, or *kiai*, is supposed to contract muscles so that physical and mental energy work in unison.

Chapter
Fourteen

European Immigrants

Immigrants from European countries are the focus of these searches. Two of the searches will highlight the contributions of Europeans specifically to science and the arts. A third search will highlight immigrant achievers in all fields of endeavor. Another search will deal with immigrants' experiences as newcomers to America. A final search will focus on the Holocaust. While the Holocaust may not be considered part of American history, it did impact on the entire world. Many immigrants arrived in this country after World War II as a result of the Holocaust.

Reference List for Immigrant Achievers in Science

Many immigrants have made contributions to America in various fields of endeavor. However, immigrant contributions to the field of science are particularly noteworthy. This search highlights only a few of those contributions.

Bruno, Leonard C. *Science and Technology Firsts*. Detroit: Gale Research, 1997. 636p. $86.00. ISBN 0-7876-0256-6.
　　Twelve chapters relating to various fields of scientific endeavor such as astronomy, biology, mathematics, and transportation have been arranged in chronological order. Entries are one paragraph in length and begin with the year of discovery or breakthrough in boldface and provide details. There are also several black-and-white photographs and illustrations. Cross-references exist only within a particular chapter; however, an extensive index helps readers locate information pertaining to more than one area of science. There is also a bibliography. Written for students and general readers, this work is also appropriate for science buffs in grade 5 and above.

Bullock, Allan, ed. *Great Lives of the 20th Century*. Secaucus, NJ: Chartwell Books, 1988. 184p. ISBN 1-55521-305-7.

More than 250 brief biographical sketches are arranged alphabetically. Most sketches are two to three paragraphs in length and include dates of birth and death, field of endeavor, place of birth, and when applicable, place of residence. This is helpful in identifying those who immigrated to this country. Included in sketches is information on the subject's early life, career highlights, and honors and awards. The introduction discusses omissions as well. There are color and black-and-white photographs on each page. Written for general readers, but appropriate for grade 5 and above.

Grolier Library of International Biographies. Danbury, CT: Grolier Education Corp., 1996. 10 vols. $299.00. ISBN 0-7172-7527-2.

Twentieth-century achievers from various fields of endeavor are profiled in this 10-volume set. Each entry provides personal information ranging from childhood events to career highlights to values and beliefs. Achievements are detailed as well. Written for students, this work is written in clear, straightforward language. Each volume is devoted to a particular field of endeavor, covering areas such as scientists, performing artists, writers, and explorers. Boldface is used to indicate that the word and its definition will be found in a glossary specific to each volume's subject area. Black-and-white photographs, bibliographies, and indexes for each volume and a general index by subject, country, and name are included. Recommended for grade 5 and above.

Katz, William Loren. *The Great Migrations: 1880s–1912*. (A History of Multicultural America). Austin, TX: Raintree Steck-Vaughn, 1993. 96p. $8.95. ISBN 0-8114-6278-1.

Katz has written several works for students. This work, part of an excellent series on multicultural Americans, deals specifically with a period of American history during which a large number of immigrants arrived. The entire series, however, describes obstacles faced as well as the contributions of all immigrants to America. Katz has interwoven the story of America with that of the ordinary and extraordinary people who came here. This particular volume consists of chronologically arranged chapters dealing with specific groups, such as the Baltic peoples; Czech, Slovak, and Polish Americans; and immigrants from India. Included as well are the chapters Sweatshops and Survival, The Journalists, and Progress Through Inventive Genius. There are several black-and-white photographs, sidebar articles, a brief bibliography, and an index. Recommended for grade 5 and above.

Reeves, Pamela. *Ellis Island: Gateway to the American Dream*. New York: Barnes and Noble, 1998. 144p. $19.95. ISBN 0-517-05905-3.

Reeves traces the history of Ellis Island from its opening in 1892 to its present-day status as a national monument. A brief introduction provides an overview of topics discussed at length in the book. Reeves presents details of the process immigrants were required to go through at Ellis Island as well as changes to the social and political climate in America during its use as an immigration center. The story of Ellis Island is told chronologically from its opening to the fire that destroyed it and through its revival and decline and finally its restoration. There are several black-and-white and full-color photographs on each page. Reeves uses firsthand accounts as well as factual information, resulting in a very moving book. Special features include Chronology of the Restoration, U.S. immigration figures from 1892 through 1954, and information for tracing one's ancestry through Ellis Island. There is also a list of famous immigrants, noting their year of arrival and country of origin. Included as well are a bibliography and an index. Recommended for grade 5 and above.

Saari, Peggy, and Stephen Allison, eds. *Scientists: The Lives and Works of 150 Scientists*. Detroit: Gale Research, 1996. 3 vols. $105.00. ISBN 0-7876-0960-9.

Biographical information in this work focuses on personal life as well as on scientific contribution. Each sketch includes black-and-white photographs or illustrations of the scientist, dates of birth and death, early life, contributions, and an Impact box that details the scientific discovery and its impact on the world. There are also bibliographies on each subject and biographical boxes of major influences on a particular scientist's life. The scope of the work is from the Industrial Revolution to the present day. Each volume begins with a complete list of Scientists by Field of Specialization, a Timeline of Scientific Breakthroughs, and Words to Know. There is also a general index. Written for students, this is an excellent reference for grade 5 and above.

Simmons, John. *The Scientific 100: A Ranking of the Most Influential Scientists, Past and Present*. New York: Citadel Press, 1996. 504p. $29.95. ISBN 0-8065-1749-2.

Scientific writer Simmons ranks the top 100 scientists of all time according to their overall influence on the world. Sketches are two to three pages in length and begin with a black-and-white photograph of the subject, field of endeavor, and dates of birth and death. Details of early life and education are presented, but sketches focus on career highlights and achievements. Simmons also discusses why each subject was chosen and ranked. Also included is an essay, Inexcusable Omissions, Honorable Mentions, and Also Rans, a bibliography, and an index. Written for general readers, but appropriate for grade 6 and above.

Search for Immigrant Achievers
in Science

Name_____ Class_____ Date_____

Use the Reference List for Immigrant Achievers in Science to find the answers to these questions. For some questions, you may find the answers in more than one of the sources on the list.

1. Elijah McCoy, the son of fugitive slaves, was born in Canada and educated in Scotland. McCoy invented a lubricating cup for engines. What was the purpose of this invention?

    _____

    _____

    _____

2. What branch of mathematics was founded in 1944 by Hungarian American mathematician John von Neumann?

    _____

    _____

    _____

3. How did Polish-born cosmetics tycoon Helena Rubenstein revolutionize face powder?

    _____

    _____

    _____

4. Serbian American inventor Nickola Tesla was first employed by another immigrant when he arrived in the United States. Name Tesla's first employer.

    _____

    _____

    _____

5. When is Albert Einstein's birthday?

    _____

    _____

    _____

6. Which scientific theory attributed to Danish-born physicist Niels Bohr became a scientific first in 1913?

_____

_____

_____

7. Polish-born Bronislaw Malinowski is renowned in what scientific field of endeavor?

_____

_____

_____

8. When Italian-born physicist Enrico Fermi won the Nobel prize in 1938, he and his family traveled to Stockholm, Sweden, to accept the prize. Why did Fermi and his family then head for the United States?

_____

_____

_____

9. What was invented by Irish immigrant John Holland in 1898?

_____

_____

_____

10. In what year did scientist-author Isaac Asimov enter the United States through Ellis Island?

_____

_____

_____

Reference List for
Immigrant Contributors to the Arts

Immigrants have greatly influenced the arts in America. Several great American films have been directed by immigrants. America's finest dance companies and orchestras have risen to greatness under the direction of immigrants. This search highlights only a few of those achievers.

Bullock, Allan, ed. *Great Lives of the 20th Century*. Secaucus, NJ: Chartwell Books, 1988. 184p. ISBN 1-55521-305-7.
　　More than 250 brief biographical sketches are arranged alphabetically. Most sketches are two to three paragraphs in length and include dates of birth and death, field of endeavor, place of birth, and when applicable place of residence. This is helpful in identifying those who immigrated to this country. Included in sketches is information on the subject's early life, career highlights, and honors and awards. The introduction discusses omissions as well. There are color and black-and-white photographs on each page. Written for general readers, but appropriate for grade 5 and above.

Di Franco, J. Philip. *The Italian Americans*. (The Immigrant Experience). New York: Chelsea House, 1996. 96p. $19.95. ISBN 0-7910-3353-8.
　　Part of a series written especially for students, this work focuses on the Italian-immigrant experience in America. Chapter One presents an overview of the topic. This is followed by a section on Italian history. Also provided are details of the economic and social conditions that led to immigration and the policies of both Italian and American governments regarding immigration. Subsequent chapters include Picture Essay: A Cultural Tapestry, Italian Catholics in America, and Italian American Contributions. There are several black-and-white photographs throughout, with full-color photographs in the picture essay. The Italian-immigrant experience is traced from pre-Colonial times to the present. Included as well are a bibliography and an index. Recommended for grade 5 and above.

Grolier Library of International Biographies. Danbury, CT: Grolier Education Corp., 1996. 10 vols. $299.00. ISBN 0-7172-7527-2.
　　Twentieth-century achievers from various fields of endeavor are profiled in this 10-volume set. Each entry provides personal information ranging from childhood events to career highlights to values and beliefs. Achievements are detailed as well. Written for students, this work is written in clear, straightforward language. Each volume is devoted to a particular field of endeavor, covering areas such as scientists, performing artists, writers, and explorers. Boldface is used to indicate that the word and its definition will be found in a glossary specific to each volume's subject area. Black-and-white photographs, bibliographies, and indexes for each volume and a general index by subject, country, and name are included. Recommended for grade 5 and above.

Katz, William Loren. *The Great Migrations: 1880s–1912.* (A History of Multi-cultural America). Austin, TX: Raintree Steck-Vaughn, 1993. 96p. $8.95. ISBN 0-8114-6278-1.

Katz has written several works for students. This work, part of an excellent series on multicultural Americans, deals specifically with a period of American history during which a large number of immigrants arrived. The entire series, however, describes obstacles faced as well as the contributions of all immigrants to America. Katz has interwoven the story of America with that of the ordinary and extraordinary people who came here. This particular volume consists of chronologically arranged chapters dealing with specific groups, such as the Baltic peoples; Czech, Slovak, and Polish Americans; and immigrants from India. Included as well are the chapters Sweatshops and Survival, The Journalists, and Progress Through Inventive Genius. There are several black-and-white photographs, sidebar articles, a brief bibliography, and an index. Recommended for grade 5 and above.

Monos, Dimitris. *The Greek Americans.* (The Immigrant Experience). New York: Chelsea House, 1996. 112p. $19.95. ISBN 0-7910-3356-2.

Monos presents a brief overview of Greek immigration followed by a chapter on Greek history that includes social and economic causes for immigration. There is also a brief photo essay presented in full color. Greek immigration is discussed chronologically. Also included are chapters detailing contributions made by Greeks to American culture. Several facets of Greek-immigrant life are presented, including obstacles faced, Greek social clubs, and the impact of classical Greek architecture on America. Part of an excellent series written for students, this work is recommended for grade 5 and above.

Watts, J. F. *The Irish Americans.* (The Immigrant Experience). New York: Chelsea House, 1996. 112p. $19.95. ISBN 0-7910-3366-X.

Written for students, this work traces the history of the Irish in America. As with other works in this series, there is a photo essay in full color. A brief history of Ireland and a discussion of the economic conditions, including the potato famine, is provided. Watts also discusses the rise of the Irish in religion and politics in America. Included as well is a discussion of the impact of the current political situation in Ireland. There are several black-and-white photographs, a bibliography, and an index. Recommended for grade 5 and above.

Wigoder, Geoffrey. *The Dictionary of Jewish Bibliography.* New York: Simon & Schuster, 1991. 568p. $83.50. ISBN 0-13-210105-X.

Nearly 1,000 biographical sketches have been alphabetically arranged in this work. Notable figures from the past 4,000 years from all walks of life have been included. Only the living have been excluded. Sketches range from a half page to two pages. Dates of birth and death, details of early life, education, contributions, and honors and awards are provided. Several black-and-white photographs are included. A special feature is the inclusion of boxed inserts with quotations or anecdotes by or about the subjects. Sketches are clearly written, making this work appropriate for grade 6 and above.

Search for Immigrant Contributors to the Arts

Name_____ Class_____ Date_____

Use the Reference List for Immigrant Contributors to the Arts to find the answers to each of these questions.

1. Polish-born concert pianist Arthur Rubinstein was not initially a success in America. How many appearances did he make at Carnegie Hall before he received a favorable review?

   _____

   _____

   _____

2. Israel Baline came to America and lived in New York's Lower East Side. He is widely known for his contributions in the field of music under what other name?

   _____

   _____

   _____

3. Film director and Sicilian immigrant Frank Capra made three Oscar-winning films and wrote an autobiography. What was the title of his autobiography?

   _____

   _____

   _____

4. George Ballanchine came to the United States at the invitation of Lincoln Kirstein. Together they opened the School of American Ballet, which produced dancers for a company that became widely known and respected. What is that company called today?

   _____

   _____

   _____

5. Name the work by Irish-born writer Brian Moore that deals with the immigrant experience.

   _____

   _____

   _____

6. Greek-born Dimitris Mitropoulos, a principal conductor for the New York Philharmonic, originally wished to become a Greek Orthodox monk. What changed his mind?

_____

_____

_____

7. Sol Hurok, a native of Russia, became an impresario. What exactly did he do?

_____

_____

_____

8. French-born artist Marcel Duchamp created a painting called *Mona Lisa's Moustache*. Describe this work.

_____

_____

_____

9. Name the immigrant who organized the comedy film stars the Marx brothers. What kind of act did they form originally?

_____

_____

_____

10. Elia Kazan, a Greek who came to America from Turkey, cofounded the Actors Studio and directed two Oscar-winning films. Name them.

_____

_____

_____

Immigrant Achievers

Immigrants have made many contributions and innovations in the fields of business, politics, education, and invention. This search highlights some of those achievements.

Reference List for Immigrant Achievers

Di Franco, J. Philip. *The Italian Americans*. (The Immigrant Experience). New York: Chelsea House, 1996. 96p. $19.95. ISBN 0-7910-3353-8.

Part of a series written especially for students, this work focuses on the Italian-immigrant experience in America. Chapter One presents an overview of the topic. This is followed by a section on Italian history. Also provided are details of the economic and social conditions that led to immigration and the policies of both Italian and American governments regarding immigration. Subsequent chapters include Picture Essay: A Cultural Tapestry, Italian Catholics in America, and Italian American Contributions. There are several black-and-white photographs throughout, with full-color photographs in the picture essay. The Italian-immigrant experience is traced from pre-Colonial times to the present. Included as well are a bibliography and an index. Recommended for grade 5 and above.

Hoobler, Dorothy, and Thomas Hoobler. *The Jewish American Family Album*. (American Family Album Series). New York: Oxford University Press, 1995. 128p. $25.00. ISBN 0-19-508135-8.

As with other books in this series, this work details the story of an ethnic group in America. The arrangement is according to topic, some of which include Departure, A New Life, and Putting Down Roots. Within the topics, several aspects of Jewish life in America are discussed. For example, the Part of America section discusses entertainment, communities, and traditions followed by a profile of a Jewish American family. There are several black-and-white photographs, sidebar profiles of famous Jewish people, and a sidebar feature called As Others Saw Them, which presents observations by contemporaries. Much of the text consists of firsthand accounts of experiences and hardships faced by Jewish people in America. There is a Jewish American Timeline, a bibliography, and an index. Written especially for students, this work is appropriate for grade 5 and above.

Katz, William Loren. *The Great Migrations: 1880s–1912*. (A History of Multicultural America). Austin, TX: Raintree Steck-Vaughn, 1993. 96p. $8.95. ISBN 0-8114-6278-1.

Katz has written several works for students. This work, part of an excellent series on multicultural Americans, deals specifically with a period of American history during which a large number of immigrants arrived. The entire series, however, describes obstacles faced as well as the contributions of all immigrants to America. Katz has interwoven the story of America with that of the ordinary and extraordinary people who came here. This particular volume consists of chronologically arranged chapters dealing with specific groups, such as the Baltic peoples; Czech, Slovak, and Polish Americans; and immigrants from India. Included as well are the chapters Sweatshops and Survival, The Journalists, and Progress Through Inventive Genius. There are several black-and-white photographs, sidebar articles, a brief bibliography, and an index. Recommended for grade 5 and above.

McGill, Alyson. *The Swedish Americans*. (The Immigrant Experience). New York: Chelsea House, 1997. 111p. $19.95. ISBN 0-7910-4551-X.

After presenting an overview of Swedish immigration and settlement in the United States, McGill traces Swedish history and then presents details of Swedish immigration from Colonial times to the present. The Swedish introduced log cabins to America. A number of Swedish immigrants were pioneers who settled in the Midwest and the Pacific Northwest. A section of the book titled The Picture Essay: A Pioneer Community is a montage of full-color photographs that portray the pioneer spirit of Swedish Americans. Other chapters include Strangers in a Strange Land and Famous Swedish Americans. There are several black-and-white photographs, a bibliography, and an index. Part of an excellent series written for young adults, this book is recommended for grade 5 and above.

Monos, Dimitris. *The Greek Americans*. (The Immigrant Experience). New York: Chelsea House, 1996. 112p. $19.95. ISBN 0-7910-3356-2.

Monos presents a brief overview of Greek immigration followed by a chapter on Greek history that includes social and economic causes for immigration. There is also a brief photo essay presented in full color. Greek immigration is discussed chronologically. Also included are chapters detailing contributions made by Greeks to American culture. Several facets of Greek-immigrant life are presented, including obstacles faced, Greek social clubs, and the impact of classical Greek architecture on America. Part of an excellent series written for students, this work is recommended for grade 5 and above.

Shapiro, Michael. *The Jewish 100: A Ranking of the Most Influential Jews of All Time*. New York: Citadel Press, 1994. 387p. $22.95. ISBN 0-8065-1492-2.

As with the other "100" books in this series, this work ranks its subjects according to degree of impact. Shapiro's list consists of Jewish people who influenced the world as well as those whose influence may have only been felt by Jewish people themselves. Included are Jewish people from all walks of life and those from the Bible. There are black-and-white photographs or illustrations, dates of birth and death, and a two- to three-page sketch for each entrant. Sketches provide details of childhood, education, contributions, and honors and awards. Shapiro also provides a brief explanation of each entrant's rank on the list. There is an index. Recommended for grade 5 and above.

Search for Immigrant Achievers

Name_____ Class_____ Date_____

Use the Reference List for Immigrant Achievers to find the answers to these questions.

1. German-born political cartoonist Thomas Nast created which two popular political images?

   _____

   _____

   _____

2. Name the company founded by Italian immigrant Marco Fontana. By what name is the company known today?

   _____

   _____

   _____

3. In 1906, Jewish immigrant Golda Meir and her family arrived in the United States. Where did they live? What was her name then?

   _____

   _____

   _____

4. What political office did German immigrant John Peter Altgeld hold in 1892?

   _____

   _____

   _____

5. What famous American ship was built by Swedish-born ship designer John Ericsson during the Civil War?

   _____

   _____

   _____

6. Greek immigrant Michael Anagnostopoulos, who shortened his name to Anagnos, became a leading educator for children with special needs. Name a famous student taught by him.

_____

_____

_____

7. Jewish immigrant Emile Berliner improved on the inventions of Edison and Bell and devised an invention of his own. What were these devices?

_____

_____

_____

8. Amadeo Obici, an Italian immigrant, operated a fruit stand that grew into what famous company?

_____

_____

_____

9. Swedish-born Carl Swanson's company is credited with creating what popular American innovation in food?

_____

_____

_____

10. Swedish immigrant Walter Hoving started in the business world working at Macy's Department Store. He quickly moved on to run two other prestigious stores. Name them.

_____

_____

_____

The Immigrant Experience
in America

Immigrants came to America for various reasons. Some came to escape religious or political persecution. Some truly believed the streets were paved with gold and brought their families here for what they believed would be a better life. Still others were seeking adventure. Even though many eventually excelled in their chosen field of endeavor, those who arrived with little initially faced a harsh introduction to America.

Reference List for the Immigrant Experience in America

Hoobler, Dorothy, and Thomas Hoobler. *The Italian Americans*. (American Family Album Series). New York: Oxford University Press, 1994. 128p. $19.95. ISBN 0-19-508126-9.

The appeal of this series is that the story of immigrants is presented in their own words and pictures. There are two or more black-and-white photographs on most pages. Beginning with details of life in the old country, the book then traces the trip to America, life and work in America, and identifies Italian contributors to American society. There is also a question-and-answer section that focuses on one Italian American family's experiences. Another special feature is an Italian American time line. There is also an index and a bibliography. Recommended for grade 5 and above.

Hoobler, Dorothy, and Thomas Hoobler. *The Jewish American Family Album*. (American Family Album Series). New York: Oxford University Press, 1995. 128p. $25.00. ISBN 0-19-508135-8.

As with other books in this series, this work details the story of an ethnic group in America. The arrangement is according to topic, some of which include Departure, A New Life, and Putting Down Roots. Within the topics, several aspects of Jewish life in America are discussed. For example, the Part of America section discusses entertainment, communities, and traditions followed by a profile of a Jewish American family. There are several black-and-white photographs, sidebar profiles of famous Jewish people, and a sidebar feature called As Others Saw Them, which presents observations by contemporaries. Much of the text consists of firsthand accounts of experiences and hardships faced by Jewish people in America. There is a Jewish American Timeline, a bibliography, and an index. Written especially for students, this work is appropriate for grade 5 and above.

Katz, William Loren. *The Great Migrations: 1880s–1912.* (A History of Multicultural America). Austin, TX: Raintree Steck-Vaughn, 1993. 96p. $8.95. ISBN 0-8114-6278-1.

Katz has written several works for students. This work, part of an excellent series on multicultural Americans, deals specifically with a period of American history during which a large number of immigrants arrived. The entire series, however, describes obstacles faced as well as the contributions of all immigrants to America. Katz has interwoven the story of America with that of the ordinary and extraordinary people who came here. This particular volume consists of chronologically arranged chapters dealing with specific groups, such as the Baltic peoples; Czech, Slovak, and Polish Americans; and immigrants from India. Included as well are the chapters Sweatshops and Survival, The Journalists, and Progress Through Inventive Genius. There are several black-and-white photographs, sidebar articles, a brief bibliography, and an index. Recommended for grade 5 and above.

Reeves, Pamela. *Ellis Island: Gateway to the American Dream.* New York: Barnes and Noble, 1998. 144p. $19.95. ISBN 0-517-05905-3.

Reeves traces the history of Ellis Island from its opening in 1892 to its present-day status as a national monument. A brief introduction provides an overview of topics discussed at length in the book. Reeves presents details of the process immigrants were required to go through at Ellis Island as well as changes to the social and political climate in America during its use as an immigration center. The story of Ellis Island is told chronologically from its opening to the fire that destroyed it and through its revival and decline and finally its restoration. There are several black-and-white and full-color photographs on each page. Reeves uses firsthand accounts as well as factual information, resulting in a very moving book. Special features include Chronology of the Restoration, U.S. immigration figures from 1892 through 1954, and information for tracing one's ancestry through Ellis Island. There is also a list of famous immigrants, noting their year of arrival and country of origin. Included as well are a bibliography and an index. Recommended for grade 5 and above.

Watts, J. F. *The Irish Americans.* (The Immigrant Experience). New York: Chelsea House, 1996. 112p. $19.95. ISBN 0-7910-3366-X.

Written for students, this work traces the history of the Irish in America. As with other works in this series, there is a photo essay in full color. A brief history of Ireland and a discussion of the economic conditions, including the potato famine, is provided. Watts also discusses the rise of the Irish in religion and politics in America. Included as well is a discussion of the impact of the current political situation in Ireland. There are several black-and-white photographs, a bibliography, and an index. Recommended for grade 5 and above.

Search for the Immigrant Experience in America

Name_____ Class_____ Date_____

Use the Reference List for the Immigrant Experience in America to find the answers for this search on the experiences of immigrants as they entered Ellis Island. Answers for some of the questions may be found in more than one source.

1. What were Irishtowns?

_____

_____

_____

2. What was Castle Garden?

_____

_____

_____

3. What was the Kissing Post at Ellis Island?

_____

_____

_____

4. What name did Italians give Ellis Island?

_____

_____

_____

5. When was the Workmen's Circle formed? What was its purpose?

_____

_____

_____

6. What happened at the Triangle Shirtwaist Factory in March 1911?

_____

_____

_____

7. Many Irish immigrants fought in the Civil War. Name the five states that had an Irish brigade.

_____

_____

_____

8. From the year it opened until it closed, which year saw the largest number of immigrants come through Ellis Island?

_____

_____

_____

9. According to Guilio Miranda, Italian and other immigrants dreaded the medical examination at Ellis Island. Doctors used chalk to mark letters on the clothing of some immigrants. What did the letters "H," "L," "X," and "E" mean?

_____

_____

_____

10. How was Ellis Island used during World War II?

_____

_____

_____

The Holocaust

While some may feel that the Holocaust is not part of American history, it did impact on the entire world. Many immigrants arrived in the United States as a result of the Holocaust, particularly after the war. This search focuses on only a few aspects of the Holocaust.

Reference List for the Holocaust

Adler, David A. *We Remember the Holocaust*. New York: Scholastic, 1989. 148p. $10.95. ISBN 0-590-76351-2.

Adler's work was written especially for young people; in fact, it came about because he wanted to explain the Holocaust to his young son. Adler interviewed survivors—many of whom live in the New York area—who were children or teenagers at the time of the Holocaust. There are many black-and-white photographs supplied by those interviewed. Nine chapters are arranged chronologically. Also included is a chronology of events from 1933 to 1945, a glossary, and an index. Adler intended his work to serve as an introduction to the Holocaust. The stories are very moving. Recommended for grade 6 and above.

Friedman, Ina R. *The Other Victims: First-Person Stories of Non-Jews Persecuted by the Nazis*. Boston: Houghton Mifflin, 1990. 214p. $14.95. ISBN 0-395-50212-8.

Friedman presents the stories of 11 survivors of the Holocaust, all of whom were persecuted for reasons other than being Jewish—one a Gypsy, another deaf, yet another a political dissident. In her introduction, Friedman explains the political climate in Germany and Hitler's concepts of the master race and world domination. For each account, there is an introduction that provides details of Hitler's persecution policy against a particular group. This is followed by the first-person narrative of a survivor from that group. Each story has a positive ending, and some of the survivors are now living in America. These are stories of courageous people, and this work is an excellent addition to a young-adult collection. Recommended for grade 5 and above.

Healey, Tom. *Secret Armies: Resistance Groups in World War II*. London: Macdonald, 1981. 48p. $22.50. ISBN 0-3560-6553-7.

Devoted entirely to the Resistance movement during World War II, Healey's work presents a fascinating study of the movement. The work consists of 22 double-page spreads on 22 aspects of the Resistance. Each section consists of clearly written text and several photographs and illustrations in color and black-and-white. Included are sections on propaganda, The Intelligence Nets, Sabotage, Codes and Ciphers, Escape Lines, Concentration

Camps, and Liberation. Healey has compiled fascinating information, such as how coded messages were rolled into cigarettes, detailed illustrations of tools and weapons used, the location of concentration camps, and reproductions of posters used during the war. This is an excellent source for grade 5 and above.

Historical Atlas of the Holocaust. United States Holocaust Memorial Museum. New York: Macmillan, 1995. 252p. $39.95. ISBN 0-02-897451-4.

The story of the Holocaust is presented here in more than 230 full-color maps and text. The work is arranged in eight sections beginning with Europe before the war. Four sections are devoted to geographical areas of Europe. One section focuses on Nazi concentration camps and includes an illustration of identification patches worn by those in the camps. Other sections focus on Rescue and Resistance, Death Marches and Liberation, and finally Postwar Europe. Other features include a glossary, a bibliography, and a gazeteer. Even though there are no photographs, this work presents a graphic vision of a truly horrific portion of modern history. It is an excellent source for anyone studying or interested in the Holocaust. Recommended for grade 7 and above.

The Holocaust Library. San Diego: Lucent Books, 1998. 7 vols. $154.00. ISBN varies for each title. The Nazis, ISBN 1-5600-60913. Nazi War Criminals, ISBN 1-5600-60972. Death Camps, ISBN 1-5600-60948.

Each of the seven volumes in this set discusses a different aspect of the Holocaust. Among them are The Death Camps, The Righteous Gentiles, The Final Solution, and The Survivors. There are six or seven chapters in each volume, and each opens with a chronology of events pertinent to that particular volume. There are several black-and-white photographs (some very graphic). Sidebar articles on related topics are also presented. Each volume also has its own index and bibliography. Several volumes also have special features. For example, Death Camps has an appendix titled The Fate of Selected Death Camp Figures. Written especially for students, this work is recommended for grade 7 and above.

Moss, Joyce, and George Wilson. *Peoples of the World: North Americans.* 1st ed. Detroit: Gale Research, 1991. 441p. $45.00. ISBN 0-8103-7768-3.

The series Peoples of the World profiles various ethnic groups. The authors have made the focus of their work the people of a country rather than the country itself. The premise of the work is that governments and other world events affect change in many countries, but culture and tradition do not change. Separate volumes have been devoted to North Americans and to Latin Americans as well as to other areas around the world. Each entry is introduced with phonetic spelling and definition. Information on population, location, language, and geographical setting is also included. Other sections for each culture include historical background and culture today. Special features include maps for each culture that indicate current location. While political and economic information may not be current, this work is a good source of cultural and historical information. Also included are black-and-white illustrations and photographs, a glossary, and an index. This set is written especially for students in junior high school, making it appropriate for students in grade 7 and above.

Nielson, Lisa Clyde, ed. *The Holocaust*. Woodbridge, CT: Blackbirch Press, 1998. 8 vols. and cumulative index. $180.00. ISBN 1-56711-213-7 (set).

Each of the eight volumes in this set is titled and edited or compiled by an expert in the field. The volumes are arranged chronologically. The editors blend narrative with primary sources to present vivid details of this incredible period of history. Each volume details a specific aspect of the Holocaust. For example, Book One, *Forever Outsiders*, provides a history of the Jews from ancient times to 1935; Book Three, *The Blaze Engulfs*, covers the period from January 1939 to December 1941; Book Six, *From the Ashes*, covers May 1945 and after; and Book Eight, *Visions and Voices*, is a collection of sources. *The Resource Guide* is an excellent multimedia list of works on the topic. The bibliography by topic—Ghettoes, Resistance, and Rescue, to name a few—is annotated, and a key indicates appropriate reading level. In addition, there are sections on illustrated books, videos, Web sites and CD-ROMs, and museum and resource centers. Each volume is 80 pages with six chapters. Black-and-white photographs accompany the text. There are occasional subject boxes with pertinent information. For example, The Angel of Death discusses Joseph Mengele in Book Five, which focuses on concentration camps. Each volume ends with Chronology of the Holocaust:1933–1945, a glossary, sources for further reading, and a bibliography. There is an index for each volume in addition to the separate cumulative index. Recommended for grade 6 and above.

Rosenberg, Maxine B. *Hiding to Survive: Stories of Jewish Children Rescued from the Holocaust*. New York: Clarion, 1994. 166p. $15.95. ISBN 0-395-65014-3.

First-person narratives recount the rescue of 14 people who were children when they were hidden from the Nazis by non-Jewish people. Each is a story of the heroism of ordinary people. Included with each account is a childhood photograph of the survivor, an account of the time spent in hiding, a postscript detailing what happened immediately after the war, and information on each person's life today. A current black-and-white photograph is also included. Each account is very moving, making this book hard to put down. Recommended for grade 7 and above.

Search for the Holocaust

Name_____ Class_____ Date_____

Use the Reference List for the Holocaust to find the answers to the following questions. For some questions, the answers will be located in more than one source on the list.

1. As a result of World War II, how many Jewish people came to America?

    _____

    _____

    _____

2. Klaus Barbie, an extremely cruel Gestapo chief also known as the Butcher of Lyons, was found working in Europe in 1947, two years after the war. What type of work was he doing?

    _____

    _____

    _____

3. Aviva Blumberg was hidden as a child during World War II. Today she lives in the United States. What is her occupation?

    _____

    _____

    _____

4. What happened on March 27, 1933?

    _____

    _____

    _____

5. During the German occupation of Poland, only elementary schools were permitted. However, immigrant Zbigniew Zawadzki attended a secret school. What kind of school was it?

    _____

    _____

    _____

6. According to one chronology of events pertaining to survivors, December 22, 1945, marked a special day. What happened on this day?

_____

_____

_____

7. Find a map of escape routes from German-occupied Europe in 1942. To which neutral countries did escape routes from France lead?

_____

_____

_____

8. Witold Pilecki, a soldier in the Polish army, volunteered for an unusual mission in World War II. What was it?

_____

_____

_____

9. Who was David Niles?

_____

_____

_____

10. Why were the six Nazi death camps all located in Poland?

_____

_____

_____

Answer Key for Immigrant Achievers in Science

1. In Katz. With McCoy's device, engines could be oiled without turning them off. This resulted in both timesaving and money-saving operation.
2. In Bruno. von Neumann invented game theory.
3. In Bullock. Rubenstein was the first to color face powder to match skin tones.
4. In Saari and Allison. Tesla first worked for Scottish-born Thomas Edison.
5. In Simmons. Einstein was born on March 14, 1879.
6. In Bruno. Bohr developed the quantum theory of the atom in 1913.
7. In *Grolier*. Malinowski was a pioneer in the field of social anthropology.
8. In Saari and Allison. Anti-Semitism was spreading rapidly in Europe. Because Fermi's wife was Jewish, they felt it necessary to defect to the United States.
9. In Katz. Holland developed the first submarine.
10. In Reeves. Asimov arrived at Ellis Island in 1923.

Answer Key for Immigrant Contributors to the Arts

1. In *Grolier*. Rubenstein did not receive favorable reviews until his third appearance.
2. In Katz. Israel Baline was better known as Irving Berlin.
3. In Di Franco. Capra's autobiography was *The Name Above the Title*.
4. In Bullock. Ballanchine's company became the New York City Ballet.
5. In Watts. Moore's work is *The Luck of Ginger Coffey*.
6. In Monos. The monks prohibited the use of musical instruments.
7. In Wigoder. Hurok presented talent at concerts, organized performances, and eventually specialized in presenting foreign talent in America.
8. In *Grolier*. Duchamp reproduced the *Mona Lisa* and drew a moustache and beard on the face of the portrait.
9. In Wigoder. Their immigrant mother, Minnie, originally organized them into a singing act.
10. In Monos. Kazan's Oscar-winning films were *Gentlemen's Agreement* and *On the Waterfront*.

Answer Key for Immigrant Achievers

1. In Katz. Nast created the Republican elephant and the Democratic donkey.
2. In Di Franco. Fontana founded the California Fruit Packing Corporation, which is known today as Del Monte.
3. In Hoobler and Hoobler. Meir's family settled in Milwaukee, Wisconsin. Her name then was Goldie Mabovitch.
4. In Katz. Altgeld was governor of Illinois.
5. In McGill. Ericsson built the *Monitor*.
6. In Monos. Anagnos taught Helen Keller.
7. In Shapiro. Berliner invented the gramophone, which was an improvement on Edison's phonograph, and his induction coil improved Bell's telephone. Berliner's own invention was the microphone.
8. In Di Franco. Obici's fruit stand grew into the Planter's Peanut Company.

9. In McGill. Swanson's company is famous for the TV dinner.
10. In McGill. Hoving ran Lord & Taylor and Tiffany's.

Answer Key for the Immigrant Experience in America

1. In Watts. Shanty communities of Irish-immigrant transcontinental railroad workers that sprang up along the tracks were called Irishtowns.
2. In Katz. Once a theater, Castle Garden was turned into a port of entry for immigrants before Ellis Island was built.
3. In Reeves. This was the area where those who had been detained were reunited with loved ones who were waiting for them.
4. In Hoobler and Hoobler, *Italian*. They called it *isola della lacrime*, which means island of tears.
5. In Hoobler and Hoobler, *Jewish*. Workmen's Circle was founded in 1900 to help those who were unemployed or unable to work. Many of those helped were immigrants.
6. In Katz. A fire broke out at the sweatshop. In 18 minutes, 146 Italian and Jewish immigrant women died.
7. In Watts. New York, Pennsylvania, Ohio, Indiana, and Illinois had Irish brigades in the Civil War.
8. In Reeves. In 1907, 1,004,756 immigrants came through Ellis Island.
9. In Hoobler and Hoobler, *Italian*. "H" meant possible heart trouble, "L" meant the person was lame, "X" meant possible mental defects, and "E" meant eye problems.
10. In Reeves. During World War II it was a detention center for people considered to be enemy aliens.

Answer Key for the Holocaust

1. In Moss and Wilson. From 1937 to 1948 somewhere between 200,000 and 250,000 Jewish people came to the United States.
2. In Nielson. Barbie was working as an informer for the U.S. government.
3. In Rosenberg. Blumberg is a psychotherapist.
4. In Adler. More than 5,000 protestors assembled at Madison Square Garden to threaten a boycott of German goods, forcing Hitler to limit the Nazi-proposed boycott of all Jewish-owned businesses to one day.
5. In Friedman. Zawadzki attended a secret medical school in Poland.
6. In *The Holocaust Library*. On that day, President Truman gave permission for all displaced persons, many of whom were concentration-camp survivors, to enter the United States.
7. In *Historical Atlas*. Escape routes from France led to Switzerland, Portugal, and Spain.
8. In Healey. He volunteered to get himself sent to a concentration camp to find out exactly what was happening.
9. In *The Holocaust Library*. Niles was a Russian Jewish immigrant and President Truman's assistant in charge of plans that allowed Jewish and other displaced persons to immigrate to the United States.
10. In Nielson. The greatest concentration of Jewish people lived in Poland at the time.

Index

from **Libraries Unlimited**

CORETTA SCOTT KING AWARD BOOKS: Using Great Literature with Children and Young Adults
Claire Gatrell Stephens

Hunting for great children's books and multicultural literature activities that involve the whole class? Look no further. This incredible array of outstanding children's literature is accompanied by hundreds of suggestions and ideas for using the award-winning titles. **Grades 3–8**.
ca.250p. 8½x11 paper ISBN 1-56308-685-9

TURNING KIDS ON TO RESEARCH: The Power of Motivation
Ruth V. Small and Marilyn P. Arnone

Dozens of quick, easy-to-apply techniques for planning, improving, and enhancing information skills lessons will have your students raring to learn. **Grades K–12**.
Information Literacy Series
xvi, 199p. 8½x11 paper ISBN 1-56308-782-0

THE THOUGHTFUL RESEARCHER: Teaching the Research Process to Middle School Students
Virginia Rankin

Engaging learning activities help middle and junior high students develop the skills necessary to carry out the steps of the research process. Rankin's well-written and captivating outlines of teaching techniques help you reach your own insights and conclusions about teaching the research process. **Grades 5–9**.
Information Literacy Series
xvi, 211p. 8½x11 paper ISBN 1-56308-698-0

GOTCHA! Nonfiction Booktalks to Get Kids Excited About Reading
Kathleen A. Baxter and Marcia Agness Kochel

With this book you can confidently talk up hundreds of books according to topics of interest to young readers, such as great disasters and unsolved mysteries. The fresh perspectives will entice even the most reluctant readers to check out nonfiction. **Grades 1–8**.
xviii, 183p. 8½x11 paper ISBN 1-56308-683-2

TEACHING WITH FOLK STORIES OF THE HMONG: An Activity Book
Dia Cha and Norma J. Livo

Build appreciation of cultural diversity and extend learning across the curriculum with these engaging project ideas based on Hmong folktales and traditions. **All Levels.**
Learning Through Folklore Series
ca.165p. 8½x11 paper ISBN 1-56308-668-9

For a free catalog or to place an order, please contact: Libraries Unlimited/Teacher Ideas Press at 1-800-237-6124 or
- **Fax: 303-220-8843**
- **E-mail: lu-books@lu.com**
- **Visit: www.lu.com**
- **Mail to: Dept. B004 • P.O. Box 6633**
        Englewood, CO 80155-6633